# LORD AND PEASANT
# IN NINETEENTH-CENTURY BRITAIN

# Lord and Peasant in Nineteenth Century Britain

Dennis R. Mills

CROOM HELM LONDON

ROWMAN AND LITTLEFIELD TOTOWA N.J.

©1980 Dennis R. Mills
Croom Helm Ltd, 2-10 St John's Road, London SW11
ISBN 0-7099-0123-2


British Library Cataloguing in Publication Data

Mills, Dennis Richard
    Lord and peasant in nineteenth-century Britain. –
    (Croom Helm historical geography series).
    1. Great Britain – Rural conditions
    2. Social structure – Great Britain – History –
    19th century
    I. Title
    301.4'00941        HN385

    ISBN 0-7099-0123-2


First published in the United States 1980 by
Rowman and Littlefield
81 Adams Drive,
Totowa, New Jersey

   ISBN 0-8476-6806-1

Typeset by Jayell Typesetting, London
Printed and bound in Great Britain by
Biddles Ltd, Guildford and King's Lynn

# CONTENTS

# TABLES

# FIGURES

# ABBREVIATIONS

| | |
|---|---|
| Agric. Hist. Rev. | Agricultural History Review |
| BPP | British Parliamentary Papers |
| Econ. Hist. Rev. | Economic History Review |
| Scot. Geog. Mag. | Scottish Geographical Magazine |
| Scot. St. | Scottish Studies |
| TIBG | Transactions of the Institute of British Geographers |
| Welsh HR | Welsh Historical Review |

To my parents and the memory of my grandparents,
who taught me my first lessons on the nineteenth century.

# PREFACE

Readers of this book who go in search of bias will find it easier to detect if I mention that it owes a great deal to the nature of my up-bringing and subsequent places of residence. Born on a Nottinghamshire estate of Lincolnshire peasant stock, I was subject in childhood and youth to the influence of both lord and peasant. For example, the big house provided cinema tickets for *Sabu the Elephant Boy* and *Snow White and the Seven Dwarfs* and because my father was the head gardener we went to Chelsea Flower Show on members' day. I was inoculated at an early age against paternalism, however, by a strong dose of independence, which came with my mother's milk, for her father was a cottage farmer in a fenside parish, and my own father became a self-employed market-gardener.

Thirty years of wandering since I left the family homestead have taken me to many parts of Britain, where I have had the chance to study lord and peasant from the ground upwards. In south-west Leices-tershire I found the traditions of the fox-hunting squires and the frame-work-knitters an especially fascinating mixture, while in south Cam-bridgeshire the collective strength of the nonconformist smallholding tradition was something of which I felt myself part. Studies of crofting communities in Lewis, visits to countless stately homes, farm holidays far and wide, hours spent traipsing round the back streets of Nottingham, Leicester, Manchester, Bradford and Leeds and compulsory tours of the Channel coast with the Navy have all had their impact on my view of nineteenth-century Britain.

So long have I been accumulating and sifting material and ideas, it would be impossible to recall the long list of those to whom I am indebted. A very early starting point, however, was the series of lectures on agrarian history given at Nottingham University by the late Prof. David Chambers and his book *Nottinghamshire in the Eighteenth Century* (2nd edn, Frank Cass, 1966).

The staff of the libraries at Nottingham and Leicester Universities and at The Open University have borne the brunt of my searching in strange corners and I would particularly like to acknowledge the help of Mr Paul Smith. For much help with an early draft I wish to thank my colleague Prof. Michael Drake. Valuable suggestions for restructur-ing were made by Dr. James Johnston of Bishop Grosseteste College,

Lincoln. I was very pleased to have the advice of my colleagues Drs. Rees Pryce and Ian Donnachie on the chapters that relate specifically to their own countries. Dr. Alan Macfarlane and Mr Michael Havinden, of the Universities of Cambridge and Exeter, not only gave generous permission to quote their own work extensively, but also commented on parts of the text. Other acknowledgements are made within the text.

All would have been in vain had not other skills been at hand. The maps have been drawn by Mr John Hunt, cartographer at the Open University. Miss Philippa Wain made the first manuscript intelligible, while the final typescript was prepared by Miss Margaret Martin and Mrs Margaret Golby with Miss Wain coming to the rescue again. The imperfections of the final result, however, must be laid at my own door.

Cat Lane House,
Thornborough, Bucks.

# 1 SETTING THE SCENE

'The great figure in the villages of those days was the lord of the manor, for whether he was a duke or a squire, he considered it his duty to make himself responsible for the well-being of the people of his village.' Noel Streatfield (ed.), *The Day Before Yesterday* (Collins, London, 1956), p. 248.

## Introduction

The squire figures prominently in many personal models or mental constructs of English village social structure during the last century. It is true that there were more squires, more country gentlemen than there are today, but that does not mean that every village had its squire. There were lordless villages too, and had been for centuries, in which there was not only no *resident* squire but also no absentee landlord who owned over half the soil. Here the land was divided up among a multiplicity of owners of varying importance – perhaps a hundred of them might share three or four thousand acres unequally, the greatest with several hundred acres or a thousand apiece, the smallest with only a cottage and a few roods of garden.

This book is about the duality of English rural social structure, about how it compared with rural Wales and Scotland and about its implications for industrial and urban growth in the century which Britain started as four-fifths rural and finished by being four-fifths urban. I have chosen the terms lord and peasant to represent this duality, but their use is not without its difficulties. To begin with, there was a world of difference between the economic role and attitudes of the nineteenth-century squire and those of the medieval manorial lord, despite the fact that many squires still gloried in the title of 'lord of the manor'. The country gentlemen of Victorian Britain could not be described as feudal or old fashioned, either in role or outlook. They were authoritarian and patriarchal to a degree, but one of their most important functions was to modernise the countryside in technological and institutional terms. They wielded vast amounts of capital in what I have called the estate system to enhance the value and potential of their land, be it in respect of agriculture, forestry, mineral exploitation, the development of communications or, very significantly, urban development. The term 'lord', then, is a convenient indicator of wealthy and powerful men who were, if you like, monopoly capitalists in land.

There were, however, many townships in which they did not have monopoly control over land and property. Here small, independent owners and entrepreneurs were important and even modestly powerful. The upper levels of county administration and justice, it is true, were monopolised by the landed interest and their allies, the Anglican clergy. They provided the magistrates, the MPs, the lords lieutenants and colonels of militia – hence perhaps some of the feudal image. But within their own villages the smaller property-owners would set up their nonconformist chapels, vote against the local territorial magnate, defy the law on church rates, elect the officials of their own village clubs, lord it over the village schoolmaster as school managers, and so on.

To represent this alternative, which was based on independence of the estate system, I have chosen, perhaps rashly, to use the term 'peasant'. In the nineteenth century this word was little used in England and then usually of native labourers or foreign agriculturalists. 'Yeoman' was still heard in some parts of the country, especially in earlier decades, but this had too specialised a meaning for it usually referred to owner-occupier farmers who got their whole living from the land. While such men were often found in a peasant village and may even have farmed most of the parish, they were usually in a minority among entrepreneurs, for there would also be smaller farmers, both tenants and owners, as well as tradesmen, craftsmen, publicans and manufacturers. Moreover, it is sometimes futile to try to draw a line between the agriculturalists and the non-agriculturalists, for many a smallholding was combined with pub or shop and many craftsmen had small pieces of land for subsistence, or as a sideline, or as grazing for their necessary draught horses. These men were as different from the continental peasants as the nineteenth-century manorial lords were from their medieval fore-runners, yet what else can we call them but peasants? The important point is that *Lord and Peasant in Nineteenth-Century Britain* should be seen as an attempt to draw out and assess a dichotomy which existed at that time, rather than an implied comparison with earlier centuries.

## The Cultural Inheritance in England

The historical geographer, however, cannot afford to ignore the cultural inheritance which is passed down from one generation or period to the next, each modifying it in their own way. Geographical inertia (otherwise known as historical momentum) is frequently a powerful factor in explaining the cultural landscape at any particular point in time; a village site in use in the nineteenth century, for example, is more likely than not to have been first established well before the Conquest. This book is also concerned with three different nations, each heir to a different language, a different set of attitudes and values and, in the case of Scotland, a different legal system from that of England and Wales.

In terms of the basic framework of country life, England has always displayed a dazzling variety from one locality to another, if only because geology, soils, aspect and natural vegetation also vary enormously. A brutal generalisation, however, reveals two, or perhaps three major divisions which can be used in the present context (see Figure 1.1). In the central areas of England, along with certain parts of the south and east the common-field system had been well developed in the centuries before and after the Conquest. Although the common fields and wastes were almost all to be enclosed in the nineteenth century, if they had not already succumbed to this process, they were associated with other features and traditions which had a lasting effect. Felden parishes or champion country, as these areas were sometimes known, were typically farmed by families living in strongly nucleated settlements, with farmsteads flank by flank in a relatively closely built-up area. Many of these farmsteads were moved out into the fields during the eighteenth and nineteenth centuries, but the non-agricultural population and many part-time farmers and farm labourers remained in the nucleus. Despite this dispersal, champion England continued to be a land of true villages, many of them in relatively small parishes. As these villages had been heavily manorialised − subject to the strict rules of carefully run manorial courts − one question that needs to be asked is whether or not they formed a 'natural' basis for the development of the nineteenth-century estate system.[1]

To the south east and north west of champion England were areas where neither the common-field system nor the manorial system had been as strongly developed. Generally speaking, these were areas of later settlement, often colonised from nearby felden parishes by men who took advantage of the relative freedom from manorial control to work out an alternative, freer socio-economic system.[2] Arable farming was less important, with a correspondingly greater role for pastoral and woodland activities. South east of the Tees-Exe line the term wood pasture is an appropriate label for the economic bias, except in the Fens where the pasture was open as in many of the moorland areas to the north and west of the line. Although common-field agriculture was

Figure 1.1: Hamlet and Champion England

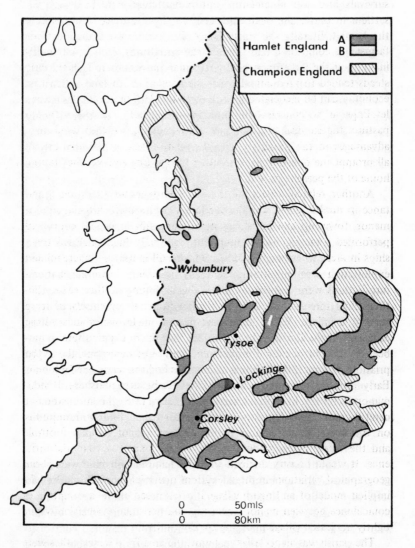

Note: Champion England as shown here corresponds to Baker's mixed farming areas. Hamlet England A is based on his wood pasture areas; and B on open pasture areas. The four villages are referred to extensively in Chs. 2 and 3.

Source: Based on A.R.H. Baker and J.B. Harley (eds.), *Man Made the Land: Essays in English Historical Georgraphy* (David and Charles, Newton Abbot, 1973), p. 66.

weakly developed, commons or wastes were extensive and large-scale survivals into the nineteenth century are frequently recorded. The settlement pattern of both open and wood pasture was dominated by the hamlet, literally the small village. Both true villages and scattered farmsteads could be found there in the nineteenth century, but except in some of the larger moorland and fenland areas where isolated farmsteads tended to predominate over the hamlets, both types of pastoral economy can be associated broadly with hamlets, hence the term 'hamlet England' to contrast with 'champion England'. The importance of pasture, the survival of commons and woodland, which offered many advantages to the peasantry, and the relative lack of manorial control all prompt the question as to whether hamlet England was the 'natural' home of the peasant system.

Another related aspect of the nineteenth-century cultural inheritance in rural England was the overlapping roles and territorial bases of manor, township and parish. Manorial lords and manorial courts still performed some significant functions, especially in unenclosed townships in areas where copyhold tenure was still in use and where mineral exploitation was important. Generally speaking, however, manorial jurisdictions were a spent force by the beginning of the century and their chief interest here is in their prior influence on the social structure of a village. Where there had been a single manor in a village, especially if the lord had been resident, one might expect there to have been close control over, for example, the use of commons, the expropriation of timber, the building of cottages and the winning of minerals. Early progress towards enclosure may also be expected here. Divided manorial control, in contrast, frequently meant that no manor exercised careful control over the community, cottages were built with impunity on the waste, population grew, nonconformity got an easy foothold and the village elders made decisions independently of manorial influence. It would be very difficult to arrive at a valid generalisation about geographical variations in the strength of manorial jurisdictions, but the implicit model of an English village is often based on the assumption of coincidence between manor, township and parish, in association with a tightly nucleated village in champion England.

The parish was an ecclesiastical unit, the area from which tithes were paid for the upkeep of a single priest and church. Parochial administration was carried out by parishioners in vestry meetings and by churchwardens on their behalf, one chosen by the incumbent, the other by the people. In southern England, East Anglia and parts of the Midlands the parish was often co-terminous with the township, the unit in which agricultural, social and fiscal administration was carried on. In champion England each township had its own set of common-fields and waste administered independently of those of neighbouring townships except for small areas of intercommon. In hamlet England this criterion is more difficult to use, but in both zones the township had its own constable, overseers of the poor, and surveyor of the highways. Where the parish and township coincided, these functions and those of the churchwardens often overlapped and the vestry meeting concerned itself with all village business. In some of the wood pasture districts and more commonly in the north and north Midlands, early population levels had been too low for each township to support a church, so that multi-township parishes were numerous.[3]

## Rural-Urban and Similar Dichotomies

The literature of industrialisation is full of descriptions which hinge upon the use of a dichotomy, or before-and-after pictures. We have already referred to Britain's transition from four-fifths rural to four-fifths urban, without concerning ourselves with the precise meanings — if there are such — of 'rural' and 'urban'. The rural-urban contrast may appear innocent enough, synonymous it may be thought to an agricultural-industrial dichotomy. It is more useful, however, to regard towns as places performing higher grade central place functions, notably those concerned with marketing. Eighteenth-century language was perhaps clearer in this respect than modern terminology, for up to that period all nucleated settlements were known as towns, while commercial centres were distinguished as *market* towns. The modern association of towns with industry was still in the future, because many country areas were important for industrial products, defining these as goods manufactured for sale outside the immediate locality. Although England was not unique in developing rural industries, the scale of production may have been a distinctive feature of English rural society and a significant factor in distinguishing between the estate and peasant systems, for the peasantry concentrated upon labour-intensive production and the estates on the exploitation of the land and its minerals by capital-intensive methods.

There have been a number of attempts by sociologists and social anthropologists to encapsulate in sociological terms the implications of the differences between rural-agricultural ways of life and those associated with towns and modern industry. Maine wrote about Status Society (old) and Contract Society (new), Spencer about the Militant (feudal) and Industrial Forms of Society. Durkheim concerned himself with the limitations of the Mechanical Solidarity which existed in undifferentiated rural communities and the opportunities offered by the Organic Solidarity of socially and economically heterogeneous populations in urban-industrial areas. Redfield has written of the Folk (traditional) — Urban (modern) continuum. Each of these dichotomies are challenged by the central thesis of this book, but none more so than the *Gemeinschaft-Gesellschaft* dichotomy of the German sociologist, Ferdinand Tönnies.[4]

He described a fundamental social divide which he believed existed between face-to-face rural communities and the specialised associations of people living in industrial society:

> There is a contrast between a social order which, being based upon consensus of wills, rests on harmony and is developed and ennobled by folkways, mores and religion, and an order which being based upon a union of rational wills, rests on convention and agreement, is safeguarded by political legislation, and finds its ideological justification in public opinion.[5]

Community is the usual English translation of *Gemeinschaft* and in this context it is to be taken as meaning a small *territorial* unit, in which face-to-face social relationships were of fundamental importance. Tönnies' harmonic consensus of wills turns out to be a euphemism for patriarchal authority, not only in the literal sense within the family and family-enterprise, but also in respect of the manorial lord in his relation to the community as a whole. A conflict between Tönnies' view of the old, traditional society of village and small town and my own distinction between the estate and peasant systems is soon apparent, for the latter dichotomy separates the manorial lord from the household-peasant enterprise. This difference of approach may result at least partially from differences between German and English society in the nineteenth century.[6]

Nevertheless Gemeinschaft is a useful concept, more particularly as Obelkevich, in a highly relevant study of religious life in nineteenth-century Lincolnshire, has made good use of Merton's derivative term *pseudo-Gemeinschaft* to describe the attempt at solidarity between the new style capitalistic farmer and his labourers.[7]

*Gesellschaft* is variously translated as association, or society, or organisation. A Gesellschaft is large scale, it is not based on any precise idea of territoriality, but upon the association of people in specialist, capitalist organisations, such as joint stock companies and professional bodies, widely scattered, in residential terms, through the industrial population in general. Agreements take the form of contracts rather than the unwritten, often unspoken understandings of traditional societies. People are less well known to each other and therefore there is mistrust where there would be confidence in a Gemeinschaft. As if in compensation, there is freedom for individuals to go their own ways in a Gesellschaft for they are no longer bound by the interdependence of the Gemeinschaft. The estate system in nineteenth-century England could be described as the cutting edge of modernisation in the countryside, representing rational will, large-scale capitalism and contract, in place of the expectation of a patriarchal society conducted on the principles of traditionalism. It will also be possible to show, conversely, that not everything in the large industrial towns fitted the Gesellschaft mould, since working-class districts frequently exhibited the Gemeinschaft-like characteristic of communal solidarity.[8]

Some readers may consider this exposure of the Gemeinschaft-Gesellschaft dichotomy as a time-wasting diversion. In the long run perhaps this is so, but for the moment consider how much of Tönnies' thinking expresses more explicitly the deeply held attitudes to rural (and urban) society of men like Streatfield whose model began this chapter. It is only fair, however, to point out that Tönnies himself recognised certain exceptions to his generalisations. Of particular interest to us are two statements each modifying one of his concepts. Gemeinschaft-like relationships could break down in rural communities in circumstances where *feudal* lords have taken advantage of their powerful positions, e.g. to appropriate areas of woodland waste for their sole use:

> In reality, Gemeinschaft-like conditions may persist where they have existed before. But pressure and resistance, which correspond to domination on the one hand and dependence on the other, will also continue and be constantly renewed if domination can assert itself by virtue of the superiority of large over small landed property.[9]

In other words, although in Gemeinschaft conditions the lord should act on behalf of the community's best interests, there was always the possibility of self-interest predominating. The best check against this tendency was for the peasantry to be owner-occupiers, thus independent of the lord's close control. Had Tönnies studied England, rather than Germany, there is a possibility, therefore, that he would have recognised the estate and peasant systems as separate entities.

Turning to his qualification of Gesellschaft-like conditions in the towns, it is significant that Tönnies remarked on their more rapid spread in economic than in social relationships, and among the upper classes compared with the working class:

> The common people are similar to women and children in that to them family life, along with neighbourhood and friendship, both of which are closely related to family life, is life in and of itself. Among . . . the educated classes . . . these relations disappear more and more as the rational freedom of the individual comes to the fore.[10]

This statement has implications for the study of working-class neighbourhoods in the great industrial towns of the late nineteenth century. Supposing that Gemeinschaft-like social relationships can be traced there, is it possible to say that these had been brought to the town from the countryside whence such large numbers of people had migrated?

**Open and Closed Villages**

To supplant a series of dichotomies long used by sociologists with yet another dichotomy, in other words the estate and peasant systems, is perhaps a hazardous procedure. Nevertheless, many nineteenth-century writers, despite their middle and upper-class origins, recognised some such distinction, especially when they had cause to write about villages (or parishes or townships). Poor law specialists were particularly fond of a model, implicit for the most part, based on the contrast between 'open' and 'close' or 'closed' villages.

Briefly expressed, this model stated that there was a dichotomy of social structure and, therefore, of poor law administration in rural England during the first six or seven decades of the century. Closed villages were those controlled by either a single landowner or a small group of like-minded men who wished to keep down the level of poor rates and exert a powerful social control over the labouring classes. Rates were not levied upon owners but, as now, upon *occupiers* of property. However, parish poor rates could rise so high as to affect the ability of tenant farmers to pay their rents or, even in extreme cases, to keep themselves in business. Landowners were motivated socially, as well as economically, for as the principal owners of cottage properties they could control not only the quantity of population, but also the *quality*, in other words only the law-abiding, deferential and morally sound of the labourers were welcome.

Open villages were those in which it was impossible for the gentry and clergy to exert a close control and to them might be added most of the towns, especially the large towns. This arose out of the division of property between a multiplicity of owners, many of whom had an incentive to put up cottage properties, either because they were engaged in the building trades or because their businesses stood, on balance, to gain from an influx of population. It is often said, though seldom substantiated in detail, that some large landowners actually demolished cottages on their estates in their pursuance of the policy of social control and the minimisation of the poor rates. However, in a period of rapidly rising population, such as 1780 to 1850, it only required the estate owners to maintain a static number of cottages for the population and poor rates of defenceless open villages to rise by leaps and bounds.

Evidence will be presented later to show that this dichotomy, so widely accepted by contemporaries, was in practice only a generalised or idealised form of reality. Poor rates did not always correlate with the number of owners in a parish. The distinction between open and closed was not always a sharp one. Circumstances varied between one period and another and, more particularly, from one part of England to another. Nevertheless, the model is a useful one because, although based initially on poor law administration, it highlights a common distinction between villages belonging to the estate system and those which were part of the peasant system. It sums up differences over a wide range of economic, demographic, social, religious and political data. There is some point, therefore, in enquiring whence the model sprang into existence.

A precise answer would require a more thorough search than has been made by the present author and this search would probably be concentrated in the first instance on the poor law literature, especially parliamentary reports and debates, in the first two decades of the century. The earliest thorough discussion of open and closed parishes in an official paper which I have found occurs in the 1834 report which led to the amendment of the poor law (but not the abolition of parish rating which continued until 1865). The context is a reference back to the Act 59 George III c. 12 (1819) which facilitated but did not originate the institution of closed or select vestries. It is stated that 'Vestries are either open, composed of all the rate-payers who choose to attend; or representative, appointed by virtue of a local Act or under the 59

George III c. 12; or self-appointed, either by prescription or a local Act.'
Under the 1819 Act, 'the inhabitants of any parish (were authorised),
in vestry assembled, to elect not more than twenty or less than five
substantial householders, who, together with the minister, churchwardens and overseers, after having been appointed by a magistrate,
are to form the select vestry of the parish'.[11]

Two important points arise out of this discussion of vestries. First,
the discussion is of vestries, not parishes or villages. The mere fact of
the vestry being select did not of itself make the parish closed, although
it could be said to facilitate it. More significantly perhaps is that select
vestries had been in operation in some parishes since 'time immemorial'
by virtue of a faculty from the diocesan bishop or through a local Act.
The Webbs even go as far as to suggest that some open vestries had
been instituted as a reaction to the closedness of select vestries.[12] As
in much of English history it becomes difficult to pinpoint changes and
developments with exactness.

Although intense discussion of poor law administration began only
at the end of the eighteenth century, the seeds of village differentiation
had been sown long before, not only because differentiation as to
ownership was a feature of centuries before the nineteenth, but also
because of the nature of the Elizabethan poor law. This encoded the
long accepted custom of the responsibility of a parish (or township) for
its own poor, a principle endorsed by the 1662 Act which began the
system of settlement certificates. These certificates made possible, at
least in theory, a greater degree of labour mobility because the home
parish promised to support the migrant should he fall on hard times in
the parish where he found work.[13] The early nineteenth-century situation, then, had such deep roots that it is no surprise to find Holderness
reporting, as one of the earliest references to close villages, R. North,
*A Discourse on the Poor* (London, 1753, but probably written before
1690), in terms which would have seemed perfectly familiar to an early
nineteenth-century reader:

> . . . Gentlemen of late years have taken up an Humour of Destroying
> their [the People's] Tenements and Cottages, whereby they make it
> impossible that Mankind should inhabit upon their Estates. This is
> done sometimes barefaced, because they harbour the Poor that are a
> charge to the Parish (p. 51).[14]

## Notes

1. Champion = Champaign (Old French, champaigne), open, unenclosed country. This paragraph and the next one are based mainly on B.K. Roberts, *Rural Settlement in Britain* (Dawson, Folkestone, 1977), pp. 15-23 and D.R. Mills (ed.), *English Rural Communities: The Impact of a Specialised Economy* (Macmillan, London, 1973), Chs. 2, 3 and 10. See also W.G. Hoskins, *The Making of the English Landscape* (Hodder and Stoughton, London, 1955), Ch. 2.

2. See, for example, J.B. Harley, 'Population Trends and Agricultural Developments from the Warwickshire Hundred Rolls of 1279' in A.R.H. Baker, J.D. Hamshere and J. Langton (eds.), *Geographical Interpretations of Historical Sources: Readings in Historical Geography* (David and Charles, Newton Abbot, 1970), pp. 55-70.

3. On the 'parish-line', dividing multi-township parishes from single-township parishes; see Dorothy Sylvester, *The Rural Landscape of the Welsh Borderland: a Study in Historical Geography* (Macmillan, London, 1969), pp. 166-7. See also R.A. Dodgshon and R.A. Butlin (eds.), *An Historical Geography of England and Wales* (Academic Press, London, 1978), pp. 100-1.

4. There is a comprehensive survey of these dichotomies in John C. McKinney's essay which appears in the introduction of the American edition of Tönnies' *Gemeinschaft und Gesellschaft* – F. Tönnies, *Community and Society* (Harper Torchbook editions, New York, 1963), translated and edited by Charles P. Loomis, pp. 12-29. Elsewhere my references are to the British edition: F. Tönnies, *Community and Association* (Routledge, London, 1955), translated and supplemented by Charles P. Loomis.

5. Tönnies, *Community and Association*, p. 261.

6. Ibid., especially pp. 3-9, 16-23, 37-9 and 43-69.

7. J. Obelkevich, *Religion and Rural Society: South Lindsey 1825-1875* (Clarendon Press, Oxford, 1976), pp. 59-60.

8. Tönnies, *Community and Association*, especially pp. 3-9, 16-23, 37-9 and 74-116.

9. Ibid., pp. 66-7.

10. Ibid., p. 193.

11. BPP 1834 XXVIII, *Reports from the Commissioners on Poor Laws*, Main Report, pp. 107 and 113.

12. S. and B. Webb, *English Local Government: English Poor Law History, Part I: the Old Poor Law* (Longman, London, 1927), pp. 173-8, 182, 189, 211 and 243.

13. V.D. Lipman, *Local Government Areas 1834-1945* (Basil Blackwell, Oxford, 1949), pp. 25-6; and T. Mackay, *A History of English Poor Law: III, 1834 to the Present Time* (P.S. King and Son, London, 1899), pp. 13 and 16.

14. B.A. Holderness, ' "Open" and "Close" Parishes in England in the Eighteenth and Nineteenth Centuries', *Agric. Hist. Rev.*, vol. 20 (1972), p. 128.

# 2 THE ESTATE SYSTEM

'Cotesbach lordship contains 1,100 acres of land, old inclosure. Robert Marriott, LL.D. owns the whole, who is lord of the manor. You see but little of this village in your approach towards it, it being shaded by a number of large trees. It consists of about 18 dwellings; there is no public house here, or tradesman an inhabitant. The Doctor, if he should chuse to govern, may give laws to all that breathe in this place, and indeed, the cattle in the field are subject to his controul; for not only all the land owns him for its lord, but every dwelling also; the patronage of the church, and the living, are all his own.' John Throsby, *Select Views in Leicestershire* (Leicester and London, 1791), vol. 2, p. 217.

This description of Cotesbach, a parish in south Leicestershire, was recorded about 1790 by John Throsby, writing inevitably for the upper-class readers who would recognise Cotesbach as the ideal estate which many country gentlemen dreamed of owning. There were no petty free-holders to ruin the totality of economic and social control; there were no tradesmen to take on labour which might be laid off onto the poor rates; there was no public house to attract poachers and other country ruffians. As Dr. Marriott was the 'squarson' there was even no parson to exercise his 'freehold' and wag a reproving finger towards the squire from the pulpit. In the length and breadth of England there were relatively few estates which gave their owners such a totality of control, but there were many which could approach this standard. This chapter analyses the estate system on a somewhat similar ideal basis: first in a very generalised fashion; then through the medium of case studies of two specific estates, those centring on Lockinge in Berkshire and Doddington Park in Cheshire (for locations see Figure 1.1).

## Analysis of the Estate System

It is important to recognise that in the estate system we are looking at a thoroughly modern institution, based on a capitalistic outlook, on profit and loss, on economies of scale. That the large landowners took their social duties seriously, gained prestige from the purchase of country estates and did not get enormous returns on their investments should not prevent us from recognising economic motives. Long before the nineteenth century, the English gentry had been playing a crucial role in the economic development of the country.[1] It might even be difficult to show that there had ever been in England the sharp social divide between gentlemen and merchants which was common in the rest of Europe.[2]

A further introductory point is that the essence of this book is to see the estate and peasant systems in constant contrast to each other. While the estates were based on the exploitation of large amounts of capital and land, the peasant system was one in which the units of ownership were very small and enterprises were very modest, if not under-capitalised. Broadly speaking, this is the same contrast as the present day distinction between big business and the self-employed. While the gentry put relatively little personal labour into the running of their estates, and this only at a higher managerial level, peasant enterprises depended to a considerable degree upon family labour as well as management. This combination of family labour and capital is a crucial criterion, for it distinguishes the peasant not only from the squire, but also from the large tenant farmer on an estate, the farm labourer and the salaried professional. The typical estate tenant, at least in corn-growing areas, was a man of substantial means whose enterprise depended on hired labour; many such farmers did little or no manual work. The labourer, like the salaried professional, did not risk his own capital; indeed the labourer generally had none to risk or otherwise he would have joined the peasantry.

Although all the principal families had town houses, mostly in London or Bath, the real centre of each estate was the country mansion. In a society in which status followed upon the acquisition of landed property until well into the nineteenth century, it was necessary not merely to buy or build a mansion, but to surround it with a great number of appendages spread out over at least one township and often more. For example, the Tollemache estate north of Ipswich extended into Framsden, Gosbeck, Ashbocking, Pettaugh and Otley as well as the home village of Helmingham.[3]

Characteristically, mansions were surrounded by parks, including, for example, the 188 places where Humphrey Repton worked in the period 1789-1817.[4] Around the biggest mansions, such as Woburn, Knowsley and Welbeck the parks are still over 2,000 acres.[5] Beyond the park there were sometimes great avenues of trees, as at Wimpole in Cambridgeshire, fox coverts, woods and many hedgerow trees in and around the tenants' fields. The model village, the lodges at the park gates, the folly or mausoleum on the hill top, the pleasure gardens, the home farm, the kitchen gardens, opportunities for hunting, shooting and fishing represented by stables, kennels, ornamental lakes and so forth, were all part of a grand design to impress visiting relatives and rivals.

It is not unusual to find that there is no village near the great house. The reason could be that the house marks the site of a lost village or a fresh start had been made well away from an old manor house site in the nearest village. Alternatively, the village may have been moved away from the house, as at Wimpole (Cambs.), Normanton (Rutland) and Canwick (Lincs.) or has been extinguished altogether, as is the case with Acton Reynold (Salop).[6] The tradition of planned villages had an impact on urban development too and a direct link has been made in Northumberland between estate villages in agricultural areas and villages for miners and forestry workers, the latter built at Byrness and Keilder by the Forestry Commission in the present century.[7]

Apart from being areas of conspicuous consumption, the estates had to be productive. The agricultural policy of the great estates during the eighteenth and nineteenth century is well known.[8] Farm sizes were gradually increased and tenant farmers with plenty of capital were selected to keep the land in good heart through rotations and other practices, such as not selling manure off the farm, that were laid down in the agreements. In return, the landlord carried out improvements to buildings, roads and other permanent features of the farm, so providing the fixed capital. The emphasis of the estate system upon the use of large amounts of capital and land is probably seen at its best in the development of large tenant farms. They presented opportunities for economies of scale, including economies in labour. This is partly because capital was used on labour-saving machinery, since, for example, many of the most labour intensive crops, such as hops, fruit, potatoes and vegetables, as well as dairying were left in large measure to small-holders, market-gardeners, cottage-farmers and cowkeepers.

The same land provided the landed classes with scope for their passion for field sports. Many upland areas of moorland were more valued for pursuits such as grouse shooting than they were for sheep farming. During the late nineteenth-century depression, they were joined by some of the poorer areas in lowland England, for instance in the Cotswolds and the Norfolk Breckland, where game and rabbits came to be more highly valued than crops.[9]

An interest in the improvement of communications, whether turnpike, river navigation, canal or railway was common to many estate owners, because such developments required the use of land and, on balance, could be seen to increase the value of the estates they served.[10] Indeed the Duke of Bridgewater's need to commission Brindley to build a canal to connect his coalmines with their market is one of the best-known episodes of the industrial revolution. Many improvements required private Acts of Parliament and even where the tradesmen of a town promoted the scheme they were dependent to some extent upon friends in Parliament. In this case the urban or commercial system of the country had to invoke the co-operation of the estate system which dominated the legislature, even after the 1832 Reform Act. The use of capital and land, as against labour, can also be noted in the improvement of communications, by comparing the weights one man and a horse could move in a barge, or three men in charge of a goods train could pull, with the maximum of about four tons in a road wagon, drawn perhaps by as many as eight horses, in the charge of two men.

Landlords like the Duke of Bridgewater were encouraged to develop the mineral resources on their estates by virtue of an oft-quoted court decision in 1568, that mineral rights were vested in landowners and not, as on the continent, in the Crown, with the exception of gold and silver.[11] Although there are a few instances of direct involvement, many landlords from the seventeenth century were leasing their mines to secondary entrepreneurs and by the nineteenth century their connection with the industry had been reduced almost to a matter of receiving royalties. Nevertheless, over a period of several centuries the landed classes actively promoted mineral exploitation on and under their estates. There is a large literature giving support to this generalisation from most of the mineralised areas of the country.[12] However, it is important to recognise that in some circumstances, such as the free-miners of the Forest of Dean, leadminers in the Pennines and squatters on commons in Shropshire, mining also represented an opportunity for small-scale enterprises within the peasant system.[13]

Timber was another important resource on estates,[14] as noted below at Lockinge. Most tree-planting schemes appear to have been the work of large landowners, a tradition probably going back to the thirteenth-century statutes which allowed manorial lords to enclose waste land.[15] The long-term nature of forestry enterprises, even after the introduction of quick growing conifers, made them suited to the entailed estates and equally unsuited to the man with little land or capital. Similarly, estates frequently contained stone quarries, clay pits used for brick and tile-making, and lime pits used for building-lime and fertiliser. Manufacturing interests were generally limited to the metal industries and other activities which were connected with the exploitation of land and minerals and it is rare to find mention of cotton mills and weaving shops.[16] A good example of vertical integration in the running of a great estate arises out of the ownership of the Swan Brewery at Buckingham by the Dukes of Buckingham. This was re-leased in 1863 to a brewer who agreed to brew not less than a given amount of ale, using not less than 200 quarters of malt, the implication being that this would encourage the use of locally grown barley. Attached to the brewery lease were the leases of eight tied houses in the town and several more in nearby villages, thus extending integration up to the eventual consumer, with some incidental benefits available at election times.[17]

The older style histories of nineteenth-century England stressed the usefulness of estates as the bases of political coercion and patronage. It is certainly the case that many aristocratic houses liked to put forward family candidates for parliamentary seats close to their estates. They usually liked to feel that the tenant farmers on these estates, small freeholders who depended on it for trade or extra fields to rent and, later in the century, labourers on the estate all voted for their preferred candidate. However, the extent of landlordly influence on the pattern of voting in small towns and even villages has been brought into question by recent writers who have shown that politics were more complicated than unthinking deference.[18]

Finally, but by no means the least, were the landowners' interests in urban development. Although based in the countryside, the landed classes took a keen interest in the growth of towns especially when they reached a stage where large amounts of land were involved. In London this stage was reached at least by the eighteenth century, where building occurred, for example, on land belonging to the Dukes of Bedford in Bloomsbury[19] and to the Russell, Grosvenor, Cavendish and Harley families in the areas which still bear these names.[20] In the nineteenth century, as urbanisation intensified and lower housing densities were achieved, exploitation of the freehold of urban land by large and small owners alike became a commonplace.[21]

One of the disadvantages of a general survey such as this is the difficulty of differentiation between large and small estates, different levels of the gentry and aristocracy and so on. The function of the two accounts of individual estates which follow is partly to make some inadequate compensation; but it is also an opportunity to create a more concrete image of the estate system. The two estates have been chosen with the deliberate aim of achieving some contrast between different parts of the country and especially between champion and hamlet England.

## The Lockinge Estate

This description is based on a single source, the book *Estate Villages* written by Michael Havinden and his colleagues in the 1960s, in which they also describe the estate as it was in the twentieth century down to the time of their investigations.[22] I have, however, rearranged their data to suit a different purpose and made use of a series of topic headings, similar to those found also in Chapters 3 and 5.

The Lockinge estate is situated on the Berkshire Downs, where township boundaries create long, narrow north-south rectangles of land each containing portions of clay vale, malmstone (greensand) and chalk. The estate took in the greater part of the six townships which comprised the parishes of Ardington and Lockinge (Figures 2.1 and 2.2). Even after enclosure the majority of the population continued to live in the larger nucleated settlements of East Lockinge and Ardington and the smaller nuclei of West Lockinge and West Ginge.

### The Land

One atypical feature of the estate was that its formation did not occur until the middle of the nineteenth century. In this part of champion England, enclosure also came late, to Lockinge in 1853 and Ardington in 1811, and may have been held up by the survival of significant numbers of small owners. Equally, one could argue that they owed their survival to the absence of a leading manorial lord bent on enclosure.

Passing over the earlier history of landownership, the nucleus of the Lockinge estate was established when Lewis Loyd, a London banker and his son, Samuel Jones Loyd (later Lord Overstone), bought some land there as an investment in 1854. It was Overstone's daughter's marriage in 1859 to Colonel Lindsay, later Loyd-Lindsay and Lord Wantage, which set the family on the path of major land acquisition. The chief acquisitions were the Ardington estate in 1861 and the Betterton estate in 1890 (Figure 2.2), which lay between the two main blocks of the original estate. With other similar purchases Lord Wantage became the sole owner of a contiguous area of about 5,500 acres. The total area owned by Lord Wantage in Berkshire in 1873 was 20,500 acres, the largest estate, occupying about one twentieth of the county.[23]

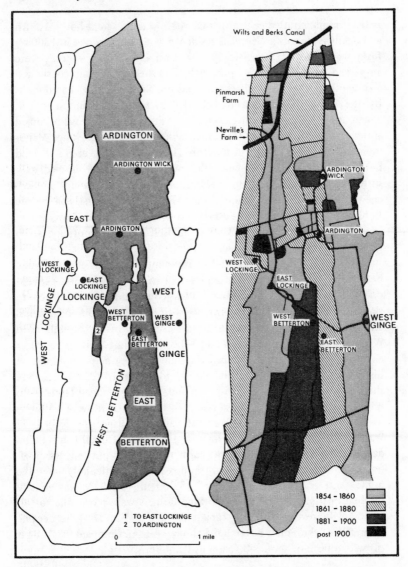

Figure 2.1: (left) The Lockinge Estate, Berkshire. Township boundaries and Domesday manors
Source: Based on Map 12 of M.A. Havinden, *Estate Villages* (Lund Humphries, London, 1966). Drawn by Brian Loughborough. Copyright Reading University.

Figure 2.2: (right) The Lockinge Estate, Loyd Purchases
Source: Based on Map 15 of Havinden, *Estate Villages*. Drawn by Brian Loughborough. Copyright Reading University.

The administrative centre of this estate was the great house known as Lockinge Manor, a Georgian residence, with wings added in 1860 by Lord Wantage. Characteristically, the central parts of the estate were emparked, giving the family privacy behind shelter belts and copses and a romantic backcloth to the house and the social activities based on it. By the 1880s the parks were extended to form a continuous block, which appears from the current Ordnance Survey map to have occupied about half a square mile. This block links the site of Lockinge Manor (demolished 1947) with Ardington House, acquired in 1861, and Betterton House (1890), now the owner's residence. Immediately surrounding the manor there were probably pleasure grounds and kitchen gardens, for there were already four gardeners in 1851 before Lord Wantage came. Over the estate as a whole game would have had an importance, although Lord Wantage himself did not shoot, and seven gamekeepers were still employed in 1961.[24]

While it has been suggested that country landowners put game before agriculture and were often content to get a return of 2 per cent on their investment,[25] nevertheless it was common practice for them to revise the tenancies of their farms so as to acquire a group of progressive tenant farmers, thus ensuring a better return on capital. Lord Wantage's smaller predecessors had been pursuing this policy. For example, Robert Vernon reduced the number of principal holdings on his Ardington estate from eight in 1831 to four in 1842, at which date the 13 principal farms in Ardington and Lockinge ranged from 70 to 830 acres, with a median of about 260. In 1854 there were 14 farms in the hands of 11 men, but from 1863 and more especially 1879 Lord Wantage began to take land in hand to farm himself. As the depression deepened, he extended his home farm rather than put tenants on an uneconomic rent. This was an unorthodox policy, particularly when the home farm reached an acreage of 15,000 in 1895. He was equally unusual in thinking that small working farmers were more able to survive the depression than big tenant farmers and in 1885 he became chairman of the Small Farm and Labourers' Land Company, starting it off with a farm of about 400 acres at Lambourn.[26]

## Population

In 1851, the population of Lockinge and Ardington was 728, representing a density of about 84 persons per square mile. No comparable figures are available for surrounding villages, but the average for a broadly similar area in Lincolnshire was over 120 persons per square mile, suggesting that the Lockinge estate was below average, but not as thinly populated as the many estates situated in lost village country. So far as trends are concerned, the estate was typical of much of rural England. From a total of 650 in 1801 it climbed to 850 in 1881, with an earlier sub-maximum in 1841, and from 1891 it declined continuously to 1961.[27]

*Occupations*

In 1851 the occupations of Lockinge men were overwhelmingly agricultural, with 206 farmworkers, 12 farmers and only 24 craftsmen and traders. This shows a high ratio of labourers to farmers (17:1) as one would expect on an estate of large farms and the small range of non-agricultural occupations which was also a typical feature. The picture was changed by the establishment of an estate yard at Ardington, which employed more than 100 men in 1907.[28] This activity helps to explain why the population recovered from its downward trend after 1841. It is important to recognise that the craftsmen employed by the estate were not running their own independent businesses, as was the case in many open villages. Instead, they were employees of the estate, who undertook construction and repair work all over the property of Lord Wantage, in some cases using home-produced materials, such as timber. The estate yard emphasises the central place function of Ardington and Lockinge within the 20,000 acres of the whole estate.

*Housing*

A visit to the Lockinge estate today reveals cottage styles characteristic of many estates, especially in the village of East Lockinge. Here part of the village was removed from the street close to the manor house and the land which had been cleared was turned into a picturesque rock garden in the Romantic tradition. In this way the privacy of Lord Wantage was increased and the landscaping of his grounds was improved. The old houses were replaced with model cottages on the west side of Lockinge Street. Men from the estate yard rebuilt most of the ten villages on the estate and even in the 1920s the housing conditions were still good by the standards of the day, mostly containing three good-sized bedrooms.[29]

*Poor Rates and Settlement Laws*

By the middle of the nineteenth century, when the Lockinge estate proper was formed, both the controversies over the poor and the population increases which exacerbated them had spent most of their force. Consequently, there is very little data to be gained from this corner of Berkshire on this subject. However, it is worth recording the fact that Lady Wantage, true to the style of this type of family, always sent soup and milk puddings to anyone who was ill. This kind of benevolence also had the advantage of keeping down the poor rates.[30]

## Religion

It was usual for estate owners to take an active interest in their parish church and to do their best to exclude nonconformity. There is evidence of both these policies at Lockinge.

Lord Wantage was eventually able to buy both advowsons, which had formerly been non-resident cures. At East Lockinge he acquired the advowson from All Souls' College in 1873 and presumably installed a resident clergyman of his own choice. At Ardington there was a resident vicar from 1840 onwards, when Christ Church College built a vicarage, but the living was poorly endowed until it was bought by Lord Wantage and augmented in 1885. Having provided regular services, Lord and Lady Wantage expected estate residents to attend church twice each Sunday.

On dissenting chapels, Havinden states plainly that none could be built in either village, presumably because Lord Wantage would neither sell nor lease any land for this purpose. Interestingly, as late as 1961, only two inhabitants said they were nonconformist and one other a Roman Catholic, the remainder being nominal or practising Anglicans.[31]

## Social Activities and Social Services

Havinden records a considerable amount of information under this heading, which can be summarised quite briefly to make one main point: that the initiative in this field was monopolised by Lord Wantage. He built a new school in each village in 1861. Lockinge had no public house and one of the two in Ardington was closed, while the other one was taken over by Lord Wantage and the publican replaced by a manager on a fixed salary. From the profits, street-lighting was provided, at what must have been a remarkably early date for a village of this size, and the more usual facility of a reading room. A savings bank was set up, no doubt partly to meet a practical need, but also with a sharp eye to moral possibilities. In 1873 this was supplemented by a sub-agency of the Berkshire Friendly Society, which proved very popular in an age long before the welfare state. Another important welfare scheme was the provision of allotments; in 1889 there were 1,360 allotments on the *whole* estate, averaging a quarter of an acre each.

All these social activities were part of the usual stock-in-trade of the good resident landlord of the time, but Lord Wantage had further, unorthodox and, in some ways, radical ideas about improving rural life. We have already noted his desire to set up small farms where possible. At the other end of the scale, on his own huge farm, he introduced a system of bonus payments in 1887, the general principle of which is still used on the estate. He also started a village co-operative society with his own capital, but otherwise operating on the Rochdale system. It provided the villages with good quality meat, groceries, coal and its own bread. Here again he anticipated later developments, for although the co-operative system was well known by this time, he could see that the small independent village shopkeeper would be hard put to compete with large urban firms. While many village shops were sinking in a sea of debt, Lord Wantage took effective action to provide a viable alternative.[32]

## Politics

Despite some radical views, Lord Wantage was an active Tory, a Berkshire MP from 1865-1885, Financial Secretary to the War Office in Disraeli's ministry (1877-80) and a strong supporter of the Conservatives in the Lords from 1885. He was also a leader in county politics. It is not surprising that his social philosophy should attract attention from his political opponents. The Liberal *Daily News* sent their special commissioner to Ardington and Lockinge while he was producing the series of articles published as *Life in our Villages*. The article on Lockinge was printed in the issue for 25 September 1891, under the title *Arcadia Realised*.

The author acknowledged that the life of the village was on a material plane well above the usual experience of rural England at that time. But the spirit of benevolent Toryism was criticised and it was suggested that, instead, the people ought to be able collectively to manage their own affairs and welfare. Where the capital was to come from was not explained. However, there is little doubt about the conclusion that practically every elector voted for Lord Wantage and his party and that the social control exercised by him and his bailiff, while benevolent, was very real. In view of the landowner's monopoly, it could hardly have been insubstantial and in this sense Lockinge was characteristic of many other estates at that time.[33]

Figure 2.3: Parish of Wybunbury, Cheshire

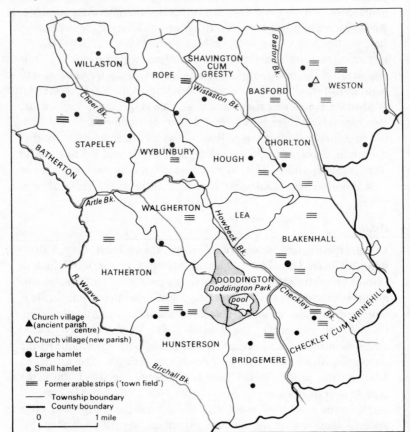

Note: This map shows the townships at the time of the Tithe Survey *c.* 1840

Source: Based on D. Sylvester, *The Rural Landscape of The Welsh Borderland* (Macmillan, London, 1969), Figure 37.


## The Doddington Park Estate

This Cheshire estate differed from the Lockinge estate, not only by being in wood pasture country, but also because it had been built up by the Delves-Broughtons from their purchase of Doddington itself as early as 1353. Miss Sylvester's study based on the tithe surveys of about

1840 revealed that by that date they owned solid blocks of land
amounting to nearly 6,000 acres in the townships of Doddington,
Batherton, Blakenhall, Chorlton, Hunsterson, Lea and Rope in which
they were the sole owners. They were also the principal owners in the
642-acre township of Basford and owners of varying scale in all the
remaining ten townships which made up Wybunbury parish in that
period (see Figure 2.3).[34]

Miss Sylvester states that the main perceptible effect of the Delves-
Broughton family was:

> . . . in the great park at Doddington, which occupies the greater
> portion of Doddington township and extends into Hunsterson,
> Walgherton and Bridgemere. It is a characteristic Cheshire park in
> that it is predominantly ornamental, containing a large lake and
> some grazing herds. The rest of Doddington township includes the
> Home Farm, the Mill, two Lodges, another farm and a few small
> holdings. There is no estate village and no indication of there ever
> having been a community or communal land organisation, though
> both may have existed and been swamped by the landowning
> interest, for the Town Fields of Walgherton and Hunsterson are
> traceable within the bounds of the park on the Tithe Map. In every
> sense, the pattern of the Estate type of township is clear and dis-
> tinctive. The same type is common in Cheshire and found especially
> on the margins of the woodland zone.[35]

As at Lockinge, it was the central part of the estate which had been
emparked. Another common characteristic was the way in which the
estate spread over several townships. It is important to recognise that
many of the larger family seats required much more for their support
than a single township, even a relatively big one of several thousand
acres. Consequently there were many townships which had an absentee
landlord, though when he lived at only a short distance his influence is
likely to have been far greater than when he lived in another county,
which was not unusual.

The absence of a village at Doddington is also worth remarking
upon. In this instance there is some possibility that neither a village nor
a hamlet (i.e. a town in the old terminology) had ever existed. Even in
areas where 'towns' had been founded, it is not out of the ordinary to
find that they had disappeared before the nineteenth century, though
whether the building up of an estate was the cause or the result is an
entirely different question.

Finally, Miss Sylvester's comment about the apparent correlation between estates and the margins of the woodland zone should be noted, especially as she has cited Calveley, Peckforton and Hurdsfield as other Cheshire examples.[36] It could be that wood-pasture areas presented equal opportunities to both medieval estate owners and the peasantry. Where the gentry settled they may have been able to rid themselves of responsibilities to an orthodox manorial community, just as the peasantry could cast off their servile status. If this is the case, it would support Macfarlane's thesis concerning the early origins of individualism.[37]

## Notes

1. This theme has been developed by a number of recent writers including: H. Perkin, *The Origins of Modern English Society 1780-1880* (Routledge, London, 1969), p. 74; E. Kamenka and R.S. Neale (eds.), *Feudalism, Capitalism and Beyond* (Edward Arnold, London, 1975), especially pp. 6 and 93; and G.E. Mingay, *The Gentry: The Rise and Fall of a Ruling Class* (Longman, London, 1976), pp. 97-107. See also D. Cannandine, 'Aristocratic Indebtedness in the Nineteenth Century: the Case Re-opened', *Econ. Hist. Rev.*, vol. 30 (1977), pp. 624-50.

2. A. Macfarlane, *The Origins of English Individualism* (Blackwell, Oxford, 1978), especially pp. 195-9 and H.E. Hallam, 'The Medieval Social Picture' in Kamenka and Neale, especially pp. 40 and 46. The two-century 'gap' between feudalism and capitalism is one of the problems discussed in P. Sweezy et al., *The Transition from Feudalism to Capitalism* (Verso, London, 1978) and there are indications that the role of the countryside – and therefore landowners and farmers, as opposed to merchants – is being recognised as a significant factor in the development of capitalism (see especially pp. 64-5, 147-8 and 195).

3. G.E. Evans, *Where Beards Wag all: The Relevance of the Oral Tradition* (Faber, London, 1970), p. 132. On the gentry estates as centres of conspicuous consumption see Mingay, *The Gentry*, pp. 140-53 and 178-84. For geographical analyses of the landscape of estates see H.C. Prince, 'The Changing Landscape of Panshanger', *East Hertfordshire Archaeological Society Transactions* 4 (1959), pp. 42-56 and H.A. Fuller, 'Landownership and the Lindsey Landscape', *Annals of the Association of Americal Geographers* 66 (1976), pp. 14-24. J.T. Ward, *East Yorkshire Landed Estates in the Nineteenth Century* (East Yorkshire Local History Society, no. 23, 1967) gives some useful geographical data, especially pp. 22-5 for the Constable estate which was based on Burton Constable.

4. For information on parks landscaped by Repton and others see H.C. Prince, 'Parkland in the English Landscape', *Amateur Historian*, vol. 3 (1958), pp. 332-8 and 'Georgian Landscapes' in A.R.H. Baker and J.B. Harley (eds.), *Man Made the Land: Essays in English Historical Geography* (David and Charles, Newton Abbot, 1973), pp. 153-66.

5. W.G. Hoskins, *The Making of the English Landscape* (Hodder and Stoughton, London, 1955), p. 131.

6. Ibid., p. 133-4; D.R. Mills (ed.), *English Rural Communities: The Impact of a Specialised Economy* (Macmillan, London, 1973), p. 93; and T. Rowley, *The Shropshire Landscape* (Hodder and Stoughton, London, 1972), pp. 133-5.

7. R. Newton, *The Northumberland Landscape* (Hodder and Stoughton, London, 1972), pp. 131-6.

8. See, for example, G.E. Mingay, *The Gentry*, pp. 84-5 and 'The Size of Farms in the Eighteenth Century', *Econ. Hist. Rev.*, vol. 15 (1961-2), p. 475.

9. J. Sheail, *Rabbits and their History* (David and Charles, Newton Abbot, 1971), p. 113.

10. F.M.L. Thompson, *English Landed Society in the Nineteenth Century* (Routledge, London, 1963), pp. 157 and 256-63; Mingay, *The Gentry*, pp. 99-103 and J.D. Chambers, 'The Vale of Trent 1670-1800: A Regional Study of Economic Change', *Econ. Hist. Rev.*, Supplement no. 3 (n.d. but *c.* 1957), p. 36.

11. J.U. Nef, *The Rise of the British Coal Industry* (Routledge, London, 1932, 2 vols.) vol. 1, pp. 277-318.

12. See in particular the summaries in J.T. Ward and R.G. Wilson (eds.), *Land and Industry: The Landed Estate and the Industrial Revolution* (David and Charles, Newton Abbot, 1971) and Mingay, *The Gentry*, pp. 98-9.

13. Rowley, *Shropshire*, p. 151-3; W. Cooper, *Laws and Customs of the Miners in the Forest of Dean in the County of Gloucester* (W. Cooper, printer, London, 1687), pp. 4 and 15 and A. Raistrick, *The Pennine Dales* (Eyre and Spottiswode, London, 1969), p. 116 referring mainly to the seventeenth century.

14. Mingay, *The Gentry*, p. 98; see Fuller, 'Lindsey Landscape' for forestry on the Brocklesby estate near Grimsby, pp. 19 and 22.

15. W.E. Tate, *The English Village Community and the Enclosure Movements* (Gollancz, London, 1967), p. 60.

16. Mingay, *The Gentry*, p. 101, gives a sole example in a long list of the industrial and mining activities of the gentry.

17. D.J. Elliott, *Buckingham: The Loyal and Ancient Borough* (Phillimore; London and Chichester, 1975), p. 202.

18. See, for example, R.J. Olney, *Lincolnshire Politics, 1832-1885* (Oxford UP, 1973), especially p. 135 and Mingay, *The Gentry*, p. 119.

19. H.J. Habakkuk, 'Economic functions of English landowners in the seventeenth and eighteenth centuries', *Explorations in Entrepreneurial History*, vol. 6 (1953), p. 98.

20. G.E. Mingay, 'The Large Estate in Eighteenth-Century England', *First International Conference of Economic History, Stockholm* (Moulton, Paris, 1960), p. 382.

21. Ward and Wilson, *Land and Industry*, pp. 38-45.

22. M.A. Havinden, *Estate Villages* (Lund Humphries, London, 1966). This is also undoubtedly the best book on the economic and social history and historical geography of an English estate. I should like to record my thanks to the University of Reading, as copyright holders. Mr. Havinden kindly read this chapter and commented on it. Other examples not already quoted are H. Thorpe 'The Lord and the Landscape' in Mills, *English Rural Communities*, pp. 31-82 which describes the development from early times down to 1963 of Wormleighton, Warwickshire; and A. Harris, *The Rural Landscape of the East Riding of Yorkshire* (2nd edn, S.R. Publications, Wakefield, 1970), especially pp. 73-7 for Sledmere and Howsham. See also D. Roberts, *Paternalism in Early Victorian England* (Croom Helm, London, 1979).

23. Havinden, pp. 31 and 11-12.

24. Ibid, pp. 90 and 137.

25. Thompson, *Landed Society*, p. 252: 'An industrial capitalist who survived for many years with no return on his fixed capital, and eventually began to receive under 2½ per cent would have been a great curiosity in mid-Victorian England.'

26. Havinden, p. 55 and Table 5, pp. 78-9 and 88.

27. Ibid., pp. 98-9; D.R. Mills, 'The Poor Laws and the Distribution of Population, *c.* 1600-1860, with Special Reference to Lincolnshire', *TIBG*, no. 26 (1959), p. 188.

28. Havinden, pp. 62, 69 and 127. On the latter page a figure of 60-70 is quoted.

29. Ibid., pp. 68-9, 95 and 127.

30. Ibid., p. 95.

31. Ibid., pp. 70-1 and 193.

32. Ibid., pp. 68 and 84-9.

33. Ibid., pp. 75-81.

34. D. Sylvester, 'Rural Settlement in Cheshire', *Transactions of the Historic Society of Lancashire and Cheshire*, vol. 101 (1949), pp. 12-17 and *The Rural Landscape of the Welsh Borderland: A Study in Historical Geography* (Macmillan, London, 1969), p. 166-7.

35. Sylvester, 'Rural Settlement in Cheshire', p. 17.

36. Ibid., p. 14.

37. Macfarlane, *Individualism*, p. 163 especially.

# 3

## THE PEASANT SYSTEM

'In my roamings about the downs it is always a relief — a positive pleasure in fact — to find myself in a village which has no squire or other magnificent and munificent person who dominates everybody and everything, and, if he chooses to do so, plays providence in the community.' W.H. Hudson, *A Shepherd'd Life* (1910, Compton Press ed., Tisbury, Wilts., 1978), p. 185.

### Analysis of the Peasant System

In taking the description and analysis of the peasant system a stage further, it is worth repeating that the most important point is not the use of the term 'peasant', but the distinction between the large entrepreneurs, who were part of the estate system, and the small ones who stood outside it within an independent socio-economic system. Once this vital distinction is accepted, there is less difficulty in regarding small cultivators and rural non-cultivators as part and parcel of the same system, with a common set of attitudes.

Nevertheless, it is also necessary to appreciate what is *not* meant by the peasant system, for the simple reason that the word 'peasant' has until recently been used too loosely in the context of English history. For most of the present century economic and social historians have been discussing when and why the English peasantry disappeared, but this debate has been thrown into an entirely different shape by Macfarlane's challenging argument that England may never have had a peasantry, at least not since the thirteenth century.[1] Obviously, such a challenge depends greatly on a careful definition of 'peasantry' and Macfarlane has gone much further by setting up a model of a 'true' peasantry as a yardstick against which various socio-economic systems can be measured and judged. While all the features of the model are unlikely to be found in any one peasantry, the realisation that many were lacking in medieval England makes it all the more necessary to appreciate the special use of the term 'peasant' in relation to nineteenth-century rural England.

Summarised very briefly the twelve features of an idealised peasantry can be described as follows:

(1) Property belongs to households and not to individuals.
(2) Farm labour is family labour.
(3) Commercial life and agricultural life exist as separate systems.
(4) Land seldom comes on the open market.
(5) Every effort is made to keep the family name on particular areas of land.
(6) Geographical mobility is severely limited, being confined mainly to movement from village to town (and not between villages).
(7) Kinship is, therefore, an important characteristic of peasant communities.
(8) Households have a tendency to extend beyond the nuclear group.
(9) They are regulated by a patriarch who is both head of the family and leader of the enterprise.
(10) Despite the large female contribution to the enterprise, female status is low.
(11) Marriage is near-universal, early and 'arranged', the labour supply and the maintenance of family property being dominant over the idea of romantic love.
(12) Peasant societies are less differentiated than capitalist societies.

Items 1, 3, 4, 5, 8, 10 and 11 did not apply to the nineteenth-century English peasant system. In fact, in most cases the reverse applied, e.g. there was a brisk market in small parcels of land in peasant villages. Williams has stressed the very wide difference between family farming communities in England and Wales on the one hand and peasants in Ireland and on the continent on the other. In England and Wales, little importance was attached in most families to keeping the name on the land.[2] The remaining items are partially applicable, in particular item 2, where the family was relatively important as a source of labour. Item 6, geographical mobility, was also probably of some relative significance because families with property in a village had an incentive to stay there longer than either tenant farmers or labourers. It follows that item 7, kinship, might also be important in peasant villages because of relative immobility, as Martin found in such communities in Warwickshire: 'Village society remained closely knit; the unifying factor of family relationship cut across the dividing lines of occupation, status and income.'[3]

Item 9, in principle, must be significant if family labour is also significant, but the degree of patriarchal control is debatable in a society where geographical mobility was so easy, and hiring oneself for

for wages presented possibilities for independence of the family patriarch. The socio-economic differentiation of families in village communities in England (item 12) varied considerably and it is probably a fair generalisation that peasant villages, more especially those in Wales and Scotland, were characterised by lesser degrees of differentiation than villages belonging to great landlords.

It is clear that the Macfarlane model did not, on the whole, apply to the nineteenth-century English peasant system as defined in this book, yet it is helpful to note on which of his indices nineteenth-century entrepreneurs were peasant-like. Likewise, the Chayanovian model based on the late years of Imperial Russia is also useful. It is part of both Macfarlane's and Chayanov's thesis that in a society in which social mobility and social differentiation are lacking, we should not expect to observe a progressive concentration of property into the hands of smaller and smaller numbers of owners. A rough estimate made by Macfarlane is that possibly 50 per cent of English land was in the hands of owner-occupiers in 1600, reducing to 30 per cent in 1700 and about 10 per cent in the nineteenth century. These are circumstances in which the small men are being bought out and the estate system is expanding.

In a peasant society, on the other hand, there is an expectation of a cyclical change in individual peasant holdings, with stability throughout a district or the country as a whole. The young couple starting off without children, or labour other than their own, need a relatively small area for their own subsistence and are unable to cultivate a large area. When the oldest children are of such an age to help, both subsistence needs and labour supply will be greater. Especially in thinly populated areas such as Imperial Russia, it was possible for the family to take on progressively more land as time passed. Older families where the young were leaving the household would be reducing the area they had taken into cultivation, thus making land available for the expanding families in the community. Instead of capital being regarded as a fixed factor of production relative to land and labour as in the capitalist system, 'In a typical peasant economy, labour, proportionate to the size of the family, is the stable element which determined the change in the volume of capital and land.'[4]

In principle, it is possible that some cyclical features could be traced at a general level in English peasant villages in the nineteenth century. Certainly individual instances of rise and decline can be found.[5] For one English parish as a whole, Williams has described how family continuity and the structural instability of farm boundaries have worked to complement each other. This study was particularly concerned with changes at the point of inheritance and the problems of finding holdings for non-inheriting sons. These problems were solved only by virtue of the English disregard for keeping the name on the land. Where farmers had no one in their elementary family to follow them, the tenancy or the land itself came on the market, providing opportunities for non-inheriting sons, labourers and outsiders to enter farming in the parish. This process was accompanied by many alterations in farm boundaries, presumably to shape the holdings to the requirements of incoming occupiers.[6]

What is really required, however, is research on the Chayanovian pattern, in which demographic trends are plotted against the changes in the size and productivity of holdings. Although not impossible, English nineteenth-century data are unhelpful because of the general absence of detailed answers to the question 'who worked for whom?' In a capitalist economy, wage labouring makes it impossible to assume the labour supply available to a peasant family from the statement made to the census enumerator. Further than that, the mixture of labouring work and independent entrepreneurship within a family, or in the case of an individual either seasonally or over his career (or both) was one of the notable features of the English peasant system as here described in the last century.

It is clear then that we cannot expect to find anything approaching a classical peasant economy even on a local basis within nineteenth-century England. Nevertheless a few peasant-like characteristics in the economy of small entrepreneurs who stood outside the estate system lend a distinctiveness to it which can probably be best encapsulated in the term 'peasant system'. For example, while the peasant enterprises were part of the prevailing capitalist system, production for home consumption was relatively more important than in the bigger enterprises.

In addition to using 'peasant' in a particular agricultural sense, an important thesis in this book is the unspecialised nature of the peasant system, for included within it are rural entrepreneurs who were entirely, or at least primarily *non*-agricultural. The inclusion of agricultural and non-agricultural enterprises within the same bracket is justified on the pragmatic grounds that it is very difficult to distinguish clearly between them. Dual occupations were very common in peasant villages and the most frequent combination was that between a smallholding and a non-agricultural pursuit.[7]

To look at these peasants through urban spectacles, classifying them as bricklayers, publicans, 'farmers', cowkeepers, shopkeepers and so forth, would be to miss the point of the unspecialised peasant system. The crucial feature of this system was that units of production were small, whether they got their main income from farming, craftsmanship or the retail trades, or from some combination of occupations. And the unit of production was necessarily small because the amount of capital it could command was also small.

This was sometimes invested in a small piece of property which acted as a base for the peasant enterprise, hence the frequent interest of historians in the owner-occupiers. Close study of the records of a peasant village often reveals, however, that many small properties were not occupied by their owners, who prove to be persons in many walks of life, such as urban shopkeepers, clergymen, distant farmers and, quite often, retired men or single women living on annuities and rents. Thus the small farmer could build up a larger holding, as his family labour and capital expanded, by renting fields and homesteads scattered about the parish. It is also common to find small properties were mortgaged and this may have been a common way of raising liquid capital. The relative cost of the stock-in-trade of a village craftsman should not be underestimated. For example, in 1887, when the property of Joseph Moss, wheelwright of North Collingham, Nottinghamshire, was surveyed for insurance purposes, the wood in stock was valued at £330, while his house was worth only £200.[8]

Characteristically, the nineteenth-century peasant enterprise survived longest in lines of activity where a suitable balance could be struck between labour and capital. When a craft was debased into dispersed wage slavery, as in the wellknown cases of handloom weaving and framework knitting, the factory was not far round the corner and with it the urbanisation of the industry concerned. Some rural crafts survived in their peasant form until they were replaced by more modern equivalents, for example, the wheelwright and the blacksmith; indeed in some cases a modern garage or agricultural engineering business has grown up on their premises.

On the land, the peasant farmer frequently sought out labour-intensive products, because general farming ceased to provide a living on small acreages unless he was able to diversify into a second occupation. For example, the increase of fruit, flower, potato and vegetable growing in the second half of the century was associated with the small-holdings of the Fens. The importance of labour-intensive crops to the freeholders in Oxfordshire has been noted[9] and the splitting-up of large general farms in the Vale of Evesham was one of the factors that contributed to the growth of fruit and vegetable production in that area.[10]

In the grassland areas of the country, where stock raising and dairying were carried on, the size of farms was in any case generally lower than in the areas of general farming with a substantial arable element.[11]

Independence was an important attitude of mind in peasant families. It was noticed, for example, that in the depression of the late nineteenth century, many smallholders in the Fens held on when big tenant farmers were going out of business, even if it sometimes meant net returns less than a labourer's wage.[12] Independence is a word that recurs, for example, in accounts of late nineteenth-century smallholders in the countryside around Evesham[13] and is to be seen in contradistinction to the benevolence, the enlightened despotism of the estate system.

## Local Studies

Although there have been no general studies of the English peasant system in the nineteenth century to compare with the work of Thompson on the landed gentry,[14] there have been more local studies from which to draw material for the present purpose. Ignoring studies of particular aspects of the peasant system — for example, politics and protest — which figure prominently in Chapter 6, the four best documented villages are Headington Quarry near Oxford, Melbourn in Cambridgeshire, Corsley in Wiltshire and Tysoe in Warwickshire.

Headington Quarry was undoubtedly a classic open village but because it was also a squatting settlement of very late origin, it is not a particularly good counterpoint to the other examples chosen. Furthermore, Samuel's study is easily available having been published only in recent years,[15] while the preferred work on Corsley has not been reprinted since 1909.[16]

A similar consideration pointed the way for a choice between Melbourn and Tysoe, both of them in champion England. While my own work on Melbourn has appeared in a number of recent publications,[17] two of the three studies by the Ashbys on Tysoe are inaccessible except through a good library.[18]

## Tysoe

This Warwickshire village lies at the foot of the Edgehill escarpment in a township of about 4,600 acres, stretching westwards from the marlstone scarp face into the Lias clay vale below, also known as the

Vale of the Red Horse. The settlement pattern is clearly nucleated, with few scattered farms, but there are three nuclei, Upper and Middle (Church) Tysoe closely adjacent to each other and Lower (Temple) Tysoe separated from them by about half a mile of open country (see Figure 3.1). In the northern corner of the township is the lost village site of Westcote, while to the south the next parish contains Compton Wynyates, the seat of the Earl (Marquis) of Northampton.[19]

## The Land

With 36 voting freeholders in 1774 Tysoe had more electors than all but two townships (Warwick and Tanworth) out of the 47 in the hundred of Kineton. The land tax assessments reached down below the level of the forty shillings franchise and recorded the rather larger number of 65 proprietors in 1775, 56 in 1778 and 1785 and 69 in 1800. The number of *occupying* owners was 27 in 1795 and 40 in 1800, a very substantial number by any standards.

Nevertheless, the Marquis of Northampton was lord of the manor of Upper and Church Tysoe during the middle of the nineteenth century, and at the enclosure in 1796 the Marquis had been allotted nearly 1,000 acres out of the 2,600 acres allotted by the award. It was not unusual for an absentee landlord to have considerable interests in an open village, just as many estate villages contained a few independent proprietors. Margaret Ashby pointed out that although the Marquis' family were great folk they had never overshadowed or alarmed Tysoe because they were never sole owners, they had frequently been absent and had never held more than two of the four manors in Tysoe.[20] It may be significant that by the standards of its district Tysoe was late in the date of enclosure. Within a radius of 12 miles, 26 parishes had been enclosed in the period 1731-96. 'As a factor determining the date of enclosure, the sub-division of landownership would affect the general development of agriculture, therefore the conditions of life and labour, and, not improbably, those of Settlement as well.'[21]

## Population

A.W. Ashby drew a useful contrast between Tysoe and Compton Wynyates. With a multiplier of 4.5 persons per family, the Domesday population of Compton was 105 and that of Tysoe 374. In 1801 the populations were 41 and 891; one had been more than halved, the other had more than doubled, though of course this does not take account of intermediate fluctuations.

Figure 3.1: Tysoe: the Three Nuclei, from the Enclosure Award Map, 1796

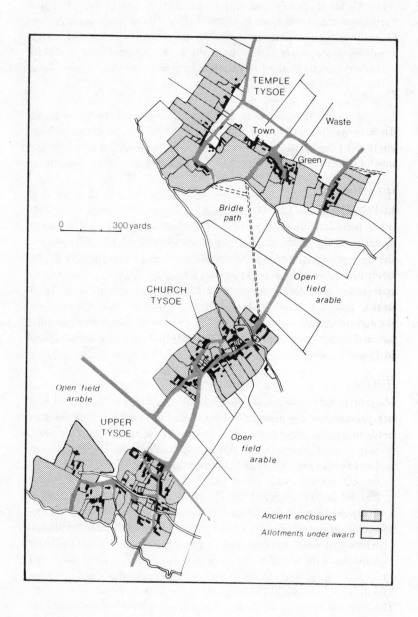

Compton was entirely owned by the Earl of Northampton, lord of the manor of Tysoe, and it seems as though its population was at some period deliberately removed or checked. In spite of the fact that Compton was over one fifth of the size of Tysoe and contained excellent agricultural land under full cultivation, it had practically no labouring population and no heavy poor rate. Thus there can be little doubt that the labour used in the cultivation of Compton came from Tysoe and that in times of unemployment or sickness its poor levies were derived from the same source.[22]

Thus Compton was a small township with a population density of about 30 persons per square mile and Tysoe was a large one with the much higher density of 120 persons per square mile.

## Occupations

In 1826, 30 of the 124 ratepayers in Tysoe were following occupations other than agriculture; there were 91 agriculturalists and three professional persons.[23] *Kelly's Directory of Warwickshire* for 1928 brings out the long-standing contrast between Tysoe and Compton. While the latter had no resident tradesmen or craftsmen, at Tysoe there were two coal merchants, two grocers, a builder, baker, wheelwright, cattle dealer, publican, butcher, boot-maker, blacksmith, boot-repairer and the following dual occupations: carrier and greengrocer; and grocer and cab and garage proprietor. The estate carpenter for Compton also lived in Tysoe.

## Housing

Margaret Ashby described the wretched cottage in which she lived with her parents in the eighties and nineties and summed up the difference between estate cottages and most of those in open villages as follows:

> Landowners and 'smock frock' landlords might be contrasted. Landowners' cottages were of fair size and in good repair, but the tenant had no liberty of mind; the fellow working man who had perhaps inherited a couple of cottages could neither repair his property nor wait for his rent. But he was chiefly to be met with in larger villages where one could hope to change one's cottage, and could call one's mind one's own.[24]

## Poor Rates and Settlement Laws

The contrast between Tysoe and Compton has already been noted for the early nineteenth century; but even in the period around 1890 sharp contrasts between neighbouring villages could be found and some of these were summed up by Joseph Ashby: 'Pauperism is higher in large than small villages', though the full picture in his part of Warwickshire was more complex by that date. It is interesting to note, however, that Tysoe had a Select Vestry in the early part of the century, comprising the 20 biggest farmers, and the shopkeepers were definitely excluded from serving as overseers. A great deal more research could be usefully done on Vestry politics in English villages.[25]

## Religion

Tysoe was a stronghold of nonconformity. A.W. Ashby states that in 1735 a licence was granted for a house in Middle Tysoe to be used as a Quaker meeting house. At the end of the eighteenth century the Methodists were strong and in 1835 there were 135 pupils at the Methodist Sunday School, compared with 86 at the parish church. These children probably went to the Wesleyan Methodist Chapel, but a Primitive Methodist Chapel was also built and in 1898 a meeting room for Plymouth Brethren. Margaret Ashby explains that the 'labourers who could and dared make claims for themselves and their children were Primitive Methodists'. We are left in no doubt that the gentry, large farmers and submissive dependants went to the parish church, the living of which was in the hands of the Marquis of Northampton. The independent ones were nonconformists, Wesleyans in the case of the middling sort of folk, Primitives in the case of the labourers.[26]

## Social Activities and Social Services

In the second half of the century, when memories of Captain Swing faded and as labourers often became literate and hopeful of a modestly better future, friendly societies became more numerous and active. The two main societies in Tysoe were the Court Greenwood Tree of the Foresters, established in 1842 and the Tysoe Club founded in 1857, but following in an older tradition of Sick and Divvi Clubs.

The Tysoe Club was run by the trustees, drawn from the honorary members who all paid a guinea subscription, a figure which excluded the labouring members and put the vicar and the large farmers in control. Its prosperity was recognised, but was accredited to the Marquis' subscription and the interest from the Feoffees' Estate. The annual Club Day coincided with the Saturday before the church's patronal festival, a date on which native Tysoe people returned home from far and wide.

Although it thus identified itself with the whole village, the Club had stiff opposition from the Foresters, an independently minded group of men led, among others, by a master wheelwright. Some of their strength came from affiliation to a national organisation, but much of it was due to the sincerity of their cause. One of their pamphlets argued that 'Dukes and bishops and farmers wanted labourers fed, but not independent. Labourers must lie very low before they could be helped. Gifts might be ropes to tie you down.'

Some of this argument was related to the size of allotments the labourers might be allowed to have, for there were those who feared the labourer might use up his strength there, rather than on his employer's farm. Margaret Ashby tells the story of how in 1893 Tysoe acquired land, not without long years of struggle, to make the Smallholdings and Allotments Association a going concern. It had taken the Compton family many years to be convinced, by Joseph Ashby among others, that the labourer might responsibly feed his family from his own crops.[27]

## Politics

It is important to recognise the benevolence and foresight of men like Lord Wantage, while remembering the downright rottenness of others in his class and among their tenant farmers, but the labourers and small masters saw things from a different point of view. They experienced first hand the grinding poverty of the age, an age in which their towns-men contemporaries appeared to go from strength to strength. The landlord and the labourer looked out on the same landscape, but saw it with different eyes. An acre of land was not particularly important to a marquis who had thousands more, except that he would be careful not to part with it too easily, for how else had his family acquired such a large estate if not by extending it when the opportunity arose? To the labourer, however, an acre allotment, instead of one of ten poles, meant four times as much land and an infinitely better chance of keeping his family fed. It meant independence of charity and poor relief: 'They must never trust another class to do justice without having to.'[28]

Lockinge and Tysoe are well matched, for in their different ways they both sustained important politicians. Joseph Ashby was a labourer who became a small farmer, a Methodist lay preacher, a member of the Court Greenwood Tree, leader of the allotments movement, a trade unionist with Arch,[29] a councillor and, most of all, a Radical. Village leaders like Ashby, Arch and Edwards had far less control over their village than a squire over his, they had to be real leaders of men, earning their support, rather than buying it. They had to convince other leaders in the same village of the rightness of their cause; only in this way could they overcome the always latent village feuds and make progress in a particular direction.

In the early nineties, during his journeys with the Land Restoration League's Red Van in Warwickshire and neighbouring counties, Joseph Ashby observed the social differences between villages:

> He described villages where the labourers never changed into a decent coat, desecrated the Sabbath with leap-frog and tip-cat, where they consented to live in cottages for which they paid six-pence a week, and they not worth it! And others, how different, with smallholdings, associations, temperance clubs, branches of the Union, gay and fruitful gardens.[30]

In close villages they had many unfriendly, even rough receptions, which reminded him of Joseph Arch's visit to Tysoe in 1872, when the vicar and the marquis' agent had made their opposition clear, even to the point of threatening not to employ any union men. On a similar occasion Lord Wantage warned his employees about the specious promises being made from the Red Van in Berkshire.[31]

### Corsley

This was the parish of 3,056 acres in the western corner of Wiltshire, about three miles from Westbury and Warminster, in which Maude Davies did her classic survey of rural life at the turn of the twentieth century. In 1901 it had a population of 824 scattered through no less than nine hamlets and other isolated dwellings (see Figure 3.2).

> These hamlets are sometimes fairly compact groups, such as Corsley Heath or Leighs Green; sometimes they are scattered and straggling dwellings, such as Dartford or Whitbourne Moor. None deserves the name of a village. There is however, one village situated on high ground to the north of the parish, named Chapmanslade. Curiously enough this typical village, consisting mainly of a long row of houses on either side of the village street, is not a distinct parish at all, but is divided up among three or four neighbouring parishes.[32]

Since 1909 Chapmanslade has become a separate parish, so it is no

longer a boundary settlement, but the area is still easily recognisable as
a part of 'hamlet' England and presents a sharp contrast to Tysoe, despite the latter's trio of nuclei.

Figure 3.2: Corsley, Wiltshire

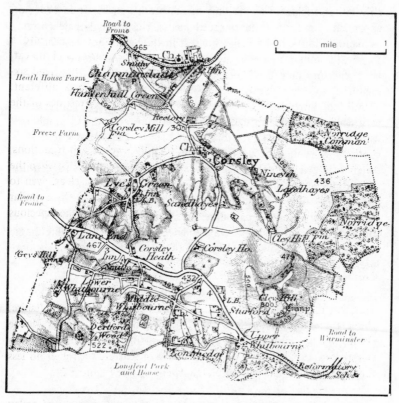

Source: Reproduced from the One Inch Ordnance Survey Map of 1809

## The Land

One striking fact about rights in land at Corsley is that there were
several medieval manors, as at Tysoe, and in 1909 there were seven,
four of which lay wholly within the parish. Despite land acquisition by
the Thynne family in the sixteenth and seventeenth centuries, landownership remained fragmented and at the time of enclosure in 1783
there were said to be many freeholders.

The common fields were situated in the eastern half of the parish, in which there were no hamlets. The western half had been inside the bounds of the royal forest of Selwood until the seventeenth century and Davies ascribed the formation of most of the hamlets to late settlement within the forest or on the heath. Figure 3.2, in fact, shows a marked difference between the western and eastern halves of the parish. Corsley Heath, Whitbourne Moor, Leighs Green and Longhedge probably either originated at the time of the heath's enclosure in 1741, or expanded from former squatter settlements. The nearby Longleat estate, as manorial lords, had a major interest in the heath, but 27 other persons had common rights, so the conversion of these rights into freehold landownership may have been a major encouragement to new settlement in the western part of the parish.

Another important feature of Corsley's agricultural history is the very wide range of farm sizes (see Table 3.1). Among the smallholdings were many which had probably existed since at least the seventeenth century, when dual occupations begin to enter the records, but some owed their origin to the local response to the late nineteenth-century agricultural depression. This response was to convert arable to pasture and to break up some of the large farms, probably tenant farms of the kind that Lord Wantage had taken over to make up his home farm. The soil, being rich and sandy, was said to be very suitable for smallholdings, that is, it would grow a wide range of crops, many of them labour-intensive.[33]

Table 3.1: Sizes of Holdings in Corsley, Wilts., *c*. 1906

| Acreage | Number |
|---|---|
| 400 plus | One |
| 300 plus | One |
| 200 plus | Two |
| 100 plus | One |
| 75-100 | Four |
| 50-75 | Nil |
| 25-50 | Seven |
| 10-25 | 12 |
| Market gardens under 10 acres | 12 |

Source: Davies, *Life in an English Village*, pp. 110-14

*Population*

The population of Corsley in 1731 was estimated at 700 and in 1760 at 1,200-1,300. The peak of 1,729 was reached in 1831, from which there was a continuous decline to 824 in 1901. At the peak, the population density was 360 persons per square mile. Even in 1901 it was 170, a figure higher than that at Tysoe and far higher than such places as Compton and the Lockinge estate.[34] Much of the explanation lies in industrial occupations.

*Occupations*

The widespread nature of rural industry in early nineteenth-century England has already been noted, and a fine woollen area had developed in West Wiltshire and neighbouring parts of Gloucestershire and Somerset at least as early as 1500.[35] Records of the industry begin in Corsley with references in the parish registers to broad weavers and cloth makers in the second half of the seventeenth century. All the processes from woolpicking to finishing were represented and under the control of several capitalist clothiers, mostly resident, the industry expanded rapidly throughout the eighteenth century. Towards the end of the century a clothworks, a dyeworks and a silk factory were established, thus limiting the former domestic nature of the industry, with a probable reduction in the number of dual occupationists. The decline in the population from 1831 is an indication that the industry was suffering from competition from the West Riding and this is borne out by the closure of all the works within the parish by the middle of the century. Clothworkers still lived in Corsley for some time after this, walking to work in nearby Rodden or Frome.

Despite the decline of industry, the tradition of smallholdings and dual occupations did not die out and the population level remained relatively high. In 1909 agriculture, market-gardening and local crafts were the main occupations left, but glove-making, building and the wagonworks were important employments. Glove-making was mainly undertaken by women, who fetched their materials from Westbury and West Leigh. A prominent employer was Mr. John Pearce who had on his books 25 carpenters, wheelwrights and painters at Corsley Heath, besides about 20 masons and other building trades workers elsewhere. The manufacture of carts must have been encouraged by the existence of numerous farmers and smallholders who engaged in haulage work, particularly of timber from the Longleat estate to the Radstock coalmines. On their return journey they carried loads of coal.

Maude Davies's occupational survey appears in Table 3.2 and confirms the relative lack of dependence on agriculture, but the figures must be interpreted in the light of her explanation that:

It is the exception rather than the rule for each man to depend on one source of income alone . . . The public-housekeepers are all either farmers or artisans. Artisans are sometimes also small farmers. Most labourers add to their earnings by selling garden produce, and the market gardeners range between people having no other source of income and the labourer working regularly at full time for another employer, with such imperceptible gradations that it is often impossible to guess whether the living is made principally from the garden or the wage.

Table 3.2: Occupations of 220 Heads of Households in Corsley, Wilts., 1905-6

| Occupations | Percentage |
|---|---|
| Agriculture | 57.7 |
| Trades | 4.5 |
| Artisans | 11.3 |
| Miscellaneous | 15.7 |
| Women heads of households | 10.8 |

Source: Davies, *Life in an English Village*, p. 105.

*Housing*

Maude Davies's motive being to emulate the urban social surveys of Booth and Rowntree,[36] she was careful to record data concerning housing and living standards. She estimated that in 1801, 1,412 persons, consisting of 388 families resided in 278 houses. It appears that the rapid growth of industry had been responsible for the multiple occupation of houses beyond that commonplace in agricultural areas and comparable, for instance, with an expanding Lancashire cotton town or Leeds at its most crowded. Field evidence suggested that the shared houses may well have included many of the three-roomed cottages still standing in Corsley in 1905. Peasant owners of one or two cottages were said to be fairly numerous and were thought to be the successors of squatters on the once extensive commons of Corsley.[37]

*Poor Rates and Settlement Laws*

Davies's survey yields nothing directly relevant to this topic, partly because it came too late, but her conclusions as to poverty were that it was on the low side. Two reasons were given for this: first, the availability of allotment land and gardens and the existence of so many by-occupations and, secondly, the relatively small child population. Thus the 12.5 per cent of the parish households which were said to be in primary poverty contained no less than 40 per cent of the children.[38] The out-migration of the second half of the nineteenth century had probably left a top-heavy population, which in 1905-6 contained many middle-aged and elderly couples whose childlessness made it possible for them to eke out a reasonable living.

## Religion

Corsley was well supplied with nonconformist chapels, as well as the parish church in the eastern part of the parish. A Wesleyan congregation was first recorded in 1769 and in 1849 the chapel at Lane End was rebuilt. This hamlet appears to have contained most of its members, a fact which is attributed to the influence of Wesleyans in Frome. The Baptist influence, on the other hand, is said to have come from Westbury, so that Chapmanslade was the best choice of site for the first chapel in 1799, another one following at Whitbourne Temple in 1811. The Congregationalists also built a chapel in Chapmanslade in 1771 and an Episcopal church was built in 1903 at Temple. Davies commented on the parish's religious geography:

> Dissent had taken a firm root in the parish, which, from its peculiar distribution in a number of scattered hamlets, was specially adapted for the formation of several small religious communities, collected round the nucleus of their chapel or church. And it is interesting to note that each of these Nonconformist settlements gained a footing in the hamlets most distant from the church, with the exception of Chapmanslade, whose nearer end is not more than a mile distant, but which is separated by a hill and a valley from the parish church of St. Margaret. At a later time . . . Church people made efforts to combat Dissent by the erection of Anglican churches in the vicinity of the two Baptist chapels.[39]

## Social Activities and Social Services

In addition to the nonconformist places of worship, Corsley appears to have had a full social life of its own; there was even a brass band at Chapmanslade. The richest development was in the tradition of clubs, going back to at least 1798. The old style sick and dividing clubs, with their annual cycle of saving and spending had been replaced before the end of the century, as in Oxfordshire and elsewhere[40] by clubs which worked on a more permanent basis. There were branches of the Ancient Shepherds, the Wiltshire Working Men's Conservative Benefit Society, the Hearts of Oak, the Oddfellows and the Foresters. Also offering insurance against sickness and death were several purely village clubs: the Corsley Gathering Club, the Corsley Mutual Provident Society (or Baptists' Club) and the Working Men's Benefit Society. In 1906 a new style social service appeared in the form of the Cley Hill Nursing Association, which, as its name implies, set out to provide more than the bare necessities of medical attention.[41] It would be interesting to know if this multiplicity of clubs was merely the outcome of peasant initiative in an open village, or whether it owed a great deal to the scattered settlement pattern and the wide range of occupations.

## Recapitulation

A sample of four parishes out of the 20,000 or so in all England is obviously inadequate on its own for the testing of a model. The four were chosen because they are well documented, bring out sharp contrasts and give the 'feel' of rural England in the nineteenth century. As the next chapter goes to the opposite extreme by assembling a wide span of quantitative data, a summary of the main points of this chapter helps to put it into focus.

The generalisations which need to be tested are as follows. Closed villages were owned by manorial lords sometimes resident in great houses surrounded by parks and large tenant farms. Population density was low, occupations were mainly agricultural, but housing standards were good. The Church of England had a spiritual monopoly, the squire made provision for social security, but he expected loyalty to his brands of religion and politics. Open villages were characterised by fragmented ownership, including owner-occupiers. The population density was high and occupations more varied, extending in some places to manufacturing industry. Housing standards were lower, but cottages were more freely available. Poor rates were high in the early years of the century and social security depended to some extent on the initiative of ordinary villagers in forming benefit clubs. In both religion and politics, a man might call his mind his own, for nonconformist chapels were plentiful and there was no heavy hand of landlordism to dampen the radical fires. The social contrast between open and closed might be summed up in the phrase 'independence v. benevolence'.

There is sufficient evidence in this chapter on which to challenge Tönnies' assumption that the more patriarchal a community the more traditional were its mores. Lord Wantage's use of his capital resources was typical of the commercial and industrial society that had developed by the second half of the nineteenth century, yet he ran his Lockinge estate on the basis of benevolent despotism. His introduction of the bonus scheme emphasised his acceptance of the cash nexus of modern economic relationships, yet alongside this he developed social security facilities which can be compared equally with the traditional duties of the pre-industrial manorial lord or to the then future welfare state.

Conversely, the peasant communities of Corsley and Tysoe cling to the last vestiges of the traditional forms of subsistence such as gardens, smallholdings and allotments and to the traditional duality of occupations, yet these villages contained subdivided property and were centres of nonconformity and radicalism, all of which challenged the higher echelons of the rural establishment. Thus the Gemeinschaft-Gesellschaft model would appear to be too simple to explain socio-spatial differences and trends in nineteenth-century rural Britain. Perhaps the open-closed dichotomy, as so far presented, is also too simple — an attempt is made to answer this question in the next chapter.

## Notes

1. A. Macfarlane, *The Origins of English Individualism* (Blackwell, Oxford, 1978), particularly pp. 17-33. Dr. Macfarlane kindly read this chapter and commented on it.

2. W.M. Williams, *A West Country Village: Ashworthy* (Routledge, London, 1963), pp. 53-9.

3. J.H. Martin, 'The Parliamentary Enclosure Movement and Rural Society in Warwickshire', *Agric. Hist. Rev.*, vol. 15 (1967), p. 28.

4. B. Kerblay, 'Chayanov and the Theory of Peasantry as a Specific Type of Economy' in T. Shanin (ed.), *Peasants and Peasant Societies* (Penguin, Harmondsworth, 1971), especially p. 154. See also Macfarlane, *Individualism*, p. 30 and R.M. Smith's editorial introduction to *Land, Kinship and Lifecycle* (Edward Arnold, London, forthcoming).

5. For instance, the striking case of Thomas Wood the elder's yeoman estate at Melbourn, Cambridgeshire, which I have described in Smith, *Land, Kinship and Lifecycle*, Ch. 13.

6. Williams, *Ashworthy*, pp. 53-9 or W.M. Williams, 'The Social Study of Family Farming', in D.R. Mills (ed.), *English Rural Communities: The Impact of a Specialised Economy* (Macmillan, London, 1973), pp. 116-33.

7. For a detailed analysis of dual occupations in one nineteenth-century peasant village see my chapter in Smith, *Land, Kinship and Lifecycle*.

8. Nottinghamshire Record Office, DD/4/110. For other examples, see B.A. Holderness, 'Rural Tradesmen, 1660-1850 — a Regional Study in Lindsey', *Lincolnshire History and Archaeology*, vol. 7 (1972), Table 1 and P. Horn, *Labouring Life in the Victorian Countryside* (Gill and Macmillan, Dublin, 1976), p. 93.

9. F. Emery, *The Oxfordshire Landscape* (Hodder and Stoughton, London, 1974), p. 177.

10. K.M. Buchanan, *Report of the Land Utilisation Survey of Great Britain: Part 68, Worcestershire* (Geographical Publications, London, 1944), pp. 634 and 649-50. Buchanan actually uses the term peasant of the nineteenth-century small-holders in the Vale of Evesham. For a later study see G.M. Robinson, *Late Victorian Agriculture in the Vale of Evesham* (University of Oxford, School of Geography, Research Paper no. 16, 1976).

11. D.B. Grigg, 'Small and Large Farms in England and Wales: Their Size and Distribution', *Geography*, vol. 48 (1963), p. 277.

12. J. Thirsk, *English Peasant Farming: The Agrarian History of Lincolnshire from Tudor to Recent Times* (Routledge, London, 1957), pp. 311-20.

13. F. Archer, *The Secrets of Bredon Hill: A Country Chronicle of the Year 1900* (Hodder and Stoughton, London, 1971), pp. 64, 75 and 77-8.

14. F.M.L. Thompson, *English Landed Society in the Nineteenth Century* (Routledge, London, 1963).

15. R. Samuel (ed.), *Village Life and Labour* (Routledge, London, 1975), Part 4. I do, of course, draw on this important essay in other ways.

16. Maude Davies, *Life in an English Village: An Economic and Historical Survey of the Parish of Corsley in Wiltshire* (T. Fisher Unwin, London, 1909).

17. Of particular relevance are 'The Quality of Life in Melbourn, Cambridge-shire in the Period 1800-50', *International Review of Social History*, vol. 23 (1978), pp. 382-404 and 'Land, Home and Kinship', in Smith, *Land, Kinship and Lifecycle*, Ch. 13.

18. A.W. Ashby, 'One Hundred Years of Poor Law Administration in a Warwickshire Village', in P. Vinogradoff (ed.), *Oxford Studies in Social and Legal History*, vol. 3 (Oxford UP, 1912); J. Ashby and B. King, 'Statistics of Some Midland Villages', *Economic Journal*, vol. 3 (1893), pp. 1-22 and 193-204 and M.K. Ashby, *Joseph Ashby of Tysoe, 1859-1919* (Cambridge UP, 1961). Joseph Ashby was born a labourer and became a small farmer and village politician; his son, A.W. Ashby became Professor of Agriculture in the University of Oxford; and his daughter Margaret wrote up his life history and with it a great deal of Tysoe history.

19. A.W. Ashby, 'Hundred Years', pp. 7 and 12.

20. M.K. Ashby, *Joseph Ashby*, p. 65.

21. A.W. Ashby, 'Hundred Years', pp. 5, 11 and 15-18.

22. Ibid., pp. 27-8.

23. Ibid., p. 27.

24. M.K. Ashby, *Joseph Ashby*, p. 160.

25. Ashby and King, p. 201; A.W. Ashby, 'Hundred Years', p. 43.

26. A.W. Ashby, 'Hundred Years', footnote p. 27; M.K. Ashby, *Joseph Ashby*, pp. 79-80 and 221; and *Kelly's Directory of Warwickshire* (Kelly's, London, 1928), p. 301.

27. M.K. Ashby, *Joseph Ashby*, Chs. 5 and 10.

28. Ibid., p. 73.

29. For comparison with Arch and Edwards, other union leaders, see J. Arch, *The Autobiography of Joseph Arch* (abridged edition, MacGibbon and Kee, London, 1967) and G. Edwards, *From Crow-scaring to Westminster: An Auto-biography* (National Union of Agricultural Workers, London, 1922). Arch lived in Warwickshire, owned the freehold of his cottage and garden and was a first rate piece worker. Edwards lived in Norfolk and was a Primitive Methodist.

30. Ashby, *Joseph Ashby*, p. 155.

31. M.A. Havinden, *Estate Villages* (Lund Humphries, London, 1966), p. 101.

32. Davies, *Life in an English Village*, p. 7.

33. Davies, ibid., pp. 8-17, 41, 53, 87. No soil, however, can be rich *and* sandy. Davies presumably meant that it was a free-working loam, which *would* make it

very suitable for many market garden crops, being 'early land' as the gardener
would say.

34. Ibid., pp. 3 and 305.

35. A.R.H. Baker and J.B. Harley (eds.), *Man Made the Land: Essays in
Historical Geography* (David and Charles, Newton Abbot, 1973), p. 75. Otherwise,
this section is based on Davies, *Life in an English Village* pp. 5, 18-26, 32-4, 41-8,
105-30. The quotation is from p. 106.

36. C. Booth, *Life and Labour of the People of London* (Williams and Norgate,
London, 17 vols., 1889-1903) and B. Seebohm Rowntree, *Poverty: A Study of
Town Life* (Macmillan, London, 1902) – the latter deals with York.

37. Davies, *Life in an English Village*, pp. 62 and 132. M. Anderson, *Family
Structure in Nineteenth-Century Lancashire* (Cambridge UP, 1971), p. 49 gives
the following figures for part of Preston in 1851: 72 per cent of the families
occupied a whole house; 12 per cent shared with another family; and 13 per cent
shared with kin or lodgers. The figures for Leeds show that five persons per
household in 1811 represents the maximum occupancy rate, about the same as in
Corsley: A. Rogers, *Approaches to Local History* (Longman, London, 2nd ed,
1977), p. 63.

38. Davies, *Life in an English Village*, pp. 62 and 132.

39. Ibid., pp. 56-9 and 89.

40. A. Howkins, *Whitsun in Nineteenth-Century Oxfordshire* (Ruskin College,
Oxford, 1973), pp. 41 and 46. See above for a similar trend at Tysoe (p. 52).

41. Davies, *Life in an English Village*, pp. 82, 250-5 and 277.

# 4 THE MEASUREMENT OF OPEN AND CLOSED

'. . . fundamental and widespread . . . was the acceptance in the Victorian countryside of two distinct kinds of village environments.' F. Emery, *The Oxfordshire Landscape* (Hodder and Stoughton, London, 1974), pp. 169-70.

## Two Approaches

The measurement of the open- and closedness of English villages is approached in this chapter on two levels. The first approach is on the local level, in which the examination of the main relevant types of document is carried out in the context of individual townships. This approach is intended partly to assist local historians to relate their work on selected communities to the generality of experience; it is also an opportunity to evaluate the documents for the purpose of larger surveys.

The second approach is at the macro-level, involving large numbers of villages seen in relationship to each other. The large-scale survey is as necessary as the local work, since it gives opportunities for the manipulation of statistical data in a way which does not arise in a parish study. Furthermore, it brings us a little nearer towards evaluating accurately the open-closed dichotomy and towards an appreciation of its variable applicability in different parts of England.

## The Documentation of Landownership

The types of document chosen for use in this section are estate surveys, enclosure awards, village surveys, tithe surveys and land tax returns. This is an approximate order of complexity, as judged from the standpoint of the present enquiry. With the exception of the first named, use will be made here only of information on ownership, as distinct from the occupation of land, mainly in order to keep the discussion within bounds and to make it relate directly to the macro-level approach of later sections.[1]

### Estate Surveys

By definition an estate survey was concerned only with the property of a single proprietor, although it is by no means unusual for information on neighbouring properties to be included. The example chosen is the Bromhead estate at Thurlby, about seven miles south-west of Lincoln, which was mortgaged at two points in the nineteenth century, 1832 and 1892.[2] This occasioned the drawing-up of the surveys, but other reasons for surveying an estate could be an impending sale, a decision to improve it and, more particularly, preparation for enclosure. Surveys may or may not have been accompanied by the drawing of a map, but map and survey do not always survive together. At Thurlby, the map made by J.S. Padley in 1828 cannot be used in conjunction with the survey of 1832, because the farms were not named in the map and the fields were not entered in the survey.

The area of the estate was about 1,400 acres, which when compared with the total township acreage of 1,847 indicates that the Bromheads controlled about two-thirds of the land and, anticipating criteria used later, this indicates that Thurlby was an estate village. Table 4.1 brings together farm acreages for 1832 and 1892 and shows that there was little change during the sixty-year interval. This does nothing to support the hypothesis that estate owners built up the sizes of their farms during this period. However, in 1832 the mean acreage of Thurlby farms was already over 100 acres[3] and some allowance should be made (a) for the absence of the Bromheads from the village, during which time the Hall was leased to tenants, and (b) for the suitability of the lower part of the parish for cowkeeping.

## Enclosure Awards

These are well-known sources of information on landownership. Like estate surveys, they relate only to individual townships, or a small group of townships, or possibly only that part of a township actually enclosed by the Act and Award in question. Unlike estate surveys, they do not usually contain information on the occupation of land, which is a serious shortcoming for those enquiring into farm sizes. Although more numerous than estate surveys, they are not available throughout the country and the majority of them were drawn up before the beginning of the nineteenth century.[4]

Notwithstanding those limitations, a great deal can be done with the information provided, although it is unfortunate that agrarian historians, unlike historical demographers, have done little to organise the data in such a way that useful comparisons can be facilitated between different townships. The size categories of owners adopted in Table 4.2 are those used by Lavrovsky in a group of Suffolk parishes in the 1930s and appear to provide as good a basis for comparison as any.[5] The comparison between Sherington (Bucks.) and Ardington (Berks.) is quite instructive because the townships were of very similar size, were enclosed within a few years of each other and were owned by similar total numbers of owners, yet there was a highly significant difference in the distribution of land between owners in the two places. At Sherington no single proprietor owned more than 300 acres (or about one sixth to one seventh of the total), whereas Ardington was well on its way to its later concentration, with 82 per cent in the hands of two big owners (see p. 67).

Table 4.1: Surveys of Lands Belonging to the Bromhead Family at Thurlby-juxta-Norton Disney, Lincs.

| Property | 1832 | | | 1892 | | |
|---|---|---|---|---|---|---|
| | A | R | P | A | R | P |
| North Farm | 231 | 3 | 14 | 185 | 0 | 07 |
| South Farm | 211 | 1 | 04 | 204 | 0 | 01 |
| River Farm | 181 | 1 | 18 | 168 | 0 | 17 |
| Halfway Farm | 75 | 3 | 21 | | | |
| Middle Farm | 150 | 0 | 26 | 122 | 2 | 19 |
| Skelmire Farm | 150 | 2 | 34 | 134 | 0 | 13 |
| Oakhill Farm | 112 | 0 | 23 | 110 | 2 | 01 |
| Wood Farm | 51 | 0 | 30 | 40 | 1 | 20 |
| Bell Lane Farm | 47 | 2 | 39 | 67 | 2 | 39 |
| Norton Lane Farm | 57 | 2 | 02 | 69 | 1 | 21 |
| Moor Lane Farm | 32 | 0 | 30 | 35 | 3 | 35 |
| Fir Holt Farm | 28 | 0 | 03 | 27 | 3 | 28 |
| Long Farm | 13 | 2 | 00 | Not entered | | |
| Green Gate Farm | Not entered | | | 103 | 3 | 06 |
| | 1,343 | 2 | 04 | 1,269 | 2 | 07 |
| Means of 13 (1832) and 12 (1892) farms | 103 | 1 | 15 | 105 | 3 | 07 |
| Hall, grounds and cottages (1832 and 1892) and woods (1832 only) | 98 | 1 | 13 | 29 | 2 | 01 |
| Total | 1,441 | 3 | 17 | 1,299 | 0 | 08 |

Table 4.2: Summary of Landowners by Sizes in Four Parishes[6]

| Category | Size (Acres) | Sherington 1797 | | Ardington 1811 | | Mareham-le-fen 1819 | | Wetheral 1840 | |
|---|---|---|---|---|---|---|---|---|---|
| | | No. | % land | No. | % land | No. | % land | No. | % land |
| 1 | Under 1 ) | | | 9 | 0.2 | 12 | 0.3 | 16 | 0.2 |
| 2 | 1-3 ) | (7) | 1.3 | 8 | 1.1 | 5 | 0.7 | 16 | 0.7 |
| 3 | 3-10 ) | (6) | 1.4 | 7 | 1.6 | 13 | 5.2 | 19 | 2.5 |
| 4 | 10-25 | 3 | 2.8 | 0 | — | 6 | 6.3 | 13 | 4.4 |
| 5 | 25-50 | 1 | 2.3 | 2 | 4.3 | 9 | 19.0 | 9 | 7.7 |
| 6 | 50-100 | 5 | 21.6 | 1 | 3.6 | 1 | 5.0 | 7 | 11.4 |
| 7 | 100-150 | 5 | 35.6 | 1 | 6.7 | 2 | 16.0 | 3 | 8.3 |
| 8 | 150-200 | 2 | 21.3 | 0 | — | — | — | 3 | 12.2 |
| 9 | 200-300 | 1 | 12.2 | 0 | — | 1 | 15.3 | 1 | 5.2 |
| 10 | 300-400 | Nil | | 0 | — | — | — | — | — |
| 11 | 400-500 | Nil | | 1 | 25.0 | 1 | 31.6 | — | — |
| 12 | Over 500 | Nil | | 1 | 57.4 | — | — | 3 | 47.5 |
| | | (30) | 1,741 acs. | 30 | 1,803 acs. | 50 | 1,583 acs. | 90 | 4,291 acs. |

(For references see Footnote 6.)

*Village Surveys*

The distinction between an estate survey and a village survey lay in the fact that while one was the product of a single owner, the other resulted from an initiative by, or at least on behalf of a whole community. One might expect to find village surveys in open villages and while they are few in number compared with estate surveys, they provide a valuable corrective to the kind of rural history which was written on the basis of documents generated by the landed classes.

The village survey chosen for illustrative purposes relates to Mareham-le-Fen, a parish in Lincolnshire about midway between Horncastle and Boston, and situated, as the name implies, where the Wolds grade down finally to the Fens. The survey provides details of both owners and occupiers and records the nature of each parcel of property in such terms as house and garden, public house, old inclosure, or the names of fields. This parish was, again, similar in size to Sherington and Ardington, but the number of owners, standing at 50, was considerable higher. The 30 smallest proprietors, however, only controlled 6.2 per cent of the area, a not uncommon characteristic of small owners even in open parishes. Nevertheless, as the greater part of this land consisted of houses, gardens and small closes, its significance in both social and economic terms was far greater than 6 per cent comprising large fields at a distance from the village would have been, for it represented a basis on which much else could be built in the peasant economy.

## Tithe Surveys

Like the Mareham village survey, the work of the tithe surveyors provides details of ownership, occupation and land use for each parcel of
property in the most meticulous, if not entirely faultless way. Tithe
surveys are often to be found for parishes in which enclosure was *not*
carried out under a Parliamentary Act, since the opportunity to commute tithe to an allotment of land for the tithe owner was often taken
at the time of enclosure. As a consequence, it is unusual to find both an
intensive enclosure survey and a similarly comprehensive tithe survey
for any particular township. The tithe surveys were commissioned in
the twenty years following the Tithe Commutation Act of 1836 in
order to commute payments in kind to a rent charge, with the option
of final redemption on payments of lump sums. The measurement,
classification and valuation of property had, therefore, to be conducted
at a very high standard.[7]

Wetheral, a village a few miles south-east of Carlisle has been chosen
to illustrate information taken from a tithe survey. Being a much bigger
parish, direct comparison with Sherington, Ardington and Mareham-le-
Fen is difficult from Table 4.2, but is more reliably done by reference
to Figure 4.1. More specifically, the ownership of 47.5 per cent of
Wetheral by three owners of more than 500 acres was not such a restric-
tion on the other 87 owners as it would have been in one of the smaller
townships. This observation suggests that large townships (by acreage)
were more likely to be open than small townships, but such a hypothesis needs careful testing. As to the processes whereby an open township might become more closed, the strength of owners in categories
5, 6, 7 and 8 was probably a crucial factor. While cottagers could be
bought out easily or ignored by the expanding squire, owners with
from 25 to 200 acres apiece could offer a much more coherent opposition if there were enough of them and they were determined. Significantly perhaps, Ardington was the odd parish out in the four, having
only 14.6 per cent of the land in the hands of such owners, compared
with 80.8 per cent at Sherington, 40.0 per cent at Mareham-le-Fen and
39.6 per cent at Wetheral.

Tithe surveys and village surveys also offer the opportunity to make
a detailed analysis of tenurial arrangements. While in the closed parish
these were usually very simple, because the estate owner controlled
most of the land and let it to tenants for whom he was the sole landlord, much more complex arrangements can be found in open villages.

Figure 4.1: Pie Diagrams Representing the Structure of Landownership in Four Townships

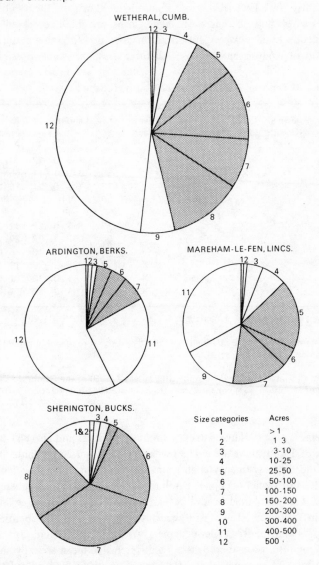

WETHERAL, CUMB.

ARDINGTON, BERKS.

MAREHAM-LE-FEN, LINCS.

SHERINGTON, BUCKS.

| Size categories | Acres |
|---|---|
| 1 | >1 |
| 2 | 1  3 |
| 3 | 3-10 |
| 4 | 10-25 |
| 5 | 25-50 |
| 6 | 50-100 |
| 7 | 100-150 |
| 8 | 150-200 |
| 9 | 200-300 |
| 10 | 300-400 |
| 11 | 400-500 |
| 12 | 500 · |

Note: The circles are proportional to the areas of the townships. Size categories 5-8 have been shaded to bring out contrasts between townships in these supposedly crucial categories of medium-sized owners. See text for full explanation and sources.

Tenants were also often freeholders and/or copyholders; landlords were also owner-occupiers and even tenants of other landlords; farmers more frequently took land from more than one landlord; and the number of both owners and occupiers was likely to be very high compared with the small, closed village. This situation cries out for some systematic method of analysis and Table 4.3 is offered as a workable possibility.

Table 4.3: Tenurial Functions in Melbourn, 1839-41

| Category | Owner-Occupr | Land-lord | Substantial Tenant * | Tenement Tenant | No. | Land owned | | | Average (mean) | | |
|----------|:---:|:---:|:---:|:---:|----|----|----|----|----|----|----|
| | | | | | | A | R | P | A | R | P |
| A | X | | | | 42 | 157 | 0 | 22 | 3 | 2 | 38 |
| B | X | X | | | 30 | 1675 | 1 | 11 | 55 | 3 | 13 |
| C | X | | X | | 13 | 198 | 0 | 21 | 15 | 0 | 38 |
| D | | | X | | 30 | Nil | | | | | |
| E | | | | X | 199 | Nil | | | | | |
| F | X | X | X | | 15 | 623 | 0 | 29 | 41 | 2 | 06 |
| G | | X | | | 56 | 1562 | 1 | 32 | 27 | 2 | 07 |
| H | | X | X | | 3 | 255 | 0 | 18 | 85 | 0 | 06 |
| J | X | X | | X | 2 | 38 | 3 | 29 | 19 | 1 | 35 |
| K | | X | | X | 1 | 1 | 0 | 12 | 1 | 0 | 12 |
| L | X | | | X | 1 | 1 | 2 | 08 | 1 | 2 | 08 |

Total owners = 163,    tenants = 264                          4512  3  22

* Substantial tenants were defined as all those renting more than a tenement and garden.

Source: this table is derived from the tithe survey (1839) of the Cambridgeshire parish of Melbourn, supplemented by data from the 1841 enumeration.[8]

Melbourn was a large parish of about 4,500 acres and an 1841 population of 1,608; there were 163 owners in 1839 and 264 tenants, including the 199 tenement tenants, mainly labourers. The four tenurial functions of owner-occupier, landlord, tenement tenant and substantial tenant were combined in no less than eleven different ways (see lines A to L in Table 4.3). The most numerous categories were the 56 absentee landlords and the 42 owner-occupiers. As might be expected from the foregoing discussion there was a big difference in mean areas owned, in fact a ratio of approximately 10 to one in favour of the landlords, who included two Cambridge colleges, the Dean and Chapter of Ely and the lord of the chief manor, who was in exile in Belgium. The most numerous categories in which combinations of tenurial function occurred were owner-occupier and landlord (A = 30 persons, 1675 acres); owner-occupier, landlord and substantial tenant (F = 15 persons, 623 acres) and owner-occupier and substantial tenant (C = 13 persons, 198 acres).

A complete explanation for the bewildering array of tenurial circumstances cannot be entered into here, but it is possible to make a useful general comment.[9] The small farmers would rent extra pieces of land from the small owners as and where they could, possible as family labour expanded after the manner described by Chayanov.[10] The many dual occupationists in the village were among those who, for example, owned a smithy or a public house and rented arable or pasture land for subsistence or for the grazing of horses. Retired owner-occupiers would keep their cottages or occasionally board with relatives, living on the rent of their 20 acres of farm land, etc. In the diverse spread of ownership and occupation, there were many combinations which were advantageous to the members of the peasantry who made up the bulk of those who undertook more than one tenurial function. The greater part of the land, as opposed to buildings, was, however, in the hands of a score or so of large farmers, some tenants, some yeomen, with acreages between about 100 and 400. Large-scale capitalist farming, therefore, co-existed with a numerous peasantry of about 60 families.[11]

## Land Tax Returns

The geographically most complete series of documents usable in the present context are the land tax returns, which are available for many counties for each year, more or less, from 1780 to 1832, or for even later dates, as in some Herefordshire and Cambridgeshire Hundreds. These returns list the names of owner and occupiers in each township, together with the amount of tax assessed, whether it had been exonerated by a lump sum payment or not. It is not possible to make direct inferences about the acreage owned from the tax assessed, because buildings put up the tax as compared with undeveloped land. However, for our purpose a property tax, which in effect was the function of the land tax, is more relevant than a tax which might have related to actual or notional agricultural use.[12]

Comparisons between land tax returns and the other types of document discussed here have, in the writer's experience, shown the returns to be a reliable and easily accessible source for classifying villages in respect of the social structure of landownership. At Melbourn, the rank order position of landowners showed a high correlation between the 1839 tithe survey and the 1841 returns. However, it was evident from the tax paid on small parcels of land that buildings were responsible for significantly raising the tax of smaller owners. For instance, William Anderson paid half a crown (12½p) on 1½ acres without buildings, while Benjamin Baker paid 5s 6d. (27p) on a similar area on which his cottage stood. A correlation test was then carried out on the 45 properties which contained no buildings and this showed that there was a significant tendency for the large owners to pay at lower rates of tax.[13]

In the second section of this chapter, the land tax returns are used to make comparisons *between* townships. Provided the assessors were reasonably consistent across a county and revised their figures to take account of major changes in land utilisation (such as industrial development), we have seen no reason to suppose that the returns will be unreliable for this purpose. Before moving on to these large-scale comparisons, it is of interest to analyse two townships in some detail to complement the analyses of other villages already mentioned. To make this small-scale comparison possible, an arbitrary series of size categories has again been adopted (compare Tables 4.2 and 4.4).

Lenton was a parish contiguous with Nottingham, but despite the development of a range of industries it was still in the hands of a relatively small number of owners, the four largest sharing over 97 per cent of the tax. These were Lord Middleton, resident at neighbouring Wollaton Hall (£15 9s), John Wright, probably of the banking firm (£46 14s), Gregory Gregory, esquire, whose name was later given to a boulevard (£86 8s) and the Duke of St. Albans, in respect of the detached area of Bestwood Park (£94 10s).[14]

Table 4.4: Land Tax Assessments Analysed in Two Townships

| Size categories by tax paid per person | Barwell, Leics., 1801 | | | Lenton, Notts., 1832 | | |
|---|---|---|---|---|---|---|
| | No. of owners | Total tax paid | Per cent of total | No. of owners | Total tax paid | Per cent of total |
| 1  Under 10s | 92 | £14.77 | 7.7 | 2 | £0.60 | 0.25 |
| 2  10s − 19s 11d | 18 | 11.90 | 6.3 | 4 | 3.36 | 1.35 |
| 3  £1 − £1 19s 11d | 11 | 14.63 | 7.7 | 1 | 1.25 | 0.50 |
| 4  £2 − £2 19s 11d | 3 | 7.62 | 4.0 | | | |
| 5  £3 − £3 19s 11d | 8 | 28.14 | 15.0 | | | |
| 6  £4 − £4 19s 11d | 2 | 9.25 | 4.8 | | | |
| 7  £5 − £9 19s 11d | 5 | 38.61 | 20.0 | | | |
| 8  £10 − £19 19s 11d | 2 | 36.08 | 18.8 | 1 | 15.98 | 6.42 |
| 9  £20 and over | 1 | 31.23 | 16.6 | 3 | 227.66 | 91.20 |
| 19s 11d = 99.5p | 142 | £192.23 | 100.9% | 11 | £248.85 | 99.72% |

Barwell was another industrial village of not dissimilar size, two miles from Hinckley and important in the production of stockings. Here the land tax returns reveal a picture comparable with that at Mareham-le-Fen, Wetheral and Melbourn, with a very large number of cottage owners at the base of the property owning pyramid. Ninety two of the 142 owners paid under 10 shillings each and only eight per cent of the total tax between them. Although she was far from being a controlling owner, the chief taxpayer, Mrs. Ashby paid more than twice the collective tax of these very small property owners. However, there was a solid core of substantial peasantry and yeomanry in size categories 5 to 7 who paid nearly 40 per cent of the tax, leaving us in little doubt that Barwell was an open village.

## Large-scale Measurement of Open- and Closedness

The first part of this chapter has given some indication of the documents which can be used in the measurement of open and closed systems of landownership and some of the possibilities for analysis on a very local scale have been discussed. However, it is also necessary to look at the problem on a larger scale, at least at a level comparable to that used by Miss Sylvester in her study of Wybunbury and the Doddington estate in Cheshire.[15] This second part of the chapter includes a detailed discussion of the land tax returns for the whole of Leicestershire, followed by briefer discussions relating to Lincolnshire, Oxfordshire, Northamptonshire, Kent and Cheshire. This assemblage of material is somewhat random, being based on pre-existing work carried out by several researchers including the writer, and therefore lacks a good balance between champion and hamlet England. In an attempt to rectify the balance a little, I have carried out a modest survey, published here for the first time, of an area of Herefordshire, neighbouring the Welsh border.

### *The Social Distribution of Landownership in Leicestershire*

Although Leicestershire was a champion county, it contained considerable contrasts between the wholly agricultural eastern part and the western and central areas where coal-mining and, more particularly, framework-knitting (the hosiery industry) were well developed activities in the countryside. Within the agricultural activities of the county, despite a predominance of grassland, the proportion of arable varied significantly, while some areas concentrated on dairying (e.g. the west and the Vale of Belvoir) rather than on stock raising.[16] Again, Leicestershire contained some great estates and was famous for the development of fox-hunting and other squirely sports, but Thompson ranked it only 27th out of 39 English counties in respect of acreage contained in estates of 10,000 acres and over. At the opposite extreme, 13 per cent of Leicestershire was in estates of 1 − 100 acres in 1870, compared with an English average of 12 per cent.[17] This county was, therefore, reasonably representative of English counties and like many more contained considerable local variations in the social distribution of land-ownership.

The land tax returns were used to discover the number of proprietors in each of the 308 rural townships in 1832, or the next nearest year available. In order to avoid some of the problems arising from wide variations in the total areas of townships, the *density of owners* was calculated by dividing the number of owners into the township acreage. The density of owners ranged from a high of only five acres per owner at industrialised Mountsorrel to a low of 2,273 acres per owner found at Stapleford, the estate village where the Earl of Harborough was sole proprietor.

The density of owners in the 308 rural Leicestershire townships has been plotted in Figure 4.2, which has a remarkably asymmetrical profile. The gentle slope on the right hand side of the diagram relates substantially to medium-sized townships, like Stapleford, in the ownership of one or two proprietors. The steepness of slope on the left hand side corresponds to the fact that there was a relative lack of minutely sub-divided townships. The modal value occurs at about 40 acres per owner, some distance along the spectrum from the median at 70 acres, thus contributing to the asymmetrical shape of the whole distribution.

Another notable feature of Figure 4.2 is its failure to divide clearly between open and closed townships. The symbols do not occur in two groups neatly separated from each other; rather, it would be fair to say that there is a statistical continuum. However, in conceptual terms, it may be acceptable to meet the problem of this continuum by enquiring into the possibility of there being significant sub-types within the definitions of open and closed villages.

The definition of 'closed' is perhaps the most crucial definition in the present context. In other words, how much land did a landowner have to own before he could be regarded as *controlling* landowner in a particular township? In practical terms, the enclosure Acts provide a good test, for enclosure was the major event in the modernisation of so many English villages. An enclosure Bill, in order to be successful,

Figure 4.2: The Frequency Distribution of Leicestershire Townships by Density of Owners and Village Types

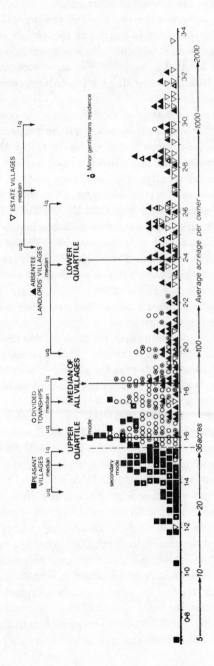

Note: A logarithmic scale has been used to compress the diagram laterally. Note the higher the density of owners, the smaller the average acreage per owner; this fact accounts for the upper quartile positions being related to smaller values than the lower quartile.

Source: Based on the land tax assessments and directories.

had to receive the support of three-quarters or four-fifths of the landowners *by acreage*.[18] In the light of this information, all the 121
Leicestershire townships in which one owner paid at least half the tax
in 1832 were labelled 'closed'.[19] With a controlling interest in half the
land, it was felt that a landlord, especially a manorial lord, would not
have much difficulty in getting the majority of owners, by acreage, on
his side.

In all but a very small number of cases, the controlling proprietor
paid not merely a half, but upwards of three quarters and often more of
the tax. There were very few borderline instances. However, a group of
13 townships were identified in which two or three *absentee* landlords
shared a controlling interest of at least two thirds of the property (or,
more properly, of the tax), without any one owner having a half share.
These were added to the original 121 to make a total of 134 closed
townships, the remaining open townships numbering 174.

The difference between a resident owner and an absentee, however,
has still to be recognised. The residential importance of the country
estate immediately suggests that any classification should recognise this
distinction, while the fact that absentee landowners included Oxbridge
colleges, large charitable trusts and other corporate owners emphasises
the rightness of the distinction.[20] Figure 4.2 indicates that townships
were more closely controlled by large landowners when they were
resident than when they were not. This is best seen by comparing the
positions of the median figure for estate villages (501 acres) with that
for absentee landlords' villages (234 acres). Whether or not the gentry
built mansions in places where they owned most land, or bought up
more land around pre-existing residences is another matter — instances
of both processes can easily be found — and does not directly affect the
interpretation of the data shown in Figure 4.2. To sum up the discussion so far, 39 Leicestershire villages were classified as estate villages
and 95 as absentee landlords' (see Table 4.5).

The 174 open villages were characterised by as much, if not more
variety than the 134 closed villages. The number of owners varied from
barely ten to well over a hundred and the density of owners ranged
from 5 acres per owner to over 200. Again, use has been made of a
combination of conceptual and statistical thinking. Thus it is possible
to consider two situations which are conceptually distinct — one in
which a large number of owners, including owner-occupiers, form the
basis of a well developed 'peasant' community, the other where the
land is merely divided between so many owners that no one of them, or
even a caucus of two or three, can be said to have a controlling interest.

Is it possible to separate divided from peasant villages in the Leicester-shire data of 1832?

Table 4.5: Classification of 308 Leicestershire Villages on the Basis of Landownership Patterns

| Classes | Number | Per cent of total | Per cent of class |
|---|---|---|---|
| Estate villages of which: | 39 | 12.7 | — |
| Estate villages belonging solely to the squire, disregarding church property | 17 | — | 43.5 |
| Absentee Landlord Townships of which: | 95 | 31.0 | — |
| Townships belonging to one absentee owner, disregarding church property | 28 | — | 29.5 |
| Townships controlled by two or three large absentee owners | 13 | — | 13.7 |
| Townships* containing seats of lesser gentry | 15 | — | 15.7 |
| Divided Townships of which: | 98 | 32.0 | — |
| Townships containing seats of lesser gentry | 31 | — | 31.6 |
| Peasant Villages of which: | 76 | 24.8 | — |
| Villages with 100 or more owners | 20 | — | 26.3 |
| Villages* with seats of lesser gentry | 15 | — | 19.7 |

* A few of these places also occurred in the sub-division immediately above.

Sources: land tax returns for c.1832, Leicestershire Record Office; and Mills, 'Landownership and Rural Population', Appendix 4.

Reference to Figure 4.2 shows that a relatively good line of statistical demarcation occurs at 36 acres per owner at a point between the mode and the only secondary mode occurring below it in the distribution. In general, peasant type villages occur below (to the left) of this line and divided villages above it. Two other considerations were added to this basic statistical division. First, a basic minimum of 20 owners was stipulated for peasant villages, which eliminated only one of the townships with a density of less than 36 acres per owner. Secondly and conversely, an arbitrary decision was taken to label any community with 50 owners or more as a peasant village regardless of the density figure. A good example is Bottesford where the very large acreage (for Leicestershire) of 4,978 was shared by 120 owners at the rate of 41 acres apiece.

On the basis of these definitions, there were 76 peasant villages in Leicestershire in 1832, leaving a residuum of 98 divided townships. The residual nature of this category is emphasised by another distribution summaried in Table 4.5 and Figure 4.2, namely the location of the lesser gentry. A comparison between the 39 estate villages defined above and lists of seats in early Victorian directories showed that the compilers of the latter recognised far more than 39 significant residences. Kelly's *Directory of Leicestershire* (1855) was chosen as giving the most comprehensive information, although it suffered from being over 20 years later than the land tax data. This listed 61 seats *outside* the estate villages and as they were not supported by the same control of land, the term lesser gentry has been used to describe them. In general the names listed in 1855 suggest that this description is reasonable, for most of them were parsons, service officers or plain esquires.

Out of these 61 seats, no less than 31 were to be found in the divided townships, where substantial blocks of property existed below the level of 50 per cent of the total. It is in these divided townships that we might expect evidence of a clash between the estate and peasant systems, as they existed side by side in the same township. Thus while in conceptual terms it can be argued that there were two types each of open and closed villages, the residual nature of the divided type emphasises the need also to think in terms of a statistical continuum. The next section is based on a recognition of this continuum.

*Landownership in Leicestershire as a Causative Factor*

The landownership data presented in Figure 4.2 were broken down into groups of villages for further analysis, which allowed a place for differences in physical geography within the county, differences which to some extent might be expected to have had a bearing on population density through the media of soils and farming. In the event, it was discovered that local differences were much wider than the differences in population density between regions.[21] As the regions were based on relative homogeneity of drift geology, variations *within* a given region must be imputed to other factors, such as landownership, farm organisation, the distribution of crafts and industries, poor law administration, and so on. What we are saying here is that the distinction between open and closed is more than a classification or dichotomy, it is a model with predictive powers. The prediction is that marked differences in the social distribution of landownership will give rise to marked differences in population density, occupations and other features of rural economy and society.

Table 4.6: Landownership as a Causative Factor in Leicestershire

| Regions | Number of† Townships | Correlations (Values of Rho) | | | |
|---|---|---|---|---|---|
| | | 1 | 2 | 3 | 4 |
| A. Coalfield | 11 | 0.68* | 0.76* | 0.71* | 0.15 |
| B. Northern Lowlands | 8 | 0.91** | 0.68 | 0.63 | 0.29 |
| C. Trent & Lower Soar Valleys | 7 | 0.93** | 0.94** | 0.83* | 0.65 |
| D. Western Fringe | 6 | 0.43 | 0.66 | – | 0.14 |
| E. Western Lowlands | 16 | 0.77** | 0.91** | 0.77** | 0.14 |
| F. Hinckley Ridge | 23 | 0.77** | 0.88** | 0.75** | 0.68** |
| G. Charnwood | 12 | 0.89** | 0.95** | 0.82** | 0.66* |
| H. Charnwood Brooks | 7 | 0.82* | 0.99** | 0.71* | 0.4 |
| J. Leicester Forest | 9 | 0.25 | – | 0.69* | – |
| K. Southern Lowlands | 19 | 0.75** | 0.86** | 0.85** | 0.69** |
| L. Soar & Wreake Valleys | 25 | 0.88** | 0.97** | 0.56** | 0.76** |
| M. Wreake Valley | 11 | 0.78** | 0.99** | 0.75** | 0.74* |
| N. Vale of Belvoir | 11 | 0.38 | 0.71* | 0.31 | 0.27 |
| O. Belvoir Ridge | 13 | 0.19 | 0.85** | 0.64* | 0.60* |
| P. Lincs Border | 9 | 0.91** | 0.80** | 0.67* | 0.44 |
| Q. Lias Plain | 77 | 0.84** | 0.93** | 0.04* | 0.68** |
| R. High Leics. | 28 | 0.72** | 0.87** | 0.57** | 0.55** |
| S. Welland Valley | 10 | 0.71 | 0.91** | 0.49 | 0.69* |

† Correct for the next column; slight variations elsewhere.

Correlation    1 = Density of owners 1832 and population density 1851
2 = Density of population 1851 and 1801
3 = Density of owners 1832 and average farm size 1867
4 = Density of owners 1832 and poor rates 1847

\* = significant at 95% level        \*\* = at 99% level.
All positive except Correlation 3.

Source: Mills, 'Landownership and Rural Population', data in Appendices 3, 4, 5, 6.

Turning to the correlation tests, by which we test the model, column 1 of Table 4.6 shows that there was a correlation between densities of owners in 1832 and densities of population in 1851 in all but four regions. In 12 of the 17 regions the correlation was significant at the 99 per cent level. Causation, of course, is another matter — did high densities of owners arise out of high population densities, or vice versa?

If population density was the causative factor, big changes in the densities of owners ought to have occurred between 1780 and 1832, on the basis that population growth was very rapid. In fact, this was not so. Comparison of the tax documents for each of the years 1780, 1801 and 1832 showed little change in township after township and for the hosiery districts of Leicestershire further correlation tests described below emphasise the comparative stability of the landownership structure in a period of rapid demographic and industrial expansion.[22] The correct inference, then, must be that fragmented ownership promoted population growth. This is confirmed by column 2 of Table 4.6 which indicates that the thickly populated townships of 1851, were by and large the same as those of 1801; most villages kept in the same position relative to their neighbours.

The next step is to seek some of the mechanisms whereby fragmented ownership sustained high population densities. This is more fully explored in the next two chapters but some of the quantitative data available for Leicestershire form a valuable underpinning of its argument. Column 3 of Table 4.6 shows that large farms in Leicestershire were found on the large estates; hence large farms, so the argument runs, must have helped to keep down the population by economies in the use of labour. However, this was certainly not the whole of the picture, partly because cottage accommodation was not always available near the labourer's work and partly because the whole population was not engaged in agriculture, even outside the industrial districts. There is also the important point that some evidence exists for thinking that small farms engaged in labour-intensive production, e.g. dairying, to a greater extent than large farms.[23]

Table 4.7: Correlations with Framework Knitting in Three Leicestershire Regions

| Frames per 100 persons 1844 correlated with: | Region F Hinckley Ridge | Region K Southern Lowlands | Region L Middle Soar and Lower Wreake Valleys |
|---|---|---|---|
| 1. Persons per sq ml 1851 | 0.88** | 0.81** | 0.76** |
| 2. Density of owners 1780 | 0.72** | 0.25 | 0.53** |
| 3. Number of voting freeholders 1719 | 0.48* | 0.51* | 0.76* |
| 4 Hearths per sq ml 1670 | 0.77** | 0.46* | 0.84** |

Source and Abbreviations: as for Table 4.6.

The shortage of cottage accommodation was reported in a number of closed townships in Leicestershire especially around Melton Mowbray and the 1851 enumerators' books give some indication that daily movements of farm labour could have occurred between neighbouring villages.[24] However, the Poor Rate Return of 1847[25] forms much the most comprehensive and convenient source of data with which to make an indirect test of the population control exercised by the large landlords. Column 4 of Table 4.6 shows that in nine mainly large regions of Leicestershire (out of 17) there was a positive correlation between the number of owners in 1832 and the level of poor rate in 1847. This point is taken up again in Chapter 6, but note for the moment that the raw data represented in this column, as in the other parts of Table 4.6, exhibited a statistical continuum, rather than a dichotomy. In this case poor rates occurred at all levels from nil up to three or four shillings in the pound.

One of the reasons for higher poor rates in some of the villages was the depressed state of the hosiery trade. This industry had overexpanded during the French Wars and had suffered ever since from lack of demand. It was still organised on a domestic or semi-domestic basis, with stocking frames (hand and foot operated machines) located in the homes of stockingers or in small groups in the workshops of small masters. Although machine-spun yarn had long been used, the knitting process was still virtually unaffected by steam power. Leicester, Hinckley and Loughborough-Shepshed were the organising centres of the trade and contained considerable numbers of frames, but the industry was also strongly oriented towards a rural labour supply.

Table 4.8: Selected Data Relating to 42 Lincolnshire Villages

| Type of Village | Peasant | Divided | Absentee | Estate |
|---|---|---|---|---|
| | N = 11 | N = 12 | N = 9 | N = 10 |
| Median Population by Size 1851 | 515 | 414 | 89 | 224 |
| Median Population Density Persons per Square Mile | 160 | 134 | 39 | 55 |
| Non-Agricultural Occupations 1889 Median Number | 27 | 18.5 | 0 | 4.5 |

Source. Mills, 'Population and Settlement', Appendices 9, 11-15, 19.

The distribution of stocking frames is shown in Figure 4.3 in conjunction with information relating to landownership. Few closed vill-

Figure 4.3: Stocking Frames and Landownership in Leicestershire

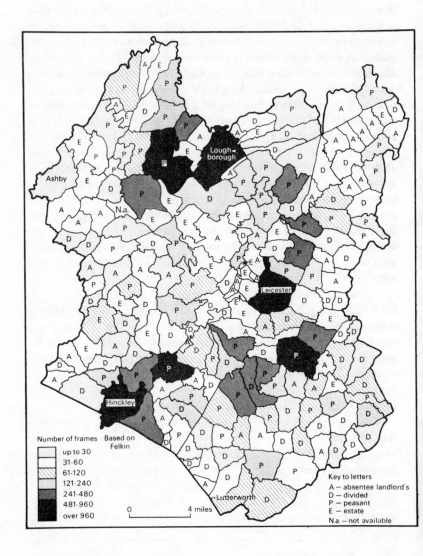

Note: Landownership as in Figure 4.2

Source: Based on the 1844 survey, W. Felkin, *A History of the Machine-wrought Hosiery and Lace Manufacturers.*

ages, whether belonging to resident or absentee landlords, contained many frames, while peasant villages were frequently characterised by a heavy dependence on the industry. Most manufacturing industries were not attractive to the landed gentry, especially where their own estates were involved; moreover the hosiery industry, in its depressed state, was particularly abhorrent because of its association with high poor rates. The broad correlation seen in Figure 4.3 is borne out in detail in Table 4.7, where it is possible to trace the correlation of high population density and fragmented landownership back to the end of the seventeenth century. This is important because the hosiery trade was being established in rural Leicestershire at that time. While general arguments about the availability of rural labour can be applied in the century from about 1750, before that date the labour supply argument must be more specific, for in the first century or so of its existence, the industry was based on stockingers who owned their own frames. In the seventeenth century a frame was an expensive item of equipment and the records of the early stockingers point to them having been men of modest substance, shopkeepers, blacksmiths, farmers, freeholders and the like and such men were much more likely to be found in peasant villages than elsewhere.[26]

## Population and Occupations in some Kesteven Villages

An earlier study by the present author in Lincolnshire confirms some of the general lines of argument developed in connection with Leicestershire, As it was not collected in a directly comparable form, and some of it has already been published, a selection of data specific to population and occupations has been made to suit the circumstances of this chapter.[27]

This selection relates to 42 townships in the former Kesteven division of Lincolnshire. Those to the south west of Lincoln were situated in an area of mixed sandy and clayey soils, the former predominating. To the south east was a group of villages located on the edge of the Witham fens, which were drained for arable farming in the early nineteenth century. The third group, between Grantham and Stamford, were situated on a limestone plateau considerable overlain by boulder clay. Circumstances therefore varied considerably, but the complete absence of domestic industries makes it possible to treat all 42 villages as one group for present purposes.

Use has been made of the four village types, two open and two closed, as a means of analysing the data and testing the open-closed model. While the raw data show the same kind of continua as in Leicestershire, calculation of the medians as shown in Table 4.8 brings out the differences between the four sub-types and more especially the two main types of village. Broadly speaking, open villages, as predicted, were larger, in fact, more than twice the size of closed villages. It is interesting to note that absentee landlord townships, as in some parts of Leicestershire contained less population than the estate villages. This is due partly to the distribution of deserted and depopulated village sites of which there were several in the nine absentee landlord townships. As there was considerable variation in township acreages, it is necessary also to consider population *density*, to eliminate the chance that small townships were predominantly those in the hands of large proprietors. The second line in Table 4.8, however indicates that this was not so; on the contrary, density of population corresponded broadly to village sizes.

One of the reasons why open villages had larger populations and higher population densities was the uneven distribution of the non-agricultural population. This consisted very largely of tradesmen and craftsmen who supplied the local services necessary to farming operations (blacksmiths, saddlers, etc.) and to the farming population more generally (food shops, tailors, builders, etc.) The bottom line of Table 4.8 shows that their numbers were disproportionately low in the closed villages. This might be explained partly in terms of the restrictions laid upon closed villages by their owners and partly by the failure of these villages to reach the threshold size necessary to support even modest service activities.

## The Leicestershire Schema Applied in South Lindsey

In his very interesting book on religion and rural society,[28] Obelkevich used the schema developed in Leicestershire as the basis for his analysis of 237 villages in south Lindsey. This study area stretches from the Trent in west to the North Sea coast on the east and from the latitude of Gainsborough and Louth in the north to the fen edge and the Witham-Foss Dyke line in the south. The relationship between the distribution of landownership and the size and density of village populations in this large area of clay vales, heath, wold and marsh closely resembles that of other areas already discussed.

The Leicestershire schema was used with one variation: the distinction between the two types of closed parishes in Obelkevich's main analysis was not based on the residence of a squire but as follows: squire's parishes were those in which one landlord owned more than half the land, while an 'oligarchic' parish was one in which a few landlords owned most of the land, but none had more than half. Out of the total of 237 villages, 130 were squire's parishes and only 27 were oligarchic, but of the 130 only 21 had a residential owner.[29] Thus, while south Lindsey had proportionately far more closed parishes than Leicestershire (66.3 per cent of the total as compared with 44.5),resident gentry were about as numerous (8.9 per cent in Lindsey and 12.6 per cent in Leicestershire).

Table 4.9: Landowners and Population in South Lindsey

| Parish Type | No. | Average acreage | Average population | Population per sq ml | Per cent increase 1801-51 |
|---|---|---|---|---|---|
| Squire's | 130 | 1,542 | 170 | 71 | 53.2 |
| Oligarchic | 27 | 1,695 | 169 | 102 | 76.5 |
| Divided | 46 | 2,008 | 418 | 133 | 94.5 |
| Peasant | 34 | 2,094 | 491 | 149 | 90.6 |

Source: Obelkevich, *Religion and Rural Society*, pp. 12-13

Table 4.9 summarises the relationship between population and ownership, which follows a pattern surprisingly similar to Leicestershire in view of the arable bias to Lincolnshire farming and a complete absence of industries other than purely local crafts. The closed parishes were smaller than the open parishes but the difference was not of very great significance − 1,600 acres compared with 2,000. Closed villages had an average population below 200 in 1851 but open parishes were more than twice as big at about 450. The densities of population showed the same kinds of contrasts, peasant townships being more than twice as thickly populated as squires'. Finally, the influence of poor law administration and the laws of settlement are inferred in the differential growth rates between 1801 and 1851, the open villages nearly doubling, the closed increasing by about two thirds.

Obelkevich adds that non-agricultural occupations, as our model predicts, were more important in open villages than closed at the 1831 census. Contrasts were greatest between the squires' and peasant villages, the oligarchic and divided villages falling between, as we have noted before. The purpose of this analysis was to lay the basis for a study of religious life and Obelkevich sums up this part of his evidence by saying that it 'strongly suggests that the structure of landownership was indeed the key variable. There were also implications for the realm of faith and morals'.[30] A return will be made to these implications in Chapter 6.

*Occupying Owners in Oxfordshire and South Lincolnshire*

The decline of the small farm gave rise to both academic and practical concern towards the end of last century, although the decline had, in fact, been started centuries before and the connection between this decline and rural depopulation was by no means well established. It was in the context of this debate that Gray made his well known study of yeoman farming in Oxfordshire. Here he defined the yeoman as 'an independent or landowning farmer (occupying owner)'.[31] This definition at least has the merit that it can be linked directly to use of land tax assessments, in which the occupying owner is identifiable.

Table 4.10: The Division of Property in Oxfordshire 1785

| Group of Townships | A | B | C | D | E | Total |
|---|---|---|---|---|---|---|
| Percentage of tax paid by occupying owners 1785 | 20 | 10-20 | 5.10 | 5 | Nil | |
| Number of townships | 48 | 54 | 36 | 68 | 90 | 296 |
| Number of occupying owners | 591 | 393 | 173 | 175 | Nil | |
| Average per township | 12.5 | 7.2 | 4.8 | 2.5 | Nil | |
| Number of townships in which ¾ or more tax paid by one man | 0 | 1 | 2 | 17 | 64* | 84 |
| do. ¾ or more paid by 2-3 men | 0 | 6 | 9 | 29 | 26 | 70 |
| do. ½ - ¾ paid by 2-3 men | 8 | 33 | 18 | 16 | 0 | 75 |
| Property much sub divided | 40 | 14 | 7 | 6 | 0 | 67 |

* Of which 20 are solely owned by one man

Source: Gray, 'Yeoman Farming', p. 302.

Gray's results are summarised in Table 4.10 in which data on 296 rural townships are brought together. Although direct comparisons with Leicestershire are prevented by Gray's concentration on the yeomen, there is sufficient evidence to support the argument that conditions in the two counties were broadly comparable. For example in 67 townships the property is described as much subdivided, a proportion similar to the 76 peasant villages of Leicestershire, out of the slightly higher total of 308 townships (refer back to Table 4.5). At the other end of the continuum comparison is less straightforward but at least the figure of 20 Oxfordshire townships where all the tax was paid by one owner is a very similar figure to the 25 instances where this occurred in Leicestershire in 1832.[32]

The survival of occupying owners in the unenclosed townships of 1755 raises questions of cause and effect in connection with enclosure which Chapter 5 articulates. The limitations of using occupying owners in this context can, however, be usefully anticipated. First, their numbers do not necessarily reflect the average size of farms, so there is no direct parallel with the inverse correlation in Leicestershire between density of owners and size of farms. Secondly, as there would be many small tenant farms, the average numbers of occupying owners per township, shown in Table 4.10, reflects truly neither the total number of small farms nor the total number of owners per township. This is the explanation for low numbers in the fifth column of the Oxfordshire table, in comparison with the many Leicestershire villages in which there were well over 50 and the twenty in which there were over 100 proprietors.

This point was taken up by Grigg who noticed that in the Holland division of Lincolnshire in 1813 the proportion of tenanted and owner-occupied farms in each size group was much the same. He ascribed the general persistence of both types of small farm, which was such a marked feature of the area, to a survival of the inheritance custom known as gavelkind, in which property was divided between surviving heirs.[33] This suggests that there were deeper cultural factors at work which need to be taken into account.

Table 4.11: Kent, Lindsey, Leicestershire and Northamptonshire Compared (Percentages)

| Parish Type | in one Hand | in a few Hands | Sub-divided | Much Sub-divided |
|---|---|---|---|---|
| Kent* | Nil | 55 | 16 | 29 |
| Lindsey | 20 | 39 | 15 | 26 |
| Leicestershire | 8 | 44 | 24 | 24 |
| Northamptonshire | 10 | 57 | 20 | 13 |

Source: Everitt, *Rural Dissent*, 76, based on Wilson, *Imperial Gazetteer*.

* See also Table 4.13.

*The Imperial Gazetteer*

Readers of the *Imperial Gazetteer* will be familiar with the information
given in that book on landownership, the usual terms being 'much
subdivided', 'subdivided', 'divided among a few' and 'property of (a
named estate)'.[34] As the first term corresponds with Gray's phraseology
and the four-fold division appears to bear a close relationship with the
four village types used in this chapter, the *Gazetteer* is clearly an important source demanding our attention, especially as it covers the
whole of England and Wales.

It has already been used by Everitt in a study of nonconformity and
Tables 4.11 and 4.13 are based on his work.[35] They repeat the now
familiar pattern of considerable variation within English counties, but a
comparison between Wilson's *Gazetteer* data and land tax data for a
sample of Leicestershire villages shows that the former should be used
with caution. This 'sample' consists of all the 55 place names beginning
with A or B for which land tax data were available. While this is not a
scientifically selected sample it will probably suffice for the inferences
made.

Table 4.12: Land Tax Assessments and *Imperial Gazetteer* Compared
as Sources of Village Classification (Sample of 55 Leicestershire Townships, Names Beginning with A and B)

| Description in Imperial Gazetteer 1870 | No. | Data from land tax assessments | |
| --- | --- | --- | --- |
| | | Range of number | Median number |
| Much subdivided | 10 | 8-134 | 60 |
| Subdivided | 7 | 20-128 | 27 |
| In few hands        )<br>Not much subdivided) | 14 | 2-64 | 26.5 |
| In one hand | 1 | 9 | 9 |
| No information | 23 | 1-59 | 11 |

Sources: Wilson, *Imperial Gazetteer* and Mills, 'Landownership and Rural
Population', Appendix 4.

The middle column in Table 4.12 shows that villages of widely varying character could be classified with the same shorthand phrase in the
*Gazetteer*. Although this disturbing discovery is mitigated by the existence of a wide difference between the medians for the much subdivided
and subdivided types, another serious problem comes to light in the
bottom two lines of the table. Only one township was listed as being in

the hands of one estate. In 1832 this township was shared by nine owners, while in the group of 23 townships for which the *Gazeteer* gave no information there were five places under single ownership in 1832. Although this group contained a significant number of estate villages and its median number of owners was lower than any other category, it is not safe to assume that all townships for which Wilson gives no data were all of the same kind. Set against these problems is the fact that we have been comparing data collected on two occasions 30 or 40 years apart. However, this was a period of general stability in landownership, if directories generally and the Leicestershire correlations described above are a reliable indication. It was not until after the First World War that the estate system, for example, began to undergo considerable modifications. Nor can the difference in dates dispose satisfactorily of the substantial number of places for which Wilson omits the relevant information.

Table 4.13: The Division of Property in Kent

| Imperial Gazetteer Description | Property | | |
|---|---|---|---|
| | in few hands | subdivided | much subdivided |
| Number of parishes | 188 | 54 | 98 |
| Average parish acreage | 1,811 | 3,514 | 4,253 |
| Divided as follows within agricultural regions — | | | |
| Weald and Forest | 9 (19%) | 10 (21) | 28 (60) |
| Chartland | 47 (54) | 16 (18) | 24 (28) |
| Downland | 59 (70) | 14 (17) | 11 (13) |
| Foothills | 55 (61) | 14 (15) | 22 (24) |
| Other areas | 27 | 3 | 9 |

Source: Everitt, *Rural Dissent*, 86, 88.

*Hamlet England*

In this last section of the chapter hamlet England can be given particular attention, albeit too briefly. First, the *Gazetteer* data are worth considering in a little more detail for Kent because they indicate significant differences between villages, and their limitations do not seem to have invalidated Everitt's general line of argument. Parishes in a few hands amounted to about half the total reported in Kent, a proportion roughly comparable with the closed villages of Leicestershire.

Many of them must have been small parishes as the average acreage was less than half that of the remaining (probably open) parishes. The lower half of Table 4.13 reveals that subdivided and much subdivided villages were particularly common in the Weald and Forest, i.e. the principal areas in which hamlets were situated. Where nucleated villages had developed from early settlement in the hartlands and downlands, open parishes were relatively rare. Thus in Kent a general division between open villages in the late areas of wood pasture settlement and closed villages in areas of early nucleated settlement appears to hold.

That this pattern cannot hold for all wood pasture areas is shown by Miss Sylvester's study of the Cheshire parish of Wybunbury, in which several townships of concentrated landownership existed without evidence of former open fields.[36] Figure 2.3 and Table 4.14 again show the diversity of circumstances which have also been revealed in counties situated in champion England. The important question to ask of medieval history may not be the date of settlement, but the circumstances in which settlement occurred – were they such that subdivision of property could develop for anyone of a multitude of reasons? All the same, it is well to mark the differences between hamlet and champion England, for they represent different socio-economic systems and different relationships between man and natural resources.

Table 4.14: The Townships of Wybunbury Parish, Cheshire

| | No. of owners c. 1840 | pop. density PPSM 1810 | 1840 average acreage per holding | 1840 No. of owner occuprs | 1860 tradesmen and craftsmen |
|---|---|---|---|---|---|
| Doddington | 1 | 74 | 45 | 1 | 2 |
| Batherton | 1 | 48 | 131 | Nil | 1 |
| Blakenhall | 1 | 91 | 50 | 1 | 2 |
| Chorlton | 1 | 69 | 32 | 1 | 2 |
| Hunsterson | 1 | 83 | 42 | 1 | 5 |
| Lea | 1 | 121 | 37 | 1 | Nil |
| Rope | 1 | 100 | 48 | Nil | Nil |
| Basford | 2 | 64 | 64 | 1 | 2 |
| Walgherton | 2 | 158 | 24 | 1 | 5 |
| Bridgemere | 4 | 122 | 27 | 3 | 4 |
| Checkley-cum Wrinehill | 11 | 69 | 38 | 6 | 5 |
| Weston | 18 | 147 | 22 | 18 | 19 |
| Hough | 19 | 158 | 19 | 6 | 14 |
| Hatherton | 21 | 152 | 18 | 21 | 10 |
| Willaston | 27 | 268 | 8 | 13 | 17 |
| Shavington-cum-Gresty | 39 | 117 | 16 | 15 | 22 |
| Stapeley | 39 | 137 | 16 | 15 | 10 |
| Wybunbury | 41 | 240 | 7 | 21 | 24 |

Sources: Sylvester, 'Rural Settlement' and (for right-hand column)
White's *Gazetteer and Directory of Cheshire*, 1860.

Finally, a simple test of the model has been carried out especially for this book in the Herefordshire Hundred of Wigmore, which lies in the north western corner of the county in the angle formed by the Radnorshire and Shropshire boundaries. The hundred contained no towns, the biggest single settlement in 1831 was Leintwardine, which with its attendant hamlets of Brakes and Heath with Jay almost reached the 500 mark. Fieldwork in 1979 suggested that true villages were few in number, the characteristic pattern of settlement being the hamlet with isolated farms. Many of the parishes contained more than one township and three of them contained half a dozen each. The land tax assessments revealed that the Earls of Oxford and Thomas Andrew Knight, esquire, were both considerable owners of land in the area. The Earls of Oxford owned land in every township and their property had included Wigmore Castle for many generations. It lay in ruins in the nineteenth century and the main Oxford residence in this period was probably at Kington, just outside the hundred. Knight was the descendant of a Coalbrookdale ironmaster and a plant physiologist trained at Oxford who had his residence at Downton Castle. There were other smaller seats in the hundred and one gains the impression that these were often based on separate small medieval manors.[37]

Despite these indications of the concentration of landownership and of a generally low population density, Table 4.15 shows clearly that there was considerable social differentiation within the area. The population size of individual census units ranged from 38 to 496 at the 1831 census, with a corresponding range in population density from 22.4 to 135.0 persons per square mile. It is true that some of these differences may reflect variations in soil fertility or the distribution of rural industry, as the study was purposely limited to demonstrate what can be achieved in a few days in reference library and record office. Where possible, the land tax assessments for 1830 were matched against the population data for the same areas (or which seemed reasonable to assume were the same areas, for in such cases of complex administrative geography the stranger could easily make mistakes). The number of owners per township (or parish) ranged from the total control by the Earl of Oxford at Letton and Newton and Evelyn Lyndon, Esq. at Upper Kinsham, to the substantial total of 46 at Wigmore, where nevertheless the Earl of Oxford paid just over 50 per cent of the tax. Similarly at Leintwardine, where there were 43 owners paying almost £30 tax, T.A. Knight, Esq. was responsible for £27. Owners of the middle range, corresponding to categories 5-8 of Table 4.2 do not seem to have been very prominent in this area. Nevertheless the density of owners correlated very closed with population density in the Hundred of Wigmore (Rho = 0.613, n = 35, confident at over 99 per cent).

Table 4.15: The Hundred of Wigmore, Herefordshire Population and Landowners

| Parish or Township | Area (Acres) | Area (sq mls) | Pop | Pop. Density (persons per sq ml) | Rank Order | No. of Owners | Density of Owners (Acs. per owner) | Rank Order |
|---|---|---|---|---|---|---|---|---|
| Adforton TP | 1,592 | 2.49 | 336 | 135.0 | 1 | 18 | 88 | 7 |
| Aston PH | 1,090 | 1.70 | 56 | 33.0 | 23 | 2 | 545 | 21 |
| Brampton Bryan PH | 3,190 | 4.98 | 249 | 50.0 | 18 | 6 | 531 | 20 |
| Buckton and Coxall TP | 1,430 | 2.23 | 120 | 53.9 | 15 | 4 | 357 | 18 |
| Burrington PH | 2,850 | 4.45 | 230 | 51.6 | 16 | est. 8 | 356 | 17 |
| Byton PH | 1,030 | 1.61 | 155 | 96.5 | 7 | est.19 | 54 | 1 |
| Combe TP | 599 | 0.93 | 101 | 108.5 | 5 | 10 | 60 | 2 |
| Downton PH | 1,170 | 1.83 | 111 | 60.5 | 13 | 2 | 585 | 23 |
| Elton PH | 1,700 | 2.66 | 85 | 32.0 | 24 | 3 | 566 | 22 |
| Lower Harpton TP | 900 | 1.41 | 68 | 48.2 | 20 | 11 | 82 | 6 |
| Lower Kinsham TP | 341 | 0.53 | 71 | 134.0 | 2 | 5 | 68 | 4 |
| Upper Kinsham PH | 1,090 | 1.70 | 38 | 22.4 | 25 | 1 | 1,090 | 24 |
| Knill PH | 550 | 0.86 | 94 | 109.1 | 4 | 6 | 92 | 8 |
| Leinthall Starkes PH | 970 | 1.51 | 127 | 84.0 | 10 | 8 | 121 | 11 |
| Leintwardine TP | 5,559 | 8.70 | 496 | 57.0 | 14 | 43 | 129 | 12 |
| Letton and Newton TP | 1,202 | 1.88 | 63 | 33.5 | 22 | 1 | 1,202 | 25 |
| Lingen PH | 2,380 | 3.72 | 298 | 80.0 | 11 | 25 | 95 | 9 |
| Litton and Cascob TP | 1,208 | 1.88 | 92 | 49.0 | 19 | 12 | 101 | 10 |
| Rodd, Nash & Lit Brampton TP | 1,934 | 3.10 | 157 | 50.5 | 17 | 10 | 190 | 14 |
| Staunton-on-Arrow PH | 2,040 | 3.19 | 393 | 123.1 | 3 | 4 | 510 | 19 |
| Stapleton TP | 1,252 | 1.96 | 156 | 79.5 | 12 | 19 | 66 | 3 |
| Titley PH | 2,030 | 3.17 | 328 | 103.6 | 6 | 14 | 145 | 13 |
| Walford TP | 1,611 | 2.52 | 212 | 84.1 | 9 | 6 | 268 | 16 |
| Wigmore PH | 3,290 | 5.15 | 476 | 92.6 | 8 | 46 | 72 | 5 |
| Willey TP | 2,095 | 3.28 | 147 | 44.8 | 21 | 10 | 209 | 15 |

## Notes to Table 4.15

### General

Owing to unresolved problems concerning acreages the following parishes and township have been excluded: Aymestry PH, Kinton TP, Marlow TP, Whitton and Trippleton TP
Acreage is from 1841 census, except where noted.
Population is from 1831 census, except where noted.
Rank order is calculated with highest population density ranking as 1, but *lowest* numb of acres per owner ranking as 1 (because the low acreage figures represent high density of owners).
Number of owners from 1830 land tax assessments (Herefordshire Record Office).

### Particular

Adforton — included Stanway, Paytoe and Grange. Acreage from *Kelley's Directory of Herefordshire* (1905).

Brampton Bryan included townships of Brampton Bryan and Beresford with Pedwardine.
Burrington — included four non-assessed owners.
Byton — included three non-assessed owners.
Combe — acreage from 1871 census.
Lower Harpton — included two non-assessed owners.
Lower Kinsham · acreage from 1871 census.
Leintwardine — includes the two separate townships of Brakes and Heath with Jay (1831 population). Land tax assessment (1826) definitely includes Brakes. Acreage is that given for Leintwardine in *Kelly's Herefordshire* (1905).

Letton and Newton — acreage from *Kelly's Herefordshire* (1905).
Litton and Cascob — acreage from 1851 census.
Rodd, Nash and Little Brampton — acreage from 1871 census.
Stapleton — acreage from 1871 census.
Walford — acreage from *Kelly's Herefordshire* (1905).
Wigmore — included Limebrook TP.
Willey — acreage from *Kelly's Herefordshire* (1905).


In a limited way, the model has been shown as valid by the Wigmore data. More particularly, the exercise is indicative of the considerable value of the land tax returns for this type of research and as these documents have survived widely the scope for future initiatives has been demonstrated. On its own, this exercise is little more than an excursion into statistical analysis, but the discussion of causes and effects elsewhere in this book, as well as the origins of village differentiation, rescue it from this emptiness.


## Summary

This summary of statistical data has established two main propositions. First, it has shown that the social distribution of landownership varied considerably from one township to the next over wide areas of England. In this respect it lends support to the thesis advanced in earlier chapters. Rural England in the nineteenth century contained two socio-economic systems which were as distinct in practice then, as they are conceptually distinct in the minds of today's historians. However, the second proposition which it supports qualifies the first, because the evidence of the existence of continua, especially in the fuller Leicestershire data, forces us to abandon the idea of the absolutely clear cut dichotomy between open and closed villages, implied in poor law literature.

The best position to adopt, in order to resolve the apparent contradiction between the two propositions, is the acceptance of a four-fold classification as the basis for a working model of English rural society in this period. A number of studies and works of reference, including those of Gray, Obelkevich, Everitt and the Imperial Gazetteer have found it satisfactory to work in terms of four types of village, thus:

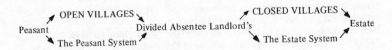

In conclusion, it is important to note that although the use of four categories is recommended, the context of evidence drawn on in the next two chapters often limits the discussion to only the two major divisions of 'open' and 'closed'. It is to be hoped that future research will lead either to the wider application of the four categories or to the use of correlation tests on the large amount of quantitative data available.

## Notes

1. Tithe and village surveys and land tax returns usually give fairly comprehensive information as to occupiers; estate surveys are also useful for information on occupiers. Enclosure awards, however, seldom give information on occupiers, but in combination with land tax returns can be made to yield some information on the occupation of land and other kinds of property. In some townships rating assessments can also be used for the analysis of ownership and occupation, but these documents are probably less plentiful for villages than towns.

2. I am indebted to Sir Benjamin Bromhead, Bart., for permission to study the family papers and to publish details therefrom. See also J.B. Harley, *Maps for the Local Historian: A Guide to the British Sources* (London, Standing Conference for Local History, 1972), Ch. 2.

3. D.B. Grigg, 'Small and Large Farms in England and Wales', *Geography*, vol. 48 (1963), p. 272, defined the small farm as *less* than 100 acres.

4. The standard reference is W.E. Tate, (ed. M.E. Turner) *A Domesday of English Enclosure Acts and Awards* (Institute of Agricultural History, University of Reading, 1978). See also W.E. Tate, *The English Village Community and the Enclosure Movements* (Gollancz, London, 1967); and Harley, *Maps for the Local Historian* Ch. 3.

5. V.M. Lavrovsky, 'Parliamentary Enclosures in Suffolk, 1790-1814', *Econ. Hist. Rev.*, vol. 7 (1937), pp. 187-208.

6. Data on Sherington, Bucks., taken from A.C. Chibnall, *Sherington Fiefs and Fields of a Buckinghamshire Village* (Cambridge University Press, 1965), p. 250 (figures in brackets estimated from Table 43); on Ardington, Berks, from M.A. Havinden, *Estate Villages* (Lund Humphries, London, 1966), pp. 53, 205-6; on Mareham-le-Fen, Lincs., from Lincs. Record Office, Chat. 3/9, ff. 3-16; and on Wetheral, Cumbs., from Cumbria Record Office, Tithe Award, T. 196. I would like to thank my mother, Mrs. Vera Mills, for transcribing the Mareham Survey and my secretary, Miss Margaret Martin, for making the necessary calculations. *White's Directory of Lincolnshire* (1856) gives the total average of Mareham-le-Fen as 1,862, the discrepancy of nearly 300 acres is probably accounted for by Mareham's share in Wildmore Fen.

7. The standard reference on tithe surveys is E.J. Evans, *Tithes and the Tithe Commutation Act 1836* (Bedford Square Press, London, 1978); see especially pp. 31-4.

8. The enumeration was used mainly to assist in the identification of owners and occupiers, whose place of residence (and therefore occupation) was unclear from the tithe survey. As this element was only a small minority, it should not be thought that the use of an enumeration is obligatory before a table such as Table 4.2 can be produced; its main features could be made out quite clearly from the tithe survey alone.

9. For further information on Melbourn see D.R. Mills, 'Land, Home and Kinship in Melbourn' in R. Smith (ed.) *Land, Kinship and Lifecycle* (Edward Arnold, London, in press) Ch. 13 and D.R. Mills, 'The Technique of House Population: Experience from a Cambridgeshire Village, 1841', *Local Historian* vol. 13 (1978), pp. 86-97.

10. See above Ch. 3 pp. 45-6 for a discussion of the Chayanovian model. As the tithe survey is the only comprehensive picture of landholding in nineteenth-century Melbourn, it is difficult to see how Chayanov's hypothesis can be tested except perhaps by using the data of the court books.

11. For other uses of tithe surveys to analyse peasant holdings see Barbara Kerr, *Bound to the Soil: a Social History of Dorset 1750-1918* (John Baker, London, 1968) pp. 57 and 256-7 and W.M. Williams, *A West Country Village: Ashworthy* (Routledge, London, 1963), pp. 21 and 27. In the Dorset village of Whitechurch Canonicorum there was a large number of labourers occupying smallholdings, perhaps an effect of the unusual structure of dairy-farming in Dorset; but also there were no less than 19 dual occupationists, combining agriculture with a trade or craft.

12. The latest and most useful statement in the discussion of the validity of the land tax returns is that by M.E. Turner, 'Parliamentary Enclosure and Landowner-ship Change in Buckinghamshire', *Econ. Hist. Rev.*, vol. 28 (1975), pp. 565-81, especially pp. 565-6.

13. The first correlation, using Spearman's Rho, gave $R = 0.968$, confident at the very high level of 99.999 per cent ($N = 163$). The second correlation (on the 45 properties with no buildings) gave $R = 0.37$, confident at about 97.5 per cent. These results are not inconsistent, as may appear at first sight, partly because they are based on rank order positions and not on absolute values. Taken together, they suggest that land tax assessments were, at Melbourn at least, carefully made and reflected true property values in an adequate way. The larger owners possibly paid at lower rates because their land was most distant from the village on the higher slopes of the chalk escarpment, with thinner soil.

Since writing this section, I have had correspondence with Mr. R.J. Grover of Portsmouth Polytechnic, who is using land tax assessments in a study of east Kent. He has found it necessary to use acreage equivalents when combining information about individual taxpayers who paid tax in more than one parish. Without this common denominator the different tax figures cannot be related satisfactorily. This procedure is based on Mr. Grover's discovery that within parishes there is a high degree of correlation between tax paid and the acreage of a holding, though with some substantial deviations for a few holdings.

14. R. Mellors, *Old Nottingham Suburbs: Then and Now* (Bell, Nottingham, 1914), Ch. 1. The land tax returns for Lenton are in the Notts. Record Office and those for Barwell in the Leics. RO.

15. See Ch. 2 pp. 38-40.

16 For further information on Leicestershire see D.R. Mills, 'Landownership and rural population, with special reference to Leicestershire in the mid-nineteenth century', unpublished PhD thesis, University of Leicester, 1963.

17. F.M.L. Thompson, *English Landed Society in the Ninteenth Century*

(Routledge, London, 1963), Tables II and VI, which relate to 1870.

18. Tate, *English Village Community*, pp. 99-100. J.A. Yelling, *Common Field and Enclosure in England 1450-1850* (Macmillan, London, 1977) – p. 8 quotes Homer (1766) to the effect that four-fifths was an appropriate legislative basis, provided the manorial lord and impropriator concurred outside this fraction.

19. See P. Grey, 'The Pauper Problem in Bedfordshire from 1795 to 1834', unpublished M.Phil thesis, University of Leicester, 1975, p. 81: in 43 per cent of Bedfordshire parishes in 1832 over half the tax was paid by one owner.

20. This point has been emphasised by H.A. Fuller, 'Landownership and the Lindsey Landscape', *Annals of the Association of American Geographers*, vol. 66 (1976), pp. 14-24.

21. See Mills, 'Landownership and Rural Population', especially Ch. 2, Appendix 2 and Figs. 1-10, 37-8 and 46-52.

22. For details see Ibid., Appendix 4. The same kind of relative stability was noted by D.B. Grigg *The Agricultural Revolution in South Lincolnshire* (Cambridge University Press, 1966), pp. 171-3. See also Turner, 'Parliamentary Enclosure'.

23. There was, however, a broad correlation between average farm size in 1867 and the density of the agricultural population in 1831: see Mills 'Landownership and Rural Population', pp. 159-62.

24. Ibid., pp. 212-16.

25. BPP, 1847-8, LIII, II, *Return Showing Population, Annual Value of Property, Expenditure, Rate in the £, Total Number of Paupers Relieved*. This return covers the whole of England.

26. See Mills, 'Landownership and Rural Population', Ch. 7.

27. The original data can be found in D.R. Mills, 'Population and Settlement in Kesteven (Lincs) *c*.1775-*c*.1885', unpublished MA thesis, University of Nottingham, 1958, mainly in the appendices. See also D.R. Mills, (ed.), *English Rural Communities: The Impact of a Specialised Economy* (Macmillan, London, 1973), Ch. 2.

28. J. Obelkevich, *Religion and Rural Society: South Lindsey, 1825-1875* (Oxford University Press, 1976), pp. 7 and 12-13. Obelkevich uses the term 'freeholders' parish', as he was following my earlier nomenclature as published in D.R. Mills, 'English Villages in the Eighteenth and Nineteenth Centuries: A Sociological Approach', *Amateur* (now *Local*) *Historian*, vol. 6 (1965), pp. 271-8, but his text indicates that he was broadly in line with my distinction between peasant and divided villages. His data are derived from the 1831 land tax returns.

29. Ibid., p. 30.

30. Ibid., p. 13.

31. H.L. Gray, 'Yeoman Farming in Oxfordshire from the Sixteenth Century to the Nineteenth', *Quarterly Journal of Economics*, vol. 24 (1909), pp. 293-326.

*32.* Mills, 'Landownership and Rural Population', Appendix 4.

33. Grigg, *Agricultural Revolution*, p. 93. He also reported very considerable variations in numbers of owners per parish, as in the other two old Divisions of Lincolnshire.

34. J.M. Wilson, *The Imperial Gazetteer of England and Wales* (6 vols., London, 1870; or two volume edition, 1875).

35. A. Everitt, *The Pattern of Rural Dissent: The Nineteenth Century* (Leicester University Press, 1974).

36. D. Sylvester, 'Rural Settlement in Cheshire', *Transactions of the Historic Society of Lancashire and Cheshire*, vol. 101 (1949), pp. 12-17 and *The Rural Landscape of the Welsh Borderland: A Study in Historical Geography* (Macmillan, London, 1969), pp. 166-7.

37. This paragraph is based partly on John Hutchinson, *Herefordshire Biogra-*

*phies* (Hereford, 1890), pp. 57 and 67; C.J. Robinson, *A History of the Castles of Herefordshire and Their Lords* (Hill, Hereford and Longman, London, 1846), pp. 8, 15-16 and 142; *Dictionary of National Biography* (*sub* Harley, the surname of the Earls of Oxford); Duncumb's Ms. History of Wigmore Hundred, *c.* 1873 (in Hereford Public Library), and more generally on Lord Rennell of Rodd, *Valley on the March: A History of a Group of Manors on the Herefordshire March of Wales* (Oxford University Press, 1958). The Herefordshire Record Office reference for 1830 Land Tax Assessments of Wigmore Hundred is Q/Rel/56/Wg/1-32. I should like to thank the staff of the library and record office for their assistance.

# 5 THE ORIGINS AND BASIS OF VILLAGE DIFFERENTIATION

> 'The typical village in the sixteenth century Midlands was one in which the ranks of society were built up from a broad base of poor wage workers with little or no land to the squire at the top. The fenland village was differentiated more at the summit than at the foundation. Its aristocracy was not a single squire and his family, but a substantial group of middling-rich yeomen.' J. Thirsk, *English Peasant Farming: the Agrarian History of Lincolnshire from Tudor to recent times* (London, Routledge, 1957), p. 47.

Although this book is primarily about the nineteenth century, the importance of geographical momentum is such that it is essential to consider, however briefly, some aspects of the prior period, during which the basis evolved for the wide local differences between villages observed in our period of study. The chapter is organised under four headings: enclosures, commons, forests, and longitudinal studies. The purpose of the first section is to show that there was no simple connection between enclosed parishes and closed villages, as is even now sometimes thought.[1] While the mode and period of enclosure depended on a wide range of other circumstances as to its influence on village differentiation, the survival of commons can be seen to have had a more straightforward effect, in favour of the survival, even the expansion, of the peasantry. The prior existence of forests – in the legal rather than the physical sense – had, like that of enclosures, a somewhat equivocal bearing on the differentiation of villages. In these first three sections discussion is confined mainly to the early modern period. The longitudinal studies are used as a specific means of demonstrating the need to look even further back for the origins of village differentiation.

## Enclosure

The literature on the history of enclosure has been coherently reviewed in the last few years by Yelling, whose book almost begins with the caution that:

. . . there is no one package of results and causes associated with enclosure, nor is the relationship with any particular feature, such as landownership, simple to describe.[2]

While Yelling concentrates on common field and examines enclosure history mainly for its own sake, his consideration of causes and effects reaches out towards our present concerns. For example, he points out the over simple view taken by many contemporaries and later writers that enclosure meant the end of the self-governing village community and to access to the land for labourers.[3] Access and self-governance had disappeared long before from many communities, while some self-governing attributes could often be found decades after enclosure. Enclosure being sometimes a sudden, traumatic event, and almost always having a visible effect on the landscape, has been taken as a scapegoat too often when explaining the supposed decline of the village from a prior period of more Gemeinschaft-like existence. Yet it cannot be ignored altogether.

A useful approach is sparked off by Yelling's remark that:

It is the nature of the economy which is the fundamental determinant of landholding patterns at the regional scale, and the effects of varying methods of enclosure are only superimposed on this.[4]

In effect this suggestion causes us to return to our earlier distinction between champion and hamlet England, for broadly speaking these represent two economies with opposite biases – respectively, arable and pasture. Furthermore, as the common field system was so firmly entrenched in champion England, its abolition was bound to have a much greater effect that in the pastoral zones, especially where common fields, rather than common wastes were concerned.

The larger settlement nuclei of felden areas involved a greater fragmentation of holdings in the common fields by virtue of the greater number of families to be fed. Piecemeal enclosure would therefore be more difficult and the cohesiveness of the peasant community would be applied to the maintenance of arable acreages. Conversely, in areas of dispersed settlement, whether in hamlets or isolated farms, there is reason to believe that the lack of identity of interests among farmers would permit piecemeal enclosure to proceed earlier and faster, especially as the fragmentation of holdings in any common fields would be less obstructive. As we shall see in a moment, the continued wide availability of pasture in hamlet England helped to maintain a large number of small farms, whereas in champion England these flourished best through the continuance of an arable regime.[5] There are, therefore, dangers of circularity of argument.

The timing of enclosure is another important aspect of the subject and it is especially necessary to distinguish in champion England between enclosure before and after about 1700, or alternatively between private and parliamentary enclosure. The earlier the enclosure, on the whole, the more likely it was to have been associated with depopulation, thus producing many of the lacunae in population maps of the nineteenth century. However, in order to appreciate fully the significance of this early enclosure in terms of village differentiation, it is necessary to have cause and effect in the correct sequence. While the final act of enclosure was frequently associated with evictions, the main direction of causation was the previous existence of a small community, for whatever reason, which provided enclosing landlords with a relatively easy opportunity to enclose the common fields and wastes of an entire township.[6] As the purpose of these enclosures was to convert arable to pasture, the effects were bound to be cataclysmic in landscape terms, as well as in terms of population change, because the economics of large scale pastoral agriculture required the encloser to have 'as great a stake in the land as possible and he needed to achieve an immediate consolidation of the farms to a level suitable for the new enterprise'.[7]

Parliamentary enclosure was a different matter, since the private Act could be used to acquire consensus where tougher methods had been necessary in the past and, in any case, there was now no necessary correlation between enclosure and conversion to pasture in large farms. In fact the seventeenth century and the earlier part of the eighteenth were a transitional period during which the peasantry were involved in amicable agreements to enclose considerable tracts of land.[8] A number of investigations have shown, again, that the timing of parliamentary enclosure was related to landownership, rather than the reverse. Hunt's work in Leicestershire and Turner's in Buckinghamshire, in particular, have indicated that, although other factors were involved, fragmentation of ownership had the effect of delaying enclosure. Moreover, enclosure in this period of rapid population growth did not lead to depopulation or the rapid decline of the small owner.[9] A whole range of other data can be shown not to relate simply to enclosure, including population density, poor rates and farm sizes.[10]

However, in respect of access to pasture the enclosure process remains a very important factor in explaining why a peasantry survived in some places and not in others. It should be noted that I have written 'access to pasture' and not the mere *existence* of pasture, for the great sheep and cattle enclosures of the Midlands were of no benefit to any farmer who was denied access. Pasture remained most accessible in hamlet England, a number of writers stressing the importance of the distinction between felden and pastoral parishes for this specific reason. Wrightson has written that 'pastoral communities tended . . . to present a greater equality in the distribution of wealth, largely because of the opportunities afforded by the existence of extensive common pastures . . .',[11] while Ravensdale states that 'On the fen edge the pastoral side of the village economies seems to have been the area in which both peasantry and gentry could most easily seek to take profit from the market.'[12] Conversely, Turner has shown for felden areas of Buckinghamshire and nearby counties before 1750, that both piecemeal enclosure and the adaptation of common field rules and regulations had 'a very close connection with the search for additional grazing lands'.[13] We pass on to consider a particular form of pasture, the common waste.

## The Importance of Commons for the Peasantry

Commons were clearly of importance to the peasant system, to those who wished to keep a little independence, for otherwise why did landlords, especially in the period from 1750, look so askance at them? The Hammonds referred to commons as the patrimony of the poor and quoted the views of certain landlords and large farmers that commons were not good for the commoners, breeding immorality — whatever that might mean — and more particularly a dislike for regular, disciplined work.[14]

It was George Sturt who gave one of the most articulate accounts of the importance of commons from actual observation and coincidentally defined the 'peasant system', using this actual term, as one in which 'people derived the necessaries of life from the materials and soil of their own countryside'. His village, Middle Bourne, was on the southernmost heathlands of Surrey, near Farnham. The 1861 enclosure of the commons was only just having an effect in the 1890s because owners had failed to fence in many of the new allotments, cottagers still making use of their rights to keep poultry, donkeys and cows and to take fuel. Sturt stressed that the old way of life was one in which subsistence was a very significant supplement to wage-earning.[15] Equally subsistence from commons could be an important supplement to a smallholding and some families benefited from all three sources of 'income'.

The subsistence which could be obtained from commons varied from one part of the country and from one common to another, but the range of possibilities included food (animals, fish, birds and fruits), fuel (peat, wood and coal), bedding for animals (bracken, for instance) building materials (reeds for thatch, clay for bricks, stone and sand and gravel) and, most obviously, grazing for geese, sheep, pigs, horses, cows and any other animals the cottager felt inclined to keep.

The inability of the ruling class to comprehend the economic signi-ficance of commons for cottage households must have been almost as great as our own inability today, unless the potential is pointed out to us,[16] for they, like us, were thoroughly accustomed to rely upon special-ists to provide their various wants. We are dealing here with a survival of some of that lack of dependence on specialists which characterised earlier economies. Commons, however, were also important in two other specific respects — in connection with squatting and the raw materials of manufacture.

The open parishes, where commons were less well regulated than where there was close manorial control, are often reported to have received an influx of population which squatted in rude cottages upon the common waste. It is not unusual to see marked on enclosure maps the occasional cottage or two on spare pieces of roadside ground and such types of squatting can be suspected on the ground today where long narrow cottage gardens pinch the width of country lanes.[17] How-ever, in some areas squatting went well beyond the surreptitious cottage or two. The rapid rise of population in the parishes of Windsor Forest (1676 — estimated 4,715; 1801 — 13,065) was attributed very consider-ably to unlicensed cottages. Similarly Enfield Chase gained about a hundred squatter houses in the period 1670-1700, where there was said to be an abundance of loose, idle and disorderly persons. Squatting was also said to be extensive in east Suffolk.[18]

One well documented area is the Weald of Sussex, which is des-cribed by Brandon as 'freer . . . than in the champion, but this was a dear-bought advantage because the land kept people poor and life generally had the uncouthness associated with pioneering frontiers for many generations' (p. 36). In this book little play has been made of the significance of physical factors, but here is an example of clear, if not deterministic influence of the physical environment on the social deve-lopment of communities. Hundreds of smallholdings and cottages are reported to have been scattered indiscriminately across Wealden wastes, such as the Heathfield-Burwash-Battle and Ashdown Forest areas. The permission of manorial lords was sometimes given, but more often one reads of attempts to get rid of squatters' cottages or to curtail their numbers. Squatter settlements like Punnett's Town lacked clear foci, except for the pubs and the nonconformist chapels. Early cabins were constructed of turf and thatch, a mode still in use for new houses as late as the 1870s. More solid buildings followed when cottages were legalised and then another local vernacular style — white weatherboard — was used. Squatters and the peasantry more generally lacked the capital to make clear breaks with traditional building methods and materials, while the landed classes were busy innovating with alien materials such as Welsh slate. The poverty of the 'free' areas is underlined by the subsistence economy of potatoes and oats, wheat as a bread grain being precluded by the lack of lime in Wealden soil.[19]

Another important study of a squatting settlement is that undertaken by Samuel at Headington Quarry, now part of Oxford, but formerly a waste area on the western edge of Shotover Common. Here he has drawn a picture of the independent labourer and craftsman working at a variety of occupations, as season, demand and family circumstances varied. Many worked in the building trades in Oxford, or as quarrymen or brickmakers, emphasising the industrial role of the countryside. Headington Quarry reflected Gemeinschaft relationships in its lack of 'real' capitalists and the importance of subsistence and barter which delayed the full onset of a money economy. Yet there was no patriarchal figure in Quarry, not even an absentee manorial lord exercising minimal control over village affairs.[20]

The absence of a large owner and the consequent dispersal of control over property were factors favourable to the maintenance of social solidarity, based on kinship networks and the relative unimportance of social 'class' distinctions. For example, cottage tenancies were taken up through local and family networks rather than through formal contractual channels in the open market. Charities were absent and in hard times the family was thrown back on the resources of its kinship network. The family was a unit of production, as well as consumption. Family businesses expanded as family size increased in accordance with the Chayanovian model. Prevalence of dissent and the development of indifference to church-going of any kind were marked features of Headington Quarry, making it comparable in this respect to the late Victorian town. Radicalism was there too, far to the 'left' of respectable Oxford Liberalism in some ways, but a form of conservatism in others: 'Quarry radicalism was a defensive affair, a matter of preserving old established rights and privileges intact' (p. 153).[21]

The name Headington Quarry is itself a reminder of the potential of commons for raw materials, in this case for brickmaking. There must have been a hazy line between materials taken for subsistence purposes and those developed for the market. Perhaps the most important material of all was fuel, especially where commons were partially covered with timber as they often were in the forest districts. In fact, it is difficult again to draw a distinction between the resources of commons and forests. Writing of the sixteenth and seventeenth centuries, Everitt has noted that two thirds of labourers leaving inventories had by-employments:

> Most of the industries were connected either with forest and woodland crafts, or with the spinning and weaving of flax, hemp and wool (p. 425). Other by-employments, such as potting, tiling, nailing, coaling and iron-smelting, which required supplies of fuel, were also centred in woodland districts (p. 427).

Once again we are told that the social structure of such areas was different from that in the champion districts, consisting often of husbandmen and labourers only, a mobile population ready to accept new ideas (which apparently did not come solely from association with the landed gentry). These places were the resorts of drovers, wayfarers, vagabonds, gypsies, bandits and millenarian sects.[22]

The final question to consider in connection with commons is to assess the effects on social structure of their enclosure. One of the remarkable facts about both Headington Quarry and Middle Bourne is the late date of survival of commons; the description of the economies of these villages around 1900 serves as a partial answer to the question, for their uniqueness depends on most other villages having lost a significant part of the basis for a peasant economy at the time of enclosure. This assertion is supported by the experience of the Hampshire village of Tadley, not far from Middle Bourne, where the enclosure act gave a common of 100 acres to *non*-freeholders, on which they could graze a beast, dig peat and collect wood. It is probably not a coincidence that there were no tied cottages in this village, where 100,000 besoms (a kind of brush) a year were produced from heather or birch, bound by withies (dried strips of the black willow).[23]

Tadley was unusual in the allocation of such a large area to non-freeholders. The three acre allotment for recreational purposes granted in the Melbourn (Cambs.) enclosure of 1839 is more typical. The general impression of enclosure commissioners' activities is that they were scrupulously careful to grant small allotments in recompense to the *owners* of common rights, provided the rights could be proved. However, for several reasons, this cannot be taken as an indication that enclosure had no adverse effect on the economic base of the lower peasantry and the labourers.

First, where the peasant was not an owner he could not automatically expect to take on the tenancy of the land granted in lieu of common rights, for that land could merely 'get lost' in the larger allotments granted to his landlord.

Secondly, as a small owner his fencing costs would be disproportionately high.

Thirdly, the destruction of the common took away the conveniences of communal pasturing of milk cows, which had then to be fetched up from the grass field twice each day for milking by each family separately.

Fourthly, a significant number of villagers had used the commons without legal rights and this practice now stopped without recompense.

Finally, it is difficult to see how there could be any recompense for the loss of fuel, building materials and the like in a landscape which was now parcelled out and tidied up, with the manorial lord and possibly the tithe owner taking large blocks of land out of the reach of the peasantry, in compensation for loss of manorial rights and the extinction of tithe. All in all, the enclosure of commons was a bad day in the annals of the peasantry, although its effects may not have been dramatic and immediate.[24]

## Forests

There are at least three channels through which forests may have affected the social structure and economy of villages lying within or near them. First is their prior influence on the settlement pattern of the area, which was not conducive to the growth of tightly controlled and tidy nuclei. Secondly, is their provision of raw materials favouring the peasant system. There is no need to say more under these heads at this point. The third channel is the institution of afforestation which was a legal status rather than a recognition of the natural vegetation cover. Afforested areas, especially those belonging to the Crown, were outside normal manorial jurisdiction during the medieval and early modern periods. Did this favour the estate system or the peasant system?

The answer appears to be that it depended on the circumstances and in a very close examination these would have to include the settlement pattern and natural resources. Discussion is limited here to the consideration of a few examples to illustrate the variety of experience. Ashdown Forest, Windsor Forest and Enfield Chase have already been mentioned as areas in which there were vast squatter populations during the seventeenth and eighteenth centuries. E.P. Thompson shows very clearly that both gentry and their inferiors could take advantage of the Crown and the natural circumstances of a woodland environment:

> The absence of compact villages, and the dispersal of foresters, made social discipline impossible: 'nothing more favours irregular and lawless habits of life among the inferior class . . . than scattered and sequestered habitations.' The gentry, also in their scattered and sequestered habitations, had decided over the previous century that enclosure was the best resource for agrarian class control . . . (so that) the 'inferior class' could then be brought in collected villages, each with a constable on patrol.

Thompson's reference is to Windsor Forest and the context is the Commission of 1809.[25]

Leicester Forest provides an example of what appears to be outright gains for the gentry. Although it might be possible to show that some of the villages standing some distance from the original outer boundary, such as Earl Shilton and Enderby gained in the strength of their peasantry through medieval common rights in the Forest, there are no such doubts about the central area of the Forest. Even in the nineteenth century, 250 years on from the last land sales, it was still an area of large farms, extra parochial areas (paying no rates) and no villages.[26] The same applies to the core area of Needwood Forest in Staffordshire, where deforestation in 1801 was followed by the creation of a characteristic post enclosure landscape of straight roads, large fields and no villages.[27] Neither the absence of villages, nor a history of afforestation are a guarantee that the peasantry were strong.


## Longitudinal Studies

The origins of village differentiation are obviously very complex. The absence of clearly distinguishable pathways of experience is one reason why so much of English local history has remained idiographic, or literally parochial. Among other factors, not already mentioned, that would have to be taken into account in any comprehensive study of the development of village differentiation are the following:

The conditions of the original settlement;
Manorial structure, both before and after the Domesday Survey;
Demesne farming;
The distribution of sokes and sokemen;
Modes of inheritance;
Monastic property;
The conversion of copyholds to freeholds.

It is also useful to note here that a statistical study of 63 Leicester-shire townships in the framework-knitting districts of the centre and south-west of the county showed significant correlations between data relating to years spread out from 1670 to 1851. Thus the density of population based on the hearth tax of 1670 showed the same spatial variation as that derived from the 1851 census, while evidence of land-ownership taken from the 1719 election (voting freeholders) and the first year of extant land tax returns (1780) fitted the same mould remarkably well. Such a degree of geographical inertia over a period approaching two centuries is reason enough to look for the origins of village differentiation long before the nineteenth and even before the seventeenth century.[28]

In order to illustrate some of the variety of local circumstances and to demonstrate the potentiality of longitudinal studies of individual parishes, the remainder of this chapter comprises five brief case studies. The investigation of the descent of a manor, or the evolution of the landscape of a parish have a value and interest of their own, but they can also be focused on specific problems of national interest. Local historians reading these case studies should bear in mind that they have been written from this perspective and they contain only the detail most relevant to this perspective. All five studies relate to Leicestershire villages, which limits the range of circumstances, but gives some coher-ence to the selection, particularly as four of the five studies are based principally on the work of G.F. Farnham, a local historian who was working in Leicestershire in the earlier part of the century.

## Whitwick

This village is situated about twelve miles north-west of Leicester in the coalfield and on the edge of Charnwood, an area which contained vast acreages of common grazing.[29] Whitwick had only one manor in 1086 and while there is evidence of temporary sub-infeudation during the twelfth century, the descent of this single manor is very straightforward. It belonged to Hugh de Grentemesnil in 1086 and passed down the Earls of Leicester and Winchester until 1264, when the splitting-up of the honor of Winchester caused Whitwick to pass to the Earls of Buchan, passing then by marriage to the Beaumonts in 1310, who lived on the manor for a very short time in the 1320s, the only paramount lords known to have done so.

The Beaumonts appear in general to have neglected their Leicestershire property in the fourteenth and fifteenth centuries and on the death of the last of the line in 1507, Whitwick manor passed to the Crown. It was granted away from the Crown at least twice in that century, but the grant by James I in 1612/3 to Henry, Earl of Huntingdon was the last one and the manorial rights remained with that family until the close of the nineteenth century.

Thus, although the manor was kept intact and, indeed, contained rights in several outlying places, continued neglect allowed tenants on the spot to better themselves. An *inquisition post mortem* of 1349 mentions 40 customary tenants, but also an unspecified number of free tenants. In 1427 12 messuages were in the lord's hands for want of tenants; this may have been the prolonged after-effects of the plagues of the previous century. In 1604 Exchequer depositions record the fact that there had been squatting on the Forest commons (part of Charnwood); and in 1609 an inquisition shows that the demesne had been split up among the villagers, but no evidence of copyholds for this property could be found.

It would be interesting to know the outcome of this inquisition, for it seems that the lords of Whitwick lost considerable ground. In 1666 the Lay Subsidy lists 61 hearths, ten of which belonged to Mr. Walter Hastings; four persons owned three, seven persons two hearths and the remaining 25 one hearth each. This suggests a fairly well developed peasant community.

When the election of 1719 occurred 18 men of Whitwick voted as well as nine others who owned a freehold in the village but lived elsewhere. In the tax returns of 1780 about 60 names are listed, in 1800 80 names and in 1832 the number reached 125. No doubt much of this later increase was connected with the development of coal-mining, but the seeds of growth had been sown much earlier.

## Stoke Golding

It would be rash to assume that Whitwick's steady development from the simple manor of 1086 to an industrial settlement was a characteristic pattern. Stoke Golding is an excellent example of the way in which the fortunes of the peasantry could fluctuate.[30] Unfortunately the early part of the story cannot be told, because Stoke Golding was considered part of Hinckley up to 1297, when the first separate mention shows that the manor was under the chief lordship of the Earl of Lancaster and Leicester, who had two sub-tenants. One of the sub-tenancies was split again into two and this might appear to have been the beginning of complete fission. Yet this was not so, for by devious means of inheritance, marriage and purchase, Sir John Harington, of Exton, Rutland, succeeded in uniting the portions in the closing years of the sixteenth century. But at this stage the fortunes of Stoke Golding took another sudden turn, for in 1603 Sir John, now Lord Harington, sold land to his 25 tenants in the village; the manor house was sold to a Basil Trumell, but the manorial rights are lost sight of completely.

The sudden disposal of land in this year is probably accounted for by the fact that enclosure took place between 1601 and 1604.[31] Lord Harington was probably content to let the farmers of Stoke Golding exercise their initiative to the full in the new system of partible husbandry and allowed them to become freeholders, instead of copyholders. In 1719 14 men, 11 of them resident, voted in respect of freeholds in this township; in 1780 there were 38 owners; in 1801, 49 and in 1832, 45, with an average of 29 acres each. Small wonder that Stoke Golding had one of the highest ratios of stocking frames to population in the county in 1844.

## Wigston Magna

No account of this nature would be complete without reference to Wigston Magna, a village now in the southern suburbs of Leicester, which is the subject of a book appropriately entitled *The Midland Peasant*.[32] Wigston is unusual in that the two parish churches originally represented two communities, one English the other Danish in origin, containing between them in 1086 31 sokemen, one priest, two knights and four Frenchmen. The presence of so many free tenants and the large total population of the two communities together constituted favourable conditions for the growth of a large peasant community. Yet in 1086 there was only one manor, in the hands of Hugh de Grentesmesnil, and this passed down the line of the Leicester earls to 1204, still intact apart from the fact that a substantial piece of property had been granted to the Croft family and this became a separate manor.

After the death of the fourth earl in 1204 the main Wigston manor passed to the Winchester honor, while the smaller manor remained in the honor of Leicester, passing later to the overlordship of the Duchy of Lancaster. About 1240 the Winchester manor passed to the Earls of Oxford, who were its overlords until 1526.

The overlords of both manors had a succession of mesne lords, none of whom, significantly, was ever resident; in the Duchy manor there was a confused period in the fourteenth century when several mesne lords followed each other rapidly. In these conditions the free tenants were able to gain ground: their share of the land was already about 40 per cent in 1086. In the twelfth and thirteenth centuries they were briskly buying and selling land, an obvious sign of a healthy peasant community, yet a feature distinguishing it from the peasantries of the continent.[33]

At the end of the sixteenth century came the final splitting up of the manors. The Turvilles had held the Duchy manor ever since 1435, but in 1586-7 they had occasion to sell out, possibly because of difficulties due to rising prices. Their land was sold in 16 lots, all except three going to Wigston men.

The break-up of the Oxford manor was not so straightforward. In 1526 the last of the Oxford male line died and this event was followed by half a century of confused administration and rapid changes of ownership. At all events, the copyholders felt their hand strong enough to test Sir John Danvers and Dame Elizabeth his wife in 1588 in the High Court of Chancery over matters of custom in the manor. The case was dismissed, but in 1606 20 copyholders bought their land, while seven of them became leaseholders.

In both manors some of the men who bought their land were already holders of other freehold land. This gave them a financial and psychological strongpoint from which to gain the freehold of their customary land. In this way Wigston entered the seventeenth century almost entirely in the hands of resident families; and although it experienced the general trend towards larger farms, this village, with about 120 owners in 1800, was one of the most divided in the county and one of the most prominent centres of the stocking trade.

## Market Bosworth

The present interest in Market Bosworth's history lies in two important facts: first, that there were two manors in 1086, including some sokemen and, secondly, that it became a small market town; yet in 1800 the village bore all the usual characteristics of an estate settlement.

The two manors were probably consolidated by the first Earl of Leicester at the beginning of the twelfth century.[34] The chief lordship of Market Bosworth passed down through the earldoms of Leicester, Winchester and Buchan to the Beaumont family, in the same way as Whitwick. It is in the record of the mesne tenants, however, that there is evidence of the sustained interest of a resident squire. The Harcourt family came into possession around the beginning of the twelfth century and they certainly held it in 1236. In 1293 Richard de Harcourt is known to have died, seised of the manor of Bosworth, which comprised, among other things, 'le Holde park' and another park called 'le South-wode', a market (charter granted 1285) and other perquisites, including rights in several outlying villages. The two parks were probably situated as today, on either side of the road leading eastward out of the village.

From the Lay Subsidies of the fourteenth century it can be seen that the village had developed into a sizable settlement, with some evidence of the existence of a commercial class. Market rights were often an important source of income to the medieval lords. It is, therefore, all the more interesting that by the eighteenth century the nobility and county gentry were in the habit of putting commerce at arm's length. Although the cattle market survives at Market Bosworth, the retail market had practically died out by 1790[35] and it is impossible to think of the village in the same bracket as nearby market towns such as Hinckley and Ashby de la Zouch.

The Harcourt family retained possession of the manor until 1509, when its sale was followed by a confused period which ended in 1571/2 with the arrival of the Dixie family, who have been continuously connected with Market Bosworth down to the present day. They bought an estate in which the manorial lord had almost complete control, all sign of the seven sokemen of 1086 having disappeared.

*Noseley*

Unlike Market Bosworth, Noseley, in the grassland area ten miles south-east of Leicester, seems never to have had the chance to develop into a community of peasant owners. Farnham's account begins with the remark that 'The manorial descent of Noseley is extremely simple.'[36] In 1086 there was one manor containing 16 villeins, eight bordars, three serfs and one priest, which belonged to Hugh de Grentesmesnil, from whom it descended through the earls of Leicester, and the earls and dukes of Lancaster to the Crown.

The mesne tenants, from 1220 if not earlier, were the Martivals, who are known to have had a capital messuage there at that date. Their preponderance as landholders is shown by the Lay Subsidy of 1327, when they paid 30s 9d. out of a total of 58 shillings. After 1332 their record dies out and in the middle years of the fourteenth century the succession is confused and incompletely known. From 1370 to 1397 the Hastings were lords and then, after another series of changes, the manor came to the Hazleriggs in or about 1430.

> In spite of all their vicissitudes this family has continued to hold Noseley until the present time, and is thus numbered among the few landed families now existing in Leicestershire, which hold property held by their ancestors before 1500 in male descent.[37]

Judging from the poll tax of 1381, Noseley was a community of 19 cottars and villeins and because there were no free tenants the Hazleriggs probably came to a village suitable for the development of a country estate. A will proved in 1544-5 shows that they had a manor house with gardens and a park. There was a memorial chapel as early as the fourteenth century; in or about 1336 it was merged with the parish church (so that Noseley became an extra-parochial place for a time) and the same building, full of Hazlerigg monuments, is used today as the parish church.

In 1504-9 the lordship was enclosed and the village partly depopulated.[38] By 1563 there were only eight households; in 1670 only one, but in 1676 the ecclesiastical census shows 20 adults. The 1801 census recorded four people; that of 1851 forty.[39] It is almost certain that these fluctuations record the comings and goings of the Hazlerigg family and its servants, for in 1719 only a Hazlerigg voted at the election and the family were the sole payers of land tax throughout a long period.

*Conclusion*

Generalisations are unlikely to emerge easily from the immense range of individual village experience illustrated by these five case histories. Noseley might look as if its fate was predetermined; but Whitwick, similarly placed in 1086, became an utterly different kind of village, even before coal-mining became important. Market Bosworth and Wigston Magna both had two manors and a number of sokemen in 1086, yet subsequent developments led off in opposite directions, to conditions which have been described, respectively, as 'that churchified and torified place' and 'a great unmanaged village'. Stoke Golding demonstrates how important a sudden turn in events could be, completely reversing what appears to have been a well established trend towards a well controlled manor. This conclusion must remain inconclusive in the sense that only a very large sample of case studies would be capable of bringing out any firm directions regarding the origins of village differentiation.

## Notes

1. For example, D.C. Moore, *The Politics of Deference: A Study of the Mid-nineteenth-Century English Political System* (Harvester Press, Brighton, 1976), p. 48: 'In the enclosed agricultural parishes (of Cambridgeshire) electoral leadership was generally exercised from the local manor house or parsonage'.

2. J.A. Yelling, *Common Field and Enclosure in England 1450-1850* (Macmillan, London, 1977), p. 2.

3. Ibid., p. 216.

4. Ibid., p. 118.

5. Based mainly on ibid., pp. 4, 43, 84 and 89-91.

6. See, for example, H.J. Habakkuk, 'Economic Functions of English Landowners in the Seventeenth and Eighteenth Century', *Explorations in Entrepreneurial History*, vol. 6 (1953), p. 96; M. Spufford, *A Cambridgeshire Community: Chippenham from Settlement to Enclosure* (Leicester University Press, 1965), pp. 53-5 and Yelling, *Common Field and Enclosure*, pp. 23-5 and 218.

7. Ibid., p. 113. For such an enterprise see Thorpe's account of Wormleighton, Warwickshire in D.R. Mills (ed.), *English Rural Communities: the Impact of a Specialised Economy* (Macmillan, London, 1973), pp. 45-60.

8. For example, see D.R. Mills, 'Enclosure in Kesteven', *Agric. Hist. Rev.*, vol. 7 (1959), pp. 85-6.

9. H.G. Hunt, 'The Chronology of Parliamentary Enclosure in Leicestershire', *Econ. Hist. Rev.*, vol. 10 (1957), pp. 265-72 and vol. 11 (1958-9), pp. 8-18 and 497-505, especially p. 501; and M.E. Turner, 'Parliamentary Enclosure and Landownership Change in Buckinghamshire', *Econ. Hist. Rev.*, vol. 28 (1975), pp. 565-81, especially p. 566. Turner's article is more concerned to demonstrate that although enclosure was accompanied by a brisk land market, the net effects in terms of the social distribution of ownership were not very considerable.

10. Yelling, *Common Field and Enclosure*, pp. 94-7, 226-7 and 230.

11. K. Wrightson, 'Aspects of Social Differentiation in Rural England c. 1580-1660', *Journal of Peasant Studies*, vol. 5 (1977), p. 35.

12. J.R. Ravensdale, *Liable to Floods: Village Landscape on the Edge of the Fens, AD 450-1850* (Cambridge University Press, 1974), p. 63, referring to the seventeenth century.

13. M.E. Turner, *Land Shortage as a Prelude to Parliamentary Enclosure* (University of Sheffield, Studies in Economic and Social History (1) 1975), p. 2.

14. J.L. and B. Hammond, *The Village Labourer* (2 vols., Guild Books edn, London, 1948), vol. 1, pp. 30-1 and 99. See also W.E. Tate, *The English Village Community and the Enclosure Movements* (Gollancz, London, 1967), pp. 163-6; G. White, *The Natural History and Antiquities of Selborne* (1st edn, 1789; Scolar Press, Ilkley, 1970), p. 19; R. Williams, *The Country and the City* (Chatto and Windus, London, 1973), p. 101; E.P. Thompson, *The Making of the English Working Class* (Penguin Books, Harmondsworth, 1968), pp. 242-3; B. Reaney, *The Class Struggle in Nineteenth Century Oxfordshire: The Social and Communal Background to the Otmoor Disturbances of 1830 to 1835* (Ruskin College,

Oxford, History Workshop Pamphlet No. 3, 1970), pp. 4, 6-7.

15. G. Bourne (= Sturt), *Change in the Village* (Chatto and Windus, London, 1912), pp. 1-4, 9, 87 and Ch. 8 'The Peasant System' more generally. See also F. Thompson, *Lark Rise to Candleford* (Oxford University Press, 1954 edn), pp. 1, 6, 57, 73-4, and 78-9.

16. Despite my country upbringing, I was abruptly reminded a few years ago of my relative lack of ability to perceive potential means of living off the country-side. My father and I were passing along a lane where the hedges contained a pro-fusion of birch and other straight-limbed saplings, upon which he remarked that they would make good sticks for his kidney bean row. *He* grew up, of course, before the day when the working man could think about buying imported bamboo canes and when his garden was a serious supplement to the household budget rather than a means of relaxation.

17. Examples of such enclosure maps are those for North Collingham, Notts. (1792) and Thornborough, Bucks. (1798) both champion parishes; examples of long narrow gardens can be seen in the lane between Chapmanslade and Corsley, Wilts. and in the lanes around Bodle Street Green in the Sussex Weald, both wood pasture areas, while the road from Baildon to Ilkley provides a number of moor-land examples of squatters' cottages set higgledy-piggledy on the rough ground.

18. E.P. Thompson, *Whigs and Hunters: The Origin of the Black Act* (Allen Lane, London, 1975), pp. 32-3 and 169 and G.E. Evans, *Ask the Fellows Who Cut the Hay* (Faber and Faber, London, 1956), pp. 251-3. See also Everitt in J. Thirsk, *The Agrarian History of England and Wales, Volume IV: 1500-1640* (Cambridge University Press, 1967), pp. 409-12.

19. P. Brandon, *The Sussex Landscape* (Hodder and Stoughton, London, 1974), pp. 194-8.

20. R. Samuel (ed.), *Village Life and Labour* (Routledge, London, 1975), pp. 15, 147, 155-61, 165-70, 184, 191-2 and 206-30.

21. Ibid., pp. 153, 156-9, 200-6 and 229-32.

22. In Thirsk, *Agrarian History IV*, pp. 411-2, 425, 427 and 462-3.

23. A. Bailey, 'Tadley, God Help Us', *Hampshire County Magazine*, vol. 16, no. 11 (September 1976), p. 41. The context suggests that besom-manufacture was carried on well into the present century.

24. Based partly on Yelling, *Common Field and Enclosure*, p. 230. See also Tate, *English Village Community*, p. 114 on fencing.

25. Thompson, *Whigs and Hunters*, pp. 239-40.

26. L. Fox and P. Russell, *Leicester Forest* (Leicester Corporation, 1948), Chs. 5 and 6 and D.R. Mills, 'Landownership and Rural Population with Special Reference to Leicestershire in the Mid-19th Century', unpublished PhD thesis, University of Leicester 1963, appendices.

27. P.H. Nicholls, 'On the Evolution of a Forest Landscape', *TIBG*, no. 56 (July 1972), especially pp. 69-73.

28. A brief discussion of these factors can be found in Mills, 'Landownership and Rural Population', pp. 240-8 and 264-73. See above, p. 80.

29. This account is based on G.F. Farnham 'Whitwick', *Transactions of the Leicestershire Archaeological Society*, vol. 16 (1927-8), pp. 231-55; also printed in G.F. Farnham, *Charnwood Forest and its Historians; and the Charnwood Manors* (privately published, Leicester, 1930).

30. G.F. Farnham 'Manorial History of Stoke Golding', *Transactions of the Leicestershire Archaeological Society*, vol. 14 (1925-6), pp. 206-27.

31. J. Thirsk in W.G. Hoskins and R.A. McKinley (eds.), *Victoria History of the County of Leicester*, vol. 2 (1954), p. 258. Information in this paragraph is also from Mills, 'Landownership and Rural Population', appendices.

32. W.G. Hoskins, *The Midland Peasant: The Economic and Social History of a Leicestershire Village* (Macmillan, London, 1957), especially Chs. 1, 2, 3 and 5.

33. A. Macfarlane, *The Origins of English Individualism* (Basil Blackwell, Oxford, 1978), p. 23.

34. Based on G.F. Farnham, 'Market Bosworth II – the Harcourt Family', *Transactions of the Leicestershire Archaeological Society*, vol. 16 (1927-8), pp. 103-23.

35. J. Throsby, *Select Views in Leicestershire* (Leicester and London, 1791), vol. 2, p. 305.

36. G.F. Farnham and A. Hamilton Thompson, 'The Manor of Noseley', *Transactions of the Leicestershire Archaeological Society*, vol. 12 (1922-3), p. 214.

37. Ibid., p. 229.

38. *Victoria History of the County of Leicester*, vol. 5 (1965), p. 266-7. This parish account generally follows that of Farnham and Hamilton Thompson.

39. *Victoria History of the County of Leicester*, vol. 3 (1955), pp. 166, 170, 173 and 195.

# 6    HOW AND WHERE THE MODEL WORKED

'Of the three classes of village, the village cared for by its lord, the village cared for by itself, and the village uncared for either by itself or by its lord (in other words, the village of a resident squire's tenantry, the village of free — or copy-holders, and the absentee-owner's village, farmed with the land) this place, Flintcomb Ash, was the third.' Thomas Hardy, *Tess of the D'Urbervilles*, Chap. 43.

**The Model**

At this point it may be useful to summarise our model of English rural society and reflect on the functions it can perform. The model rests on the validity of a dichotomy between the estate and peasant systems. A secondary and closely related feature is that these systems produced two types of village social structure and landscape, which are capable of further sub-division. Most writers have used two subdivisions of the two main types, though the methods of division do not always coin-cide. Interestingly, Thomas Hardy subdivided the closed villages but not the open, but even so he was using his model for reasons similar to twentieth century social scientists — he wished to simplify reality accurately and to predict human behaviour in a given situation.

The discussion so far has hinged on the assumption that the social distribution of landownership was the crucial causative factor in rural life, taken along with such qualifications as the settlement pattern and the survival or otherwise of commons. In other words, the model is taken to be not merely a schematic view of rural society, but also explanatory and predictive. This chapter is concerned with *how much* of rural life the model can explain. If the model is successful it should be possible to predict differentiating features of village life — social, economic, religious, political — from a knowledge of differences in the social distribution of landownership.

Within the same pages there is also an attempt to say *where* the model worked, in geographical, rather than sectoral terms. Particular attention is paid to the division of England into hamlet and champion areas. In this compass and within the prevailing state of research defini-tive answers cannot be provided to all the questions raised. Within the framework provided, however, there are many opportunities for local historians to test hypotheses which will refine the delineation of the model and add to the sum of social scientific knowledge of English rural society.

Table 6.1: Summary of Open and Closed Township Characteristics

| OPEN | CLOSED |
|---|---|
| Large populations | Small populations |
| High population density | Low population density |
| Rapid population increases *c.* 1851 | Slow population increases |
| Many small proprietors | Large estates |
| Peasant families | Gentlemen's residences |
| Small farms | Large farms |
| High poor rates | Low poor rates |
| Rural industries and craftsmen | Little industry and few craftsmen |
| Shops and public houses plentiful | Few shops and public houses |
| Housing poor, but plentiful | Housing good, but in short supply |
| Nonconformity common | Strong Anglican control |
| Radicalism and independence strong in politics and social organisations | Deference strong in politics and social organisations |
| Poachers | Gamekeepers |

*Particular Characteristics of Hamlet and Champion England*

HAMLET

| O/H | | C/H |
|---|---|---|
| Preponderance of open communities | Closed communities were relatively scarce. | |
| Large parishes and townships derived from wood pasture and moorland settlement. | Extra parochial areas common also lost villages deparochialised. | |
| Common field and manorial systems weak. | Absence of common field tradition. | |
| Late survival of commons. | Commons never existed except in special sense of grazing in royal forests, etc. | C |
| O P E N — Pasture farming and rural industries. | Pasture farming or late establishment of arable, e.g. Northumberland, Sherwood. | L O S E D |
| Mixture of open and closed. | Mixture of open and closed. | |
| Settlement Laws important. | Settlement Laws important. | |
| Large townships with nucleated villages and dispersed population. | Small compact townships, with strong manorial tradition. | |
| Parliamentary enclosure usual. | Early enclosure usual; lost villages often found. | |
| Late survival of commons. | Loss of commons, early. | |
| Arable farming often with labour-intensive specialities. | General arable farming. | |
| O/C | | C/C |

CHAMPION

The evidence presented in this chapter is arranged under headings similar to those used in Chapters 2 and 3: poor laws and population growth; occupations; housing; religion; social control; protest and politics. Table 6.1 is offered as a crude summary of the Chapters 1-6 of the book and in particular as a series of signposts for this chapter. The top part of the table is the cruder of the two, consisting of an unqualified open-closed dichotomy; the lower half is rather more subtle, taking into account also the differences between champion and hamlet England.

Table 6.2: Regional Analysis of 'Close' Parishes in England in the Mid-nineteenth Century

|  | All Townships | | | 'Close' Townships | | | |
|---|---|---|---|---|---|---|---|
|  | A | B | C | D | E | F | G |
| Region | No. of town- ships | Av. no. acres per house | Av. pop. growth, 1801-41 | No. of town- ships | % all town- ships | Av. pop. growth 1801-41 | Acres per house* |
| Essex, Herts., Cambs. | 82 | 16.3 | 45.7 | 5 | 6.1 | 2.4 | 40 (5) |
| Dorset, Som., W. Wilts. | 165 | 16.7 | 34.7 | 38 | 23.0 | 10.6 | 40(29) |
| Huntingdonshire | 98 | 21.0 | 54.4 | 22 | 22.5 | 22.4 | 45(22) |
| W. Leics., E. Warks. | 145 | 17.4 | 39.7 | 32 | 22.1 | 9.6 | 40(30) |
| N.E. Kent | 93 | 20.5 | 55.9 | 14 | 15.5 | 22.5 | 45(18) |
| Lindsey Marshes | 102 | 28.9 | 63.7 | 24 | 23.6 | 31.9 | 60(17) |
| Vale of Severn | 87 | 16.3 | 53.5 | 9 | 10.3 | 15.6 | 40(7) |
| Cotswolds (Glos.) | 199 | 15.1 | 37.7 | 56 | 28.1 | 22.8 | 40(55) |
| E. Leics., Rutl., West Kesteven | 201 | 28.7 | 30.2 | 78 | 39.8 | 16.8 | 60(47) |
| West Norfolk | 165 | 25.4 | 47.0 | 55 | 33.3 | 22.3 | 55(48) |
| East Riding Wolds | 157 | 38.4 | 61.2 | 68 | 43.3 | 32.0 | 70(51) |

*Column G gives the number of acres per house used as the demarcation line between 'close' parishes and others, and (in parentheses) the number of places in each region beyond that line. The difference between the numbers in column G and column D was supplied from information other than Census data.

Source: Holderness ' "Open" and "Close" Parishes in England', p. 135.

## Poor Laws and Population Growth (See Table 6.2)

A considerable amount of information on this subject has been summarised by Holderness, who has shown that population density and
population growth were very much lower in a sample of 401 closed
townships than in the average of all townships in his sample areas. The
average density was often two or two and a half times greater than the
density in the closed townships, while average population growth over
the period 1801-41 was often twice as high, in percentage terms, as in
the closed townships. This compares well with a more detailed study in
Bedfordshire, which reports one person per 5.61 acres in 1841 in 25
close parishes, but one person per 3.34 acres in 90 open parishes.[1]

Discarding that part of England north of the Tees and Ribble, in
which boarding in, cottage boarding and the bondager system limited
the problem of poor relief, the average number of closed townships was
about 20 per cent for the country as a whole. The local incidence, however, was uneven, rising to as much as 40 per cent in some areas and
falling away to little or none in others. It is interesting that the old
forest districts of Kent, Sussex, Surrey, Essex and Hertfordshire were
largely exempt, along with Suffolk and south Norfolk. In the Midland
Plain the problem of closed townships varied from one soil and farming
district to another. The most affected areas were in the lighter soil
districts of the East Riding, Lincolnshire Wolds, central Nottinghamshire, east Leicestershire, north west Norfolk and the Cotswolds.

While enclosure history varied, the Wolds containing many anciently
depopulated places, Sherwood Forest being an area of deforestation,
and so on, the common denominator was a predominance of arable,
mainly corn-farming, which expanded its labour force very rapidly in
the later eighteenth and early nineteenth centuries and this extra population concentrated in the open villages. Conversely, 'there was no
problem in regions where upland grass farms and family holdings predominated — in Cornwall, Wales and much of northern England', and
by implication other similar areas in Devon and the Welsh Border.[2]

An important by-product of the pattern of open and closed villages
was that open villages frequently provided labour for farms in closed
villages. The more essential workers, frequently those working with
stock, or gamekeepers, would be found cottages in closed villages, but
day labourers, especially in harvest time would be drawn in from
neighbouring open villages. This practice has been reported from widely
scattered districts, including Oxfordshire, Essex, Leicestershire,
Lincolnshire, Norfolk, the Blandford district of Dorset, the East Riding

and the Sherwood Forest district of Nottinghamshire.[3] It is a good example of integration between or the interdependence of the peasant and estate systems. The use of gangs prevalent in eastern England and elsewhere was partly related to the shortage of harvest labour in closed parishes and to unemployment in open villages. The latter was also a factor in causing labourers to walk for work into neighbouring towns, including Bournemouth, Leeds, Leamington and Oxford.[4]

## Occupations

The estate system was most characteristically associated with large farms and these were to be found in considerable numbers in the arable areas of lowland England.[5] Conversely, the family holding, apart from specialised areas such as the Fens, the Vale of Evesham and Kent, was found mainly in pastoral areas, especially those in the north and west of England, but also in areas of wood pasture in south-east England, such as the Weald and the Chilterns. This section summarises information and research on the distribution of secondary occupations in rural areas, the way in which they were linked to farming and their significance for the peasant system.

It was quite usual for village craftsmen, publicans and shopkeepers to operate from the basis of a peasant holding, as in the seventeenth century fen edge villages of Cambridgeshire.[6] Nineteenth-century examples are not difficult to find – they emerge in census studies, particularly when the 1841 or 1851 census is supplemented by a tithe award, as in studies as far apart as Dorset and the Hope Valley in Derbyshire.[7] However, in some areas of the country, whole industries can be linked with an agricultural base, frequently growing up in the sixteenth to the eighteenth centuries, and declining again in the nineteenth century as industry became more concentrated and urbanised.

Before looking at these distributions, it is important to appreciate why pastoral farming favoured the peasantry and provided a basis for industrial growth. It was less demanding on capital and could be made profitable on a smaller scale than arable farming. For instance, Barbara Kerr has contrasted the use late into the nineteenth century of *wooden* pails, churns and cheese vats with the seed drills and threshing machines required in corn farming. She has also emphasised the use of female labour in dairying, which would often be family labour, at a time when arable farming was making little use of women. In a census study contrasting arable Lincolnshire with pastoral Derbyshire, Fletcher has drawn attention to farms of several hundred acres, presumably mainly rough grazing, in the Hope Valley in 1851 which used very small amounts of hired labour.[8] The amount of expensive equipment required by arable farming is well illustrated by considering the number of horses in use and the range of implements which they drew. Even at the end of the nineteenth century, the reaper-binder, for example, required three horses, a man and a boy if it was to be used efficiently on a heavy crop.

The spread of rural industry from the sixteenth century onwards was not only based on its ability to be combined with pastoral farming during the latter's slack times, although this may have been the most important initial factor. It was also due to the greater availability of subsistence, commons and house sites in pastoral areas when population grew during the second stage of industrialisation, i.e. the stage at which the original craftsmen faded into the background as middlemen increasingly employed a scattered proletariat in order to expand production from the lowest possible outlay. This stage has been called proto-industrialisation.[9] Examples come from diverse sources and districts. In the Pennines, weavers and lead-miners often lived on small-holdings, which were an important means of subsistence in remote areas and a compensation in times of slack trade. Of the lead-mining areas Raistrick comments significantly, that it was good country for Quakers, Methodists and nonconformity generally and miners, small farmers, shepherds and artisans were prominent leaders.[10]

Lancashire was another county in which early enclosure, industry and small owners went hand in hand in the seventeenth and eighteenth centuries and the small owner was still dominant in the nineteenth century,[11] although agriculture was increasingly divorced from industry in this highly urbanised county. Cumberland, a third pastoral county, contained the example of Gosforth, where there were 50 farms in 1800, 'most of which must have ranged in size from 50 to 100 acres. Interspersed among these were the wheel-barrow farms and small patches of land farmed by men who were also inn-keepers, farm labourers and village craftsmen'.[12]

Framework knitting grew up in some of the more pastoral parts of the east Midlands in the late seventeenth century. This has sometimes been attributed to the presence of cheap labour,[13] but a more important factor in the present context is the availability of capital for the purchase of stocking frames. The early stockingers generally appear to have been substantial tradesmen or farmers and the open villages of a grassland area, lacking scope for expansion of labour consuming arable

farming, would seem to be the right sort of place to expect such inno-
vators.[14]

Dr. Joan Thirsk in a considerable survey of rural industries has
summarised their location as follows:

> With few exceptions, all the rural industries of the fifteenth, six-
> teenth and seventeenth centuries throve in pastoral areas where fresh
> reserves of labour were available on a part-time basis. And this is
> where many of them remained into the eighteenth, nineteenth and
> some even into the twentieth centuries, though the industries them-
> selves ceased to be organised on a domestic basis and moved into
> mills and factories.[15]

Eric Jones has drawn from this distribution a conclusion that comparative economic advantage led areas such as southern England and
East Anglia away from industry and into innovative arable farming,
while in the agriculturally backward pastoral areas, industrial development was the only means of economic advance. This pattern was
repeated in other areas of Western Europe, North America and Japan.
Not only did arable farming, especially corn-farming, generally consume
most of the available capital and labour, it also encouraged the growth
of large-scale urban industries related to its products. In contrast to the
marketing on the hoof of the meat produced in pastoral areas, corn
needed to be reduced in bulk near the point of production. This process
was carried out by millers, maltsters and brewers, who although not
confined to the towns, nor to big towns, were subject to an earlier
townward drift and concentration in large enterprises than, say, some
of the textile processes which used wool.[16] Langton quotes Norwich,
Witney, Worcester, much of Wiltshire and Somerset and the Vale of
Severn as examples of areas where arable or mixed farming helped to
urbanise industry.[17] In these ways the occupational structures of arable
and pastoral areas developed distinctive features and in so far as the
estate and peasant systems were associated with one or the other the
gulf between the two systems widened.

This section strongly suggests that a variation on the Chayanovian
model developed by the Soviet geographer Chelintsev may have applied
to the English peasant system from the sixteenth century. Chelintsev
recognised the limitations of Chayanov's model in areas where land was
in short supply, a factor which affected most of England. For land, he
substituted labour as a means of expanding the peasant enterprise and
suggested that labour-intensive crops would supplant labour-extensive

activities.[18] English examples could include potato-growing in the Fens and fruit-growing in a number of areas. Chelintsev does not mention industrial by-occupations, but this is clearly an alternative possibility. Likewise a drift into trades and crafts could be cited as a means of maintaining the peasant system in the face of land shortages and competition from large farms. One example is the Cambridgeshire village of Melbourn where a rapid rise in population in the early nineteenth century was absorbed mainly in non-agricultural occupations despite the absence of industry, so that in 1840 there were 50-60 peasant families compared with, at most, only 30 full-time farmers.[19] Another consideration is that pointed out by Barbara Kerr – the desperate competition among village craftsmen engendered presumably by the ease with which they could start out in business and the lack of better opportunities in the countryside. An extreme, but indicative example is the increase from two to 19 carpenters at Bere in Dorset between about 1800 and the 1841 census, an increase out of all proportion to the rise in population.[20]

Indeed Chelintsev recognised that under-employment was an important feature of the peasant economy in certain conditions of capital and prices. That this was not an occasional feature of exceptional villages, is demonstrated by Collins' study of migrant labour in British agriculture when he has pointed out that, in addition to recruiting harvest labour from grass and wood pasture districts and from domestic industrial workers:

> The third and quantitatively most important movement was that between the small-farm subsistence and large-farm capitalist sectors of British agriculture. The source areas were characterised by overpopulation, a small or unprofitable stock of by-employments, low incomes per head and a low marginal productivity of labour. Because a significant part of their active labour force could be released for most of the summer period, this category of migration was, more than any other, long-distance and long-duration. The homelands included any number of 'squatter' or small-farming communities, and at one time or another the greater part of the upland zone.[21]

## Housing

The general importance of the dichotomy between the two systems in respect of housing can be tested by two different and complementary methods. One is by reference to the considerable poor law literature summarised by Holderness and myself,[22] where in one district after another the poor housing standards of the large, overcrowded open villages are contrasted with the labourer's seventh heaven of the formally planned estate village.

The second method of approach is through present-day fieldwork. Despite the lapse of time, contrasts can still be seen in many parts of the country.[23] In the open villages the poorest housing has nearly all gone, having been swept away by improving legislation of the twentieth century. A more widespread legacy, however, is the great wealth of small and medium-sized houses built in the local vernacular, using traditional materials which are typical of literally hundreds of ordinary villages, although their collective visual impact is much greater in a smaller number of large villages where population pressure and other factors promoted a near-continuous façade down the village street. The conscious replacement of the vernacular was recorded by a topographer about 1790 when, after a glowing description of Shuckburgh Ashby's new houses at Hungarton, he remarked that 'Travellers would forget the Leicestershire dirt walls, for which our villages are famed, were they here.'[24]

Thus, estate villages not only represented good housing conditions for the tenants, for which reason much of it has survived, they also indicated the march of modernisation, the introduction of new materials and new designs imported into the landscape by the landlord's command of capital.

Interest in the contrasting conditions of open and closed villages continued up to the time of the first world war. For instance, in a considerable survey of two Poor Law Unions in Warwickshire about 1890, Ashby found the 'best cottages are generally those on large estates; the worst in villages where low rents prevail, and where the cottages are owned by comparatively poor men'.[25] (See Table 6.3.) Caird had also commented earlier on the high rents in open villages and drew out the point in relation to the Melksham Union of Wiltshire that the labourer was sometimes open to the tyranny of the small landlord who also held a quasi-monopoly of provision retailing in the same village.[26]

Table 6.3: Classification of Villages in Two Warwickshire Unions by Cottage Accommodation

| Villages | Above average | Average | Below average |
|---|---|---|---|
| Close and semi-close | 28% | 39% | 33% |
| Open | 16% | 38% | 46% |

Source: Ashby and King, 1893.

Reviewing the housing of the open villages in Norfolk, Marion Springall concluded that 'Cottages were inferior and more highly rented than those on the estates. Sanitation and water supply were frequently inadequate.'[27] However, she would have probably have agreed with Flora Thompson, who referring to Juniper Hill (Oxon), stated that 'A shilling, or two shillings a week, they felt, was not too much to pay for the freedom to live and vote as they liked and to go to church and chapel or neither as they preferred.'[28] Control over housing was indeed part of the social control exerted by the landed classes, a topic to which a return is made below.

## Religion

On the subject of religion, Gay has offered the following generalisation:

> Where the village was of the closed integrated type, the squire and parson would wield a patriarchal influence ensuring the stranglehold of the Church of England . . . In those 'miniature welfare states' there was little possibility of chapel life developing. If the village was one of the open type with no dominant landlord, independent thought and action was more possible and chapels could be easily established . . . In general an arable economy, with its nucleated settlement favoured the Church of England, while a pastoral economy with its scattered settlement favoured the Nonconformists.[29]

Figure 6.1 demonstrates for one county that Gay was substantially correct in his generalisation, for estate parks and nonconformist chapels were found overwhelmingly in different townships in Leicestershire.[30] Similarly confirmation is forthcoming from Hey's study in south Yorkshire, Obelkevich's work in Lindsey and Everitt's investigations in a large number of counties.[31] Most recently, Gilbert has reviewed the literature at the national level and confirmed Gay's conclusion.[32] This considerable amount of research can be summarised by citing circumstances in which the dependency system, to use Gilbert's term, was at its weakest. This was the system in which a strong manorial or estate structure made farmers and labourers dependent on squire and parson. It was challenged wherever a substantial peasantry or numerous freeholders existed, in large nucleated villages, in decayed market towns and more generally in the grassland areas of the north and west. Furthermore, Gilbert's statistics suggest that nonconformity was especially well supported by artisans.

Figure 6.1: Squires and Dissent in Leicestershire *c*. 1851

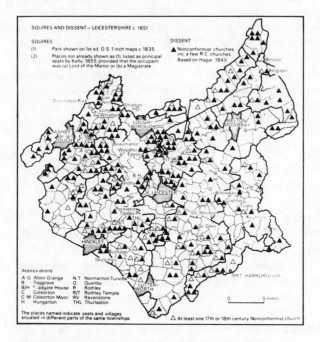

Note: Nonconformist churches were generally situated in townships without resident gentry, the latter being represented by their parks. The heavy lines are the boundaries of soil regions, within which townships contained similar combinations of soil types. Compare with Figure 4.3, which shows landownership in all but some marginal areas of the county.

## Social Control

Religion and social control were closely related aspects of rural life in the nineteenth century. Social control of the labourers by the squire and parson through the medium of the established church is perhaps fairly obvious, but it would be wrong to ignore the power of the deacons or other elders in a nonconformist church over their congregation. Thus, for example, the trustees of the Congregational Chapel at Melbourn, Cambridgeshire, in the summer of 1845 discussed the exclusion of Jonathan Stockbridge because he was in the habit of working his windmill on Sundays.[33]

However, in terms of the open-closed model of villages the important point to note is the concentration of social control in the one situation, as compared with its wider distribution in the other. The last
section has already demonstrated the choice of religious sects available
to the inhabitants of the open villages, but an equally important though
neglected point is that non-attendance (at any place of worship) was
also quite strong in open villages. Thus in Leicestershire where most
places had at least one attendance at a place of worship by 20 to 40 per
cent of the population, where there was industry or a large population,
the figure was usually below 20 per cent. The definition of a large
parish here is as low as a population of 600. Conversely, above average
attendance was experienced in parishes with a population below 200.
Commenting on the figures for Lincolnshire, which repeated the
Leicestershire correlation of size of village and non-worshipping,
Obelkevich points out that the influence on attendance of resident
squires could be traced despite the obvious fact that small parishes were
generally closed parishes.[34] In open villages, then, social control was
weak, in the sense of control exerted from above on those below and
this was not confined to church attendance and related matters,
although to the contemporary mind the root cause of lack of deference
was often seen as failure to attend church.[35]

The vertical social control of the closed village could take on a number of forms. Control of village clubs has been mentioned in Chapter
3, while control through housing has been referred to once already in
this chapter. Tenancy agreements were not uncommon vehicles of pressure as, for example, on the Tollemache estate at Helmingham, Suffolk
where tenants agreed to 'attend some place of worship once each
Sabbath day', or on the Lincolnshire estate where lodgers not agreeable
to the landowner were the cause of tenants being given notice.[36]
Gossiping women were also subject to control through housing on at
least two estates where cottages were purposely built without front
doors so that any gossiping would be out of sight.[37] A final illustration
is that houses, especially almshouses could be made to carry significant
messages from landowner to tenant, as at Budby in Nottinghamshire
where Earl Manvers took the occasion of rebuilding in 1807 to inscribe
on a cottage the following sentiments:

Hear instruction and be wise and refuse it not.

Proverbs VII v. 33

Be pious patient honest and industrious.

Such inscriptions pre-supposed a literacy which the gentry were keen to extend to their nineteenth-century tenants, at least partly because the school and the reading-room could be used as other instruments of social control. At least this was the experience of Flora Thompson in the 1880s when the parson in school 'spoke to them from a great height, physical, moral and spiritual. "To order myself lowly and reverently before my betters" was the clause he underlined in the Church Catechism'.[38] Educational establishments, like houses, might also carry messages with a social moral such as that over the door of the reading-room and village hall at Winthorpe, Notts: 'Fear God and keep his commandments.'

The seriousness of the need for social control by means now regarded as 'indirect' should not be underestimated in an age which lacked a proper police force and had only a small standing army. Descriptions of open villages as refuges for bad characters, including known burglars, have been discovered for three widely separated districts – Wheatley (Oxon.), Ampleforth (North Riding) and Egmanton (Notts.).[39] And the importance of game preservation by gamekeepers against poachers on country estates is a theme which does not need labouring, although a study of this problem in relation to the open-closed model does not appear to have been carried out for any district in the nineteenth century.

Finally in this section, the significance of the village, as against dispersed settlement, for social control is excellently brought out by the reasons given by the Earl of Radnor for building the Berkshire village of Coleshill to replace the maximum number of outlying cottages:

First       To put the inhabitants under the influence of public opinion
Second   To put them near the Church
Third      To put them near the School
Fourth    To put them near the Post Office
Fifth       To put them near the shop by which the labourer saves 15 per cent of his wages.

Lord Radnor, as to his first reason, said 'You never see a slattern in a village, nor train up a poacher there.'[40]


**Protest and Politics**

Protest and politics are closely enough related to be considered together, but because of the nature of the evidence and the narrowness of the rural franchise for most of the period, this section falls into three distinct passages. In the first, some account is given of rioting and other violent expressions of rural discontent up to the early 1830s; this is followed by a discussion of voting behaviour after 1832 and, finally, by a few remarks on agricultural trade unionism.

It is instructive to go back to the first quarter of the eighteenth century when the power of the landed classes over the Crown was being consolidated at the beginning of Walpole's long period of office. Their strength is demonstrated by the passing of the Black Act of 1723, which turned into capital offences many forms of rural protest and crime. such as deer-stalking, poaching in disguise (blacking), cutting trees and maiming cattle. While the exact reasons for the passing of this Act remain obscure, there is a clear connection with the struggle between Whig usurpers of Crown property in Windsor and other forests and the local peasantry, who resented a reduction in what they regarded as their customary perquisites that abounded in a royal forest.

This area has been mentioned before as one in which population pressure was relieved by squatting. A similar function can be allotted to the by-employments, such as lime-burning, brick-making, the getting of sand and gravel and the making of articles out of wood, all of which made use of raw materials found in the forest. There were few gentry and few nucleated villages. This was yeoman's country with many small freeholds in hamlets and dispersed settlement. Lax manorial and forest administration had permitted the growth of customary practices providing support for the economy, which was traditional, rather than market-oriented and capitalistic.[41]

As the Whigs withdrew the Hanoverian royal family from positions of effective power in the royal forest, a new class of gentry entered into forest offices, bent on capitalist exploitation and showing a callous disregard for traditional customs almost equal to those responsible for the Highland clearances (See Chapter 7). Owing to their brazen, self-seeking policies they were unable to earn the deference of the social orders below them:[42]

> Blacking (disguising oneself for poaching, etc.) arose in response to the attempted reactivation of a relaxed forest authority. This provoked resentment among foresters generally, whether small gentry (outside the charmed circle of Court favours), yeomen, artisans or labourers. The resort of deer-poachers to more organised force may be seen as retributive in character and concerned less with venison as

such than with the deer as symbols (and as agents) of an authority which threatened their economy, their crops and their customary agrarian rights.[43]

It is important to recognise that neither labourers nor known criminal types formed the core of the protest movement, which was to be found in the middling orders of the forest (i.e. the peasantry). The crisis appears to have been used by Walpole as a means of building up autocratic power through the passing of the Black Act and in due course poaching and similar offences declined but were still prevalent at the beginning of the nineteenth century. Then came the final enclosure of the forest and the extinction of common rights, which can be interpreted as the triumph of capitalism and the pure money economy.[44] Lord Radnor's philosophy is again seen in the ascendant:

> The absence of compact villages, and the dispersal of foresters, made social discipline impossible: 'nothing more favours irregular and lawless habits of life among the inferior class . . . than scattered and sequestered habitations'. The gentry, also in their scattered and sequestered habitations, had decided over the previous century that enclosure was the best resource for agrarian class control . . . (so that) the 'inferior class' could then be brought in collected villages, each with a constable on patrol.[45]

In the early nineteenth century protest expanded far beyond special cases like royal forests or the Blaxhall district of Suffolk, where it was said that smuggling was carried out by the rising class of tradesmen resentful of the domination of the landed gentry.[46] As population growth outstripped the rural demand for labour, whether from farming or industry, and poor relief demoralised the labouring classes, various forms of protest became widespread. It was ephemeral rather than organised and systematic; and for the most part has not been analysed from the present standpoint. For instance, Peacock's study of village radicalism in East Anglia 1800-50 only suggests implicitly that incendiarism and other forms of protest was most common in large, open villages.[47]

However, in their study of the Swing riots of 1830, Hobsbawm and Rudé posed specific questions about the distribution of riots. Unlike the forest disturbances, the Swing riots were well developed in low wage corn-growing areas in East Anglia and the south, although there were also significant exceptions. In order to investigate the distribution of riots at more local levels where factors such as the open-closed dichotomy could be considered, Hobsbawm and Rudé took sample areas in Norfolk, Suffolk, Hampshire, Wiltshire and, at a less intensive level, Bedfordshire, Berkshire and Kent. It is worth noting that they too found the open-closed dichotomy less clear cut than as presented by contemporary writers and worked with four sub-types similar to those described in Chapter 5 — monopoly villages, oligarchies (such as the multi-manor villages of Norfolk), mixed villages and classical open villages, such as Ixworth and Earl Soham in Suffolk and Pewsey and Ramsbury in Wiltshire.[48]

Hobsbawm and Rudé considered a wide range of data for their sample villages and discovered considerable local complexities and qualifications to the general rule. Cause and effect were by no means straightforward. For example, tradesmen were often involved in rioting, frequently as leaders, or they were numerous in places where rioting against landowners and farmers occurred. This was not so much because they had a direct grievance about farm wage levels, it was more a question of their social identification with the labouring classes, dependence on their custom (though they also depended on the custom of farmer and squire) and their general position as community leaders, owing to a superior education and knowledge of the world. The same argument can be applied to the role of nonconformity. While the chapels seldom if ever preached sedition, lay preachers were community leaders and their mere presence was a challenge to the authority of gentlemen farmers and gentry.[49]

Despite necessary qualifications it was possible to draw up a provisional 'profile' of a village disposed to riot:

> It would tend to be above average in size, to contain a higher ratio of labourers to employing farmers than the average, and a distinctly higher number of local artisans; perhaps also of such members of rural society as were economically, socially and ideologically independent of squire, parson and large farmer: small family cultivators, shopkeepers and the like. Certainly the potentially riotous village also contained groups with a greater than average disposition to religious independence. So far as landownership is concerned, it was more likely to be 'open' or mixed than the rest. Local centres of communication such as markets and fairs were more likely to riot than others, but there were too few of these to explain the prevalence of unrest. It might well contain rather more pauperism and unemployment than the tranquil village, but there is no reason to

assume that it was normally much more miserable than its miserable neighbours. We need hardly add that it was more likely to be engaged in tillage and especially grain farming, or in the production of specialised crops with a highly fluctuating demand for labour, and less likely to be engaged in pastoral farming. If it had a history of local disputes — most likely over enclosures, perhaps also over local politics and administration — this would increase its propensity to riot; and in some cases, for which no generalisations are possible, it might actually become one of those local centres of militancy whence riot radiated out over the surrounding region.[50]

This profile offers highly significant support for the model of open and closed villages, especially in corn-growing districts where the large areas controlled by major landowners and large tenant farmers threw the open villages into high relief.

Examples quoted in Chapters 2 and 3 suggest that deferential patterns of voting might well have been common in England throughout the nineteenth century and especially before the adoption of the Ballot Act which rendered voting secret. Moore, for example in connection with Cambridgeshire, has committed himself to the generalisation that party voting, especially plumping, and deferential voting tended to coincide with the big estates, whereas in freehold villages neither appeared strongly. Writing of County Durham, Nossiter has stated that the tenant's primary loyalty in voting was to the estate, rather than to a political party and only those who developed counter-loyalties, such as those to chapel or meeting house, were likely to break out of the system.[51]

Other writers, however, have warned that the balance between landlordly influence, actual coercion (e.g. eviction) and political issues varied very greatly in determining the outcome of elections. Olney has for instance recorded that in the North Lincolnshire election of 1852 only 25 out of 65 close parishes showed 'absolutely regular voting' and of 45 major landowners only 27 secured absolutely regular voting in one or more parishes on their estates. Davis points out that only 26 per cent of the electors in the rural parts of Aylesbury constituency around 1850 were tenants of great landowners, even broadly interpreted. Moreover, landlordly attitudes towards the political affiliations of their tenants varied from the strict view of Lord Carrington, who sometimes evicted recalcitrant tenants, to Dr. Lee who kept his preferences very much to himself. Moreover it has been pointed out in the context of Westmorland that complications arose when freeholders were also customary tenants of a manor where the lord entered politics and expected allegiance — hence the need to combine information from poll books with other relevant sources naming individuals.[52]

In contrast, Pelling's work on the elections of 1885-1910, which relies much more on newspaper accounts and cannot make use of known voting behaviour, suggests that political affiliation *did* fit into the pattern of the model used here. For example, in a general statement about farmers:

> . . . the political pattern . . . depended to a considerable degree upon (their) condition . . . and upon their numbers in proportion to labourers. There was, however, a law of political compensation. Where the farmers were large scale and prosperous and hence likely to be Conservative, they employed the largest proportion of labourers, who were likely on balance to be Liberal. But where, as on poor land and in the uplands, the farms were comparatively poor, there were fewer labourers, but the farmers themselves were working farmers and likely to feel themselves to be exploited by their landlords.[53]

He might have gone on and suggested links between small farmers and other small entrepreneurs, whom even Olney and Davis generally acknowledged to have Liberal tendencies.

Significantly, Pelling has drawn together some of the evidence concerning the distribution of dissent, of great estates, of rural occupations and of settlement patterns and related it to evidence of political behaviour. Examples ranging over many parts of England build up the contrasting pictures. The first is of strongly nucleated villages on great estates in arable areas where allegiance to the Established Church and the squire's politics (usually Conservative, but still occasionally Liberal from the days of Whig politics) were all interlocked in a now recognisable syndrome. Deference, to describe this picture in one word, was said to be strong in the south east region outside London; in the Devizes area of Wiltshire; Oxfordshire and the Vale of Aylesbury; the Downland areas of Dorset, Wiltshire and Hampshire; the strongly nucleated Sedgemoor villages and similar places in South Devon; around the Duke of Devonshire's Chatsworth estate in Derbyshire; in small parishes near Horncastle (Lincs) and in arable areas of strongly nucleated settlement in the north of England.[54]

Areas of 'independence', were often those of small farms, notably the Fens, Cornwall and the Dales and in the latter area the supposed

importance, in political terms, of the pastoral economy was noted.[55]
The link between dissent and Liberalism was a marked feature of
Norfolk, where it outweighed the Conservative vote from the big farms,
of Cornwall, Lincolnshire, Cheshire, many parts of Yorkshire and of the
Midlands industrial villages.[56] The lingering non-agricultural occupations of rural areas were also significant in building up the Liberal vote,
as with the fishermen of Cornwall, the miners and potters in industrial
villages of north Staffordshire and the lead-miners of the Pennines.[57]
The importance of scattered settlement patterns and large parishes was
brought out in areas such as the Chilterns, Cheshire and the Yorkshire
Wolds.[58]

Whether or not Pelling's evidence is acceptable in explaining political
behaviour may be open to the kinds of questions raised by Olney and
Davis for the period before 1885. Nevertheless it brings out certain
strengths of the model offered here for different purposes, to show, in
fact, that there were two kinds of rural England, one interwoven with
the other spatially and sectorally, yet each distinct and recognisable
both to the contemporaries who wrote the newspaper accounts and
memoirs used by Pelling and to the historian a century later.

Although election riots were not unknown after 1850, physical
forms of protest for the most part died out with the eclipse of Chartism
around the mid-century. Several decades went by in the countryside
before labourers again came together to better their lot. This movement
was known as 'The Revolt of the Field' and owed a good deal to the
worsening conditions in arable England during the agricultural depression of the last quarter of the century. It was, however, a peaceful
revolt: in place of the burning of effigies and the writing of semi-
literate messages from Captain Swing, there was a steady determina-
tion to found a permanent and powerful agricultural labourers' union.

There is some evidence that the open villages were prominent in the
movement, as at Tysoe (see above, Chapter 3). In Oxfordshire, the area
around the former forest of Wychwood was especially prominent and
in Lincolnshire union meetings occurred in large open villages such as
Normanby-by-Spital, Swineshead, Long Sutton, Binbrook, Bassingham,
Billingborough, Blyton and Heckington.[59] The connection with the
Methodist movement in Lincolnshire, Norfolk and Suffolk led to many
meetings being held in Methodist chapels[60] and as Methodist chapels
were generally located in open villages and market towns this connection strengthens the assumption that the movement was strong in the
open villages.

It has been shown that Methodist methods of organisation, Methodist support of total abstinence and Methodist education in Sunday schools all had a considerable influence on the membership of agricultural unions in Lincolnshire and East Anglia between 1870 and the end of the century. Many of the meetings were conducted not only in chapels but also with many of the features of services, such as the singing of hymns, the saying of prayers and the use of Biblical language and scriptural justifications for union policy. In the three counties studied by N. Scotland, 95 per cent of the union leaders whose religious affiliations could be established were known Methodists and of these approximately 75 per cent were Methodist office-holders. Although Primitive Methodists were the most prominent and many of the leaders were themselves labourers, both Wesleyans and non-labourers (some men were both) could be found quite easily among the ranks of union leaders.[61]

This brief account of unionism indicates the importance of the open village and the peasant system in religious, social, economic and political spheres. The quarrel of the labourers with their employers was basically economic, but their targets were the large farmers (and their allies the landlords and Anglican clergy) from whom they were so distinct socially. The founding of unions and their organisation were political activities which led the labourers into the Liberal camp at general elections. In a society which, despite the beginnings of non-attendance, was still intensely religious, union activities inevitably spilled over into the religious sphere. It is interesting that the small farmers (who often hired labourers), craftsmen and shopkeepers should provide a sympathetic background to union activity, because the latter struck at the roots of the estate system by which they too felt threatened.

## Conclusion

As Table 6.1 provides a useful summary of this chapter, the conclusion takes a different form by attempting to draw out two generalisations, one spatial, the other sociological.

The spatial generalisation is based on Thompson's data on land-ownership, in which he used the county as his level of analysis. His tables indicate the percentage of each county (excluding waste) in estates of different sizes in the early 1880s and are in turn based on Bateman's improvement of the New Domesday Book of 1873.[62] The sizes are as follows: 1-100, 101-300, 301-1,000, 1,001-3,000, 3,001-10,000 and over 10,000 acres. As estates of less than 1,000 acres could dominate a single township, only the first two categories can be safely associated with the peasantry. The middle ground of 301-3,000 acres could be expected to contain many and varied circumstances, including yeoman farmers, the estates of urban tradesmen and many non-corporate owners; but at levels of over 3,000 acres we are fairly certain to be dealing with the country gentry proper and the aristocracy above them.

Figure 6.2: English Counties by Percentage of Land in Estates of 1-300 Acres, *c*. 1870

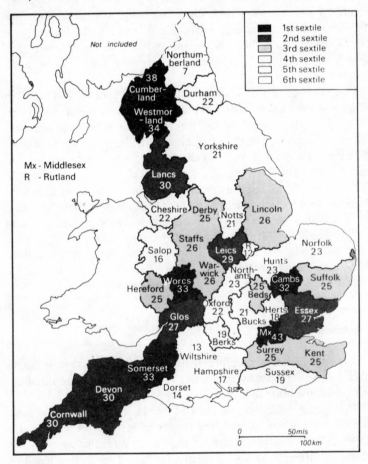

Source: Based on Table VI in F.M.L. Thompson, *English Landed Society in the Nineteenth Century* (Routledge, London, 1963).

It is of some interest, therefore, that when the list of 39 counties are placed in rank order by percentages in estates of 300 acres and less and *inversely* by percentages in estates over 3,000, there is a very close correlation (Rho = 0.82). In other words, the peasantry and the great landowners were mutually exclusive at the county level of analysis. Counties which departed most noticeably from this norm included Bedfordshire, where the great Woburn estate co-existed with peasantry of median strength; Cornwall, where the peasantry and the large estates appear to have squeezed out moderate sized estates; and Lancashire which did not rank high in the peasant list despite there being relatively few great estates.

Figure 6.2 gives only a broad indication of the areas in which the peasantry were strong because the county is too coarse a unit of analysis in such obvious cases as Yorkshire and Lincolnshire where, as we have already seen, there was room enough for the growth of the great estate without the dispossession of a strong peasantry in the Pennines and the Fens. Counties in the first and second sextiles are predominantly situated in hamlet England; in fact only two out of these 12 counties, Leicestershire and Cumberland, belonged to areas where villages were the usual form of settlement; both were grassland counties and Cumberland was not affected greatly by common-field systems.

At the other end of the scale, however, the patterns are much more complicated. Of the 12 counties in the fifth and sixth sextiles only Nottinghamshire, Rutland, and Wiltshire belonged clearly to champion England. Most of the remainder, like Hampshire, Derbyshire, Dorset and Northumberland occupy intermediate positions, but contained much hamlet territory. This broad discussion is somewhat indeterminate and is a reminder that a considerable amount of further work remains to be done in this field.

The sociological generalisation which must be attempted relates to the changing class structure in rural England and the validity of Tönnies' Gemeinschaft — Gesellschaft dichotomy. The concept of Gemeinschaft is dependent on there not being a perception of class interests, as distinct from the interests of the community. It is possible that in England's medieval past there actually existed Gemeinschaft-like relationships within a village, for there is evidence that persons of differing social status all lived 'within the community'. However, in view of Macfarlane's thesis concerning the origins of English individualism[63] even this measure of togetherness may be only relative. Nevertheless, there are numerous indications that Gemeinschaft characteristics fell away with the passage of time. The received view of the medieval castle or monastery, with everyone eating in the great hall and only the lord and lady retiring to private quarters at night is obviously much more Gemeinschaft-like than the manor houses of later time. In the nineteenth century the typical country house was separate from its village (if that had survived), hidden behind park walls and screens of trees and the lord and lady exercised themselves privately in acres of pleasure gardens walled about by immense yew hedges, as well as by bricks and mortar. Inside the house, the geography of staircases and passages was arranged so that servants and family only met in carefully controlled circumstances.

So the gentry and aristocracy withdrew from the community first, followed by the large tenant farmers whom they had created. At one time the latter had boarded their farm servants at the top of the farmhouse, like the urban merchants with their apprentices. The nineteenth century saw this practice on the wane, especially on the big farms of the south and east when high farming made many farmers into gentlemen farmers, who could afford hunters for themselves and their sons and piano lessons for their daughters. The Scottish solution was the bothy, while in England the young farm hands had to find lodgings with their married workmates or stay in their parents' homes.

There are suggestions that the peasantry remained 'in the community' for longer, since there is plentiful evidence that they fought to retain some of the customary features of village life, especially where these had an immediate economic implication. It was in their interest that commons should remain open, fens should remain undrained and forests should remain standing. As J.G. Rule has remarked:

> The conflict of custom with legal prohibition is a recurring theme of the social history of the eighteenth and early nineteenth centuries. It is clearly seen in such activities as smuggling and poaching, but it is present also in the enclosure debate and inherent in the food riot, and of course in wrecking and plundering.[64]

This conflict of custom with legal prohibition or the will of the landed classes manifests itself in many forms of village recreation. The regulation of village clubs and the suppression of feasts have already been mentioned. The old ways of celebrating Whitsun constitute another example which has been carefully studied from this angle.[65] In a most important passage, Obelkevich has analysed the suppression and revival of harvest suppers in Lincolnshire. The old style, rough and impudent behaviour at harvest home had been suppressed in one district by about 1840, but in the period of high farming the harvest festival (of the Anglican church) was introduced and the big farmers revived the harvest suppers in a more antiseptic form, taking care to underline their largesse and separateness. This event has been labelled a pseudo-Gemeinschaft by Obelkevich who interprets it in the following terms:

> . . . the old-style farmer was . . . 'naive', aware of no rift between himself and his milieu, his dependents; the new-style farmer was by contrast 'sentimental', aware of the rift, and anxious to bridge it by a deliberate act of will. The one belonged to the age of community; the other, to the age of 'labour relations' and the manipulation of morale.[66]

By extension, the term pseudo-Gemeinschaft could be used of the estate system as a whole. Evidence of very varied kinds has been used to show that the system was run on Gesellschaft-like lines, on a commercial basis, the rational replacing the traditional, in recreation as at work. Yet there is also considerable evidence of the landed classes taking an interest in the social, moral, physical and religious welfare of their tenants and labourers. This face of rural capitalism has been more widely publicised and accepted than the Gesellschaft face; paternalism has been mistaken for the fag-end of feudalism; perhaps pseudo-Gemeinschaft, false Gemeinschaft is the term which most accurately sums up what the nineteenth-century estate system stood for. Meanwhile other features of Gemeinschaft survived longer in the peasant system, most of all the importance of the family as the unit of production and a retention of some of the traditional features of community life.

This sociological analysis of the changes in rural English society during the nineteenth and earlier centuries is useful in one more respect to our evaluation of the open-closed model of villages. Mainly for the sake of brevity and simplicity, the model has been presented in a static form, in that the concentration on inter-village contrasts at given points in time has obscured the possibility of significant changes in these contrasts *over* time. The lack of suitable data to trace change over time in the many facets of the model is another reason for the relatively light treatment of change.

However, by implication many changes have been indicated, if not measured thoroughly. For example, the change from parochial to union rating for poor laws purposes was obviously of significance, while certain political issues, such as the Swing riots and disputes over church rates obviously came and went, leaving marks of varying strength on the fabric of village life. The change from community to class society was a long-term underlying shift, which began before our period and continues today. It cannot fail to be important to any model of nineteenth-century villages and village life, but there is still much research to be done along both dimensions. However, the conclusion that the relevance of the open-closed model is greatest for the history of the period 1780-1850 is likely to stand the test of time, for so many factors contributed in that period to widen village differentiation. These included the dislocation caused by war and enclosure; the build-up of overpopulation and high poor rates; the increase of country industries later replaced by urban-based production; and the rise of mass nonconformity, with the corresponding response by the Church of England personified in the gentleman vicar. Never before and never again did so many forces act in the same direction.

## Notes

1. B.A. Holderness, ' "Open" and "Close" Parishes in England in the Eighteenth and Nineteenth Centuries', *Agric. Hist. Rev.*, vol. 20 (1972), pp. 126-39 and P. Grey, 'The Pauper Problem in Bedfordshire from 1795 to 1834', unpublished M.Phil thesis, University of Leicester, 1975, p. 82. Leicestershire presents a similar picture: see D.R. Mills, 'Landownership and Rural Population with Special Reference to Leicestershire in the Mid-19th Century', unpublished PhD thesis, University of Leicester, 1963, Table 20 (p. 193) and Appendix 3.

2. Holderness, p. 134-6, see also D.R. Mills (ed.), *English Rural Communities: The Impact of a Specialised Economy* (Macmillan, London, 1973), Ch. 8 for Nottinghamshire.

3. R. Samuel (ed.), *Village Life and Labour* (Routledge, London, 1975), pp. 36, 48; Holderness, pp. 133, 137; J.A. Sheppard, 'East Yorkshire's Agricultural Labour Force in the Mid-nineteenth Century', *Agric. Hist. Rev.*, vol. 9 (1961), pp. 53-4; Mills, *English Rural Communities*, pp. 188-9 and 'Landownership and Rural Population', p. 213; P.M. Tillott and G.S. Stevenson, *North-west Lindsey in 1851* (University of Sheffield, Department of Extra-Mural Studies, duplicated 1970), pp. 4, 9; Pamela Horn, *Labouring Life in the Victorian Countryside* (Gill and Macmillan, Dublin, 1976), pp. 246-7. J.W.F. Hill, *Victorian Lincoln* (Cambridge UP, 1974), pp. 93-5, noted journeys to work of five miles in the area north of Lincoln and that several parishes in the city contained farm labourers.

4. Holderness, p. 136; Grey, p. 83; Samuel, pp. 16 and 157 and J.P.D. Dunbabin, *Rural Discontent in Nineteenth-Century Britain* (Faber and Faber, London, 1974), p. 66.

5. D.B. Grigg, 'Small and Large Farms in England and Wales: Their Size and Distribution', *Geography*, vol. 48 (1963), pp. 270-1.

6. J.R. Ravensdale, *Liable to Floods: Village Landscape on the Edge of the Fens, AD 450-1850* (Cambridge UP, 1974), p. 63.

7. B. Kerr, *Bound to the Soil: A Social History of Dorset 1750-1918*, (John Baker, London, 1968), pp. 254-7; A.J. Fletcher, 'The Hope Valley in 1851', *Derbyshire Archaeological Journal*, vol. 91 (1971), p. 176.

8. Kerr, pp. 56-7; Fletcher, p. 175.

9. R.A. Dodgshon and R.A. Butlin (eds.), *An Historical Geography of England and Wales* (Academic Press, London, 1978), p. 184; F.F. Mendels, 'Proto-industrialisation in the First Phase of the Industrialisation Process', *Journal of Economic History*, vol. 32 (1972), p. 241.

10. C.J. Hunt, *The Lead Miners of the Northern Pennines in the Eighteenth and Nineteenth Centuries* (Manchester UP, 1970), pp. 136-68; H. Heaton, *The Yorkshire Woollen and Worsted Industries* (Oxford UP 2nd edn, 1965), pp. 290-2; A. Raistrick, *The West Riding of Yorkshire* (Hodder and Stoughton, London, 1970), pp. 113-4 and ibid., *The Pennine Dales* (Spottiswoode, London, 1969), pp. 116, 127.

11. J.D. Marshall, *Lancashire* (David and Charles, Newton Abbot, 1974), pp. 40, 53, 83, 104; C.S. Davies, *North Country Bred: A Working Class Family Chronicle* (Routledge, London, 1963), pp. 10, 30, 161.

12. W.M. Williams, *The Sociology of an English Village: Gosforth* (Routledge, London, 1956), p. 6.

13. J.D. Chambers, 'The Vale of Trent 1670-1800: A Regional Study of Economic Change', *Econ. Hist. Rev.* Supplement no. 3 (n.d. *c.* 1957), pp. 13-14; J. Thirsk in W.G. Hoskins and R.A. McKinley (eds.), *Victoria History of the County of Leicester*, vol. II (Institute of Historical Research, London, 1954), pp. 227-8.

14. L.A. Parker, in *ibid.*, vol. III (1955), p. 7 and D.R. Mills, 'Landownership and Rural Population with Special Reference to Leicestershire in the Mid-19th Century', (unpublished PhD thesis, University of Leicester, 1963), p. 227.

15. In A.R.H. Baker and J.B. Harley (eds.), *Man Made the Land: Essays in English Historical Geography* (David and Charles, Newton Abbot, 1973), p. 95.

16. E.L. Jones 'Agricultural Origins of Industry', *Past and Present*, no. 40 (1968), pp. 69-70.

17. In Dodgshon and Butlin, p. 184.

18. M. Harrison, 'Chayanov and the Economics of the Russian Peasantry', *Journal of Peasant Studies*, vol. 2 (1975), p. 404-5.

19. D.R. Mills, 'The Quality of Life in Melbourn, Cambridgeshire, in the Period 1800-50', *International Review of Social History*, vol. 23 (1978), p. 390ff and D.R. Mills, 'Land, Home and Kinship in Melbourn', in R. Smith (ed.), *Land, Kinship and Lifecycle* (Edward Arnold, London, forthcoming).

20. Kerr, pp. 64-5, 132-4. Another good example, from the period around 1700 is given by M.L. Baumber, *A Pennine Community on the Eve of the Industrial Revolution – Keighley and Haworth between 1660 and 1740* (Privately published 1977), p. 34.

21. E.J.T. Collins, 'Migrant Labour in British Agriculture in the Nineteenth Century', *Econ. Hist. Rev.*, vol. 29 (1976), especially p. 45.

22. Holderness, ' "Open" and "Close" Parishes', passim; D.R. Mills 'Spatial Implications of the Settlement Laws in England' in Open University, *Poverty and Social Policy 1750-1870*, A401 Great Britain 1750-1850, Block IV (1974) pp. 18-23. An excellent and still unexploited source is BPP (1850) 1152, XXVII, 299, *Reports to the Poor Law Board on the Operation of the Laws of Settlement and Removal of the Poor*.

23. Most books dealing with the architectural evidence are concerned princi-pally with the exceptional conditions of planned estate villages, for example, T. Rowley, *Villages in the Landscape* (Dent, London, 1978), pp. 131-40 and G. Darley, *Villages of Vision* (Architectural Press, London, 1975), especially pp. vii-viii. A useful antidote is J. Woodforde, *The Truth about Cottages* (Routledge, London, 1969).

24. J. Throsby, *Select Views in Leicestershire* (Leicester and London, 1791), vol. 2, p. 132.

25. J. Ashby and B. King, 'Statistics of some Midland Villages', *Economic Journal*, vol. 3 (1893), pp. 193-4. Fifty years and more after union rating was brought in (1865), social reformers were still remarking on the contrast between open and closed villages in terms of housing conditions. See, for example, BPP (1884-5), XXX. *Royal Commission on the Housing of the Working Classes* First Report, pp. 24-7; J.L. Green *English Country Cottages: Their Condition, Cost and Requirements* (Rural World Publishing Co. Ltd., London, *c.* 1899), p. 51-2, quoting, *inter alia*, the 1893 Royal Commission on Labour; and C. Adeane and E. Savill, *The Land Retort: a Study of the Land Question with an Answer to the Report of the Secret Enquiry Committee* (John Murray, London, 1914), p. 19.

26. J. Caird, *English Agriculture in 1850-1* (Longman, London, 1851), pp. 75-6, 161, 197, 516.

27. M. Springall, *Labouring Life in Norfolk Villages, 1834-1914* (Allen and Unwin, London, 1936), p. 20. See also M.W. Barley, *The English Farmhouse and Cottage* (Routledge, London, 1961), pp. 249-50.

28. F. Thompson, *Lark Rise to Candleford* (1st edn, 1939, Penguin, Harmondsworth 1973), p. 21. For another Oxfordshire example see G.S. Stevenson, 'Open Village: Victorian Middle Barton', *Cake and Cockhorse: Magazine of the Banbury Historical Society*, vol. 6 (1975), p. 40-3, referring to a village in which tradesmen owned most of the cottages.

29. J.D. Gay, *The Geography of Religion in England* (Duckworth, London, 1971), p. 111.

30. Since this map was originally drawn, the dichotomy has been confirmed by D.M. Thompson, 'The Churches and Society in Nineteenth-century England: A Rural Perspective', *Studies in Church History*, vol. 8 (1972), p. 269.

31. D.G. Hey, 'The Pattern of Nonconformity in South Yorkshire 1660-1851', *Northern History*, vol. 8 (1973), pp. 86-7; J. Obelkevich, *Religion and Rural Society: South Lindsey 1825-1875* (Clarendon Press, Oxford, 1976), pp. 21-2 and 32; A. Everitt 'Nonconformity in Country Parishes', *Agr. Hist. Rev.*, vol. 18 (1970), pp. 188-97 (this is a supplement to the *Agr. Hist. Rev.* also available as J. Thirsk (ed.). *Land, Church and People: Essays Presented to Prof. H.P.R. Finberg*, Reading University, 1970); A. Everitt, *The Pattern of Rural Dissent: The Nineteenth Century* (Leicester UP, 1974), especially p. 44. Everitt's areas of study include Devon, Yorkshire, Lancashire, Cheshire, Warwickshire, Northamptonshire, Leicestershire, Lincolnshire, Kent and Nottinghamshire. See also R. Currie, 'A Micro-theory of Methodist Growth', *Proceedings of the Wesley Historical Society*, vol. 36 (1967), pp. 65-73 and J.C.C. Probert, *The Sociology of Cornish Methodism* (Cornish Methodist Historical Association, Redruth, 1971).

32. A.D. Gilbert, *Religion and Society in Industrial England: Church, Chapel and Social Change, 1740-1914* (Longman, London, 1976), especially pp. 67 and 98-109.

33. Cambridge University Library, W.M. Palmer Deposit, A27, pp. 54-5.

34. D.M. Thompson, pp. 269-70 and Obelkevich, pp. 154-5. The attendance figures are calculated from the 1851 Religious Census.

35. R. Parker, *The Common Stream* (Collins, London, 1975), p. 234, referring to the Cambridgeshire fens where Anglican places of worship were widely spaced.

36. G.E. Evans, *Where Beards Wag All: The Relevance of the Oral Tradition* (Faber and Faber, London, 1970), pp. 117-24 and 209-10 (note that by implication going to chapel was regarded as preferable to complete non-attendance); Obelkevich, p. 36, fn. 1.

37. On the Earl of Yarborough's estate, Brocklesby, Lincs – H.A. Fuller, 'Landownership and the Lindsey Landscape', *Annals of the Association of*

*American Geographers*, vol. 66 (1976), p. 19 and on the Duke of Rutland's estate, Aylestone, Leics. – oral tradition per Mrs Lucy Tugby.

38. F. Thompson, *Lark Rise*, p. 179.

39. F. Emery, *The Oxfordshire Landscape* (Hodder and Stoughton, London, 1974), caption to plate 24; Patrick Rowley in a letter to *Local Population Studies*, no. 3 (1969), p. 53-4 and D.R. Mills, 'Francis Howell's Report on the Operation of the Laws of Settlement in Nottinghamshire, 1848', *Transactions of the Thoroton Society of Nottinghamshire*, vol. 76 (1972), p. 51.

40. Quoted by Rev. H. McKnight (1891) in *Annales Parochiales*, a document in Silk Willoughby (Lincs.) Church Chest, in connection with the rebuilding of cottages on Lord Dysart's estate there; it also describes the parson's concern to put right the water supply when he arrived in 1879 at a time of deaths due to diptheria and scarlet fever. I am indebted to Rev. F.H. Bailey, the present incumbent, for the use of this document.

41. E.P. Thompson, *Whigs and Hunters: The Origins of the Black Act* (Allen Lane, London, 1975), especially pp. 21-2, 48, 52-3, 109, 121-2; G. White, *The Natural History and Antiquities of Selborne* (1789; Scolar Press, Ilkley, 1970), pp. 12-14, 19, 426.

42. Thompson, *Whigs and Hunters*, especially pp. 99, 108, 242.

43. Ibid., p. 64.

44. Ibid., especially pp. 91-4, 239-41; White, *Selborne*, pp. 25-6. For fictional examples see Thomas Hardy, *Under the Greenwood Tree* and *The Woodlanders*. For a study which stresses the forest areas of Kent, Forest of Dean and Northamptonshire, see P. Clark, 'Popular Protest and Disturbance in Kent 1558-1640', *Econ. Hist. Rev.*, vol. 29 (1976), pp. 365-81.

45. Thompson, *Whigs and Hunters*, p. 240.

46. G.E. Evans, *Ask the Fellows Who cut the Hay* (Faber and Faber, London, 1956), pp. 188-9. See also D. Hay *et al.*, *Albion's Fatal Tree: Crime and Society in Eighteenth Century England* (Allen Lane, London, 1975), pp. 153-4, 182, 200, 208 for many examples of non-labourers as smugglers, wreckers and poachers in several parts of eighteenth-century England.

47. Dunbabin, *Rural Discontent*, pp. 20-24 and Chapter 3 generally.

48. E.L. Hobsbawm and G. Rudé, *Captain Swing* (Lawrence and Wishart, London, 1969), pp. 172-88.

49. Ibid., pp. 62-3, 138, 181, 184, 187, 207, 242-6.

50. Ibid., p. 188-9. Hobsbawm and Rudé's general study has been confirmed subsequently by B. Reaney, *The Class Struggle in Nineteenth-century Oxfordshire: The Social and Communal Background to the Otmoor Disturbances of 1830 to 1835* (Ruskin College, Oxford, History Workshop Pamphlets, No. 3, 1970).

51. D.C. Moore, *The Politics of Deference: A Study of the Mid-nineteenth century English Political System* (Harvester Press, Brighton, 1976), p. 82; T.J. Nossiter, *Influence, Opinion and Political Idioms in Reformed England: Case Studies from the North East 1832-1874* (Harvester Press, Brighton, 1975), p. 49.

52. R.W. Davis, *Political Change and Continuity 1760-1885: A Buckinghamshire Study* (David and Charles, Newton Abbot, 1972), pp. 173-8; R.J. Olney, *Lincolnshire Politics 1832-1885* (Oxford UP, 1973), p. 135; J.D. Marshall and C.A. Dyhouse, 'Social Transition in Kendal and Westmorland *c*. 1760-1860', *Northern History*, vol. 12 (1976), pp. 140-1.

53. H. Pelling, *Social Geography of British Elections: 1885-1910* (Macmillan, London, 1967), p. 428.

54. Ibid., pp. 83, 115-9, 126-7, 139-43, 150-1, 169, 198, 219, 224, 313, 321.

55. Ibid., pp. 97, 158-64, 311, 321.

56. Ibid., pp. 103, 108, 226, 281, 311, 313.

57. Ibid., pp. 158-64, 274, 311.

58. Ibid., pp. 119, 281, 313.

59. Dunbabin, *Rural Discontent*, pp. 86-8; R.J. Olney, 'The Class Struggle in Normanby-by-Spital *c*. 1830-1900', *Lincolnshire History and Archaeology*, vol. 11 (1976) p. 39; and R.C. Russell, *The 'Revolt of the Field' in Lincolnshire* (National Union of Agricultural Workers, Lincoln, 1956), pp. 4-15, 154.

60. N.A.D. Scotland, 'Methodism and the "Revolt of the Field" in East Anglia, 1872-96', *Proceedings of the Wesley Historical Society* vol. 41 (1977), pp. 2-11 and 39-42, especially p. 8.

61. Ibid., passim, but especially pp. 4-5.

62. F.M.L. Thompson, *English Landed Society in the Nineteenth Century* (Routledge, London, 1963) pp. 32 and 113-7 and J. Bateman, *The Great Landowners of Great Britain and Ireland* (Harrison, London, 4th edn, 1883).

63. A. Macfarlane, *The Origins of English Individualism* (Blackwell, Oxford, 1978).

64. In D. Hay *et al*., *Albion's Fatal Tree*, pp. 185-6.

65. By A. Howkins, *Whitsun in Nineteenth-century Oxfordshire* (Ruskin College, Oxford, History Workshop Pamphlet, No. 8, 1973).

66. Obelkevich, *Religion and Rural Society*, p. 60. This section is much in debt to Obelkevich's Chapter 2, 'Agrarian Society: From Community to Class Society'.

# 7 RURAL SCOTLAND

'Few countries had so much power concentrated in the hands of a few great landowners whose economic, political and social power was supreme.' I.H. Adams, 'The Agricultural Revolution in Scotland', *Area*, vol. 10 (1978), p. 201.

## Introduction

Despite the appearance of books dealing with the history or geography of the whole of Britain, the three national regions have generally been studied separately rather than comparatively. There are good reasons for separate treatment, most obviously the separate cultural traditions and the domination of England, which has produced a tendency towards an inward-looking emphasis on the distinctiveness of Welsh and Scottish institutions. One of the advantages of explicit comparison is that it provides an opportunity to gain different insights into the English model presented in earlier chapters, while conversely the model itself facilitates comparison. Broadly speaking, it is argued that Wales approximated to the English peasant system, being a more developed form of peasant society, while Scotland exhibited most of the characteristics of the estate system. Moreover, these generalisations appear to have held true over wide areas, both spatially and sectorally, in contrast to the patchwork effect described in England.

Whether 1700 or 1800 is taken as the standpoint, the overwhelming impression of Wales and Scotland is of backwardness in economic and technological terms as compared with England. Industrial and commercial development came late to both countries for a variety of reasons, including the isolation of upland communities from channels of commerce, the inhospitable nature of the environment, the late pacification of the Highlands, lack of capital and the neo-colonial position of Scotland and Wales with respect to England.[1] The latter point is well illustrated by the deprivation of the Welsh 'royal' families of power in the middle ages and by the better known dispossession of the Jacobite rebels after the 1745 rebellion in Scotland.[2] However, it could be argued that economic advancement came with the penetration of English ideas through the anglicisation of the Welsh gentry and the mixing of the English and Scottish landed classes after Union in 1707.

## Village, Hamlet and Farm

According to Thorpe's work, based on post-1945 maps, most of Scotland is characterised by dispersed settlement. The northern part of the Central Lowlands, a swathe of territory running along the east coast between Forth and Moray and a third area at the northern end of the Southern Uplands form the principal exceptions. There the dispersed settlement is complemented by hamlets and villages.[3] So far as its relative lack of villages is concerned, Scotland might be thought of as comparable with hamlet England, were it not for the important fact that the settlement pattern is of comparatively recent origin and owes much to the work of improving landlords between 1700 and 1850.[4]

Turning to farm size, Geddes[5] established from his study of the nineteenth-century Statistical Accounts that large farms were frequent in south east Scotland from whence in a north-westerly direction the size of holdings decreased, with the qualification that areas to the west of this imaginary line contained smaller farms than eastern areas lying opposite. The larger farms contained high proportions of arable, while the smaller enterprises to the west depended more on a grassland economy. The sociological significance of these observations was not lost on Geddes. In the Lothians he described a threefold hierarchy of landlord, non-working farmer and farm servant, comparable with the corn-growing lands of south-east England. In the intermediate zone the farmer and farm servant were often of the same family and, in any case, worked side by side. In the crofting counties it was said that a co-operative democracy prevailed. From this it would appear that two of Geddes' three zones were free from landlord control, but this is not the case, as there was no equivalent to the English yeomen or class of owner-occupiers and it is shown below that the landed classes exerted considerable influence throughout Scotland.[6] In order to appreciate their role it is necessary to take this account back to about 1700.

## Rural Scotland at the Beginning of the Eighteenth Century

At this date a largely subsistence economy survived in most parts of the country, although it was the backwardness of the highlands and islands that attracted most attention. There the clan system was still in existence. This was based on military service, like the English feudal system, but has to be distinguished from the latter by reason of the considerable emphasis it laid on kinship, or supposed kinship. By the end of the eighteenth century the clan system had totally disappeared, but its rapid transformation into something comparable with the English estate system meant that many aspects of highland society differed from the more 'modernised' English rural society. Thus for instance, the Scottish middle class grew slowly by English standards until the second half of the eighteenth century, when it was too late to have much influence upon a rural economy already in decay. Not only in the highland zone, but throughout Scotland the lasting impression is of a landed class which carried all before it on a journey to full-blooded capitalism and outdid the English in speed and thoroughness. Caird's statement that there were *only* 8,000 considerable proprietors in Scotland implies a concentration of landownership, but so much depends on a definition of 'considerable' that it is difficult to relate this figure to Thompson's 7,000 owners who shared four-fifths of the United Kingdom. It is perhaps more evocative to record that 68 persons owned nearly half of Scotland and 580 owned over three quarters in 1878. In the highlands and islands, estates of 100,000 acres were normal and anything under 20,000 was small.[7]

The characteristic settlement of early eighteenth-century rural Scotland was the hamlet of multiple tenants known as a *ferm-toun* in the lowlands and sometimes as a *bailie* in the highlands, or a *clachan* if a church existed. In Argyllshire, for example, a clachan contained an average of three to five houses and no more than 12 has been recorded, except late in the eighteenth century.[8] In the highlands tacksmen held lands from the chiefs primarily in return for military service and let the lands in turn to tenants and sub-tenants. Payments of rent were mainly in kind and in labour until feudal tenure was abolished in 1746.

Below the tenants in the social scale were the cottars and crofters who depended considerably, as the English cottager had done, on common pastures and day labour, or on craft-work, as well as on their smallholdings. In the lowlands money rents had come in and military tenures had gone out some time before 1700, but ferm-touns were still the usual agricultural form, except in Aberdeenshire and where the Anglian settlement in south-east Scotland had left a tradition of larger nucleated settlements.[9]

## Improvement – Evolution or Revolution?

The degree of backwardness in 1700 was matched by the speed and extent of change – improvement was the usual word – after that date. Caird states that Scotland's rural landscape is 'a landscape of "revolution" rather than one of slow evolution', with geometrical lines comparable with many colonial territories. Storrie, writing of west highland settlement distinguishes between evolutionary and revolutionary processes, but Caird's generalisation still holds good if the comparison implied is with England, where new village sites were a considerable rarity after 1700.[10] Kay supports this view with these words:

> The agricultural landscape of much of Scotland was virtually remade between 1750 and 1850. So drastic and widespread were the changes in this period that few signs of previous settlements and land-use systems are visible today. Patterns then established, however, have persisted with relatively little change and many features of the present landscape can be dated to this revolution.[11]

The untidy clusters of small farmsteads typical of the old ferm-touns disappeared and were replaced by much larger, dispersed holdings equipped with large, modern farmsteads, sleeping quarters and bothies for single servants and a row of cottages for married men. The subsistence economy of run-rig (common field), peasant holdings, common pasture and a chaotic lay out of tracks and buildings were swept away and replaced by capitalist farmers and a large landless proletariat in an efficiently laid out landscape. In the crofting areas, the old style clustered settlements were replaced by separate crofts widely enough spaced to classify loosely as dispersed settlements.[12]

Contact between the Scottish lairds and their counterparts in England, following the Union of 1707, which took Scottish aristocrats and gentry to London to share in national government, is generally accepted as one of the factors promoting such thorough-going change – much more radical than in England. But the Enclosures Acts of 1661, 1685 and 1695 and the Division of Commonties Act of 1695, all passed by the Scottish Parliament, gave the Scottish landowner a much freer hand than his opposite number in England, who was required to raise a Private Act for each separate township.[13] This both implies greater concentration of landownership and, together with the general absence of long-standing customary rights in arable land, explains some of the speed and extent of landscape change. Thus even where small farms and crofts were the result, the estate system was the basis of Scottish rural society. Finally, an Act of 1770 gave the proprietors of entailed estates much greater scope and, along with the greater availability of surveyors, this helps to explain the increase in estate-surveying after this date.[14]

A recent debate among historical geographers as to whether agricultural change in Scotland amounted to a 'revolution'[15] has left those who stress the rapidity of change in a secure position, but forced to acknowledge regional variations and that there were signs of change even in the seventeenth century. Acceptance of these qualifications, however, does not detract from the argument that, compared with England, change was very rapid in Scotland. For example, fundamental change in England can be traced in some areas and parishes to much earlier dates than 1600, notably in respect of depopulating enclosures. One useful product of the debate has been to widen the scope of enquiry from a study of landscape, which was the central theme of work done in the fifties and early sixties, to include such matters as tenancies, the possibility of enclosure without the abolition of the infield — outfield system, technological changes and the effect of the work of the Forfeited Estates Commission. In the main, there has been little challenge to the view that large landowners were in a position of dominant control in the Scottish countryside.

## Planned Villages

The planned village movement was another respect in which rural Scotland approximated to the model of the English estate system, for over a hundred were built, a considerable number in view of the fact that the agricultural system had been replanned on a basis of larger, dispersed farmsteads. While some of the ideas employed in the establishment of these new villages may have been borrowed from England, the basic rationale arose out of the Scottish situation.

There was a need to have local consumption points in what was now a commercial economy, a need to provide for the victims of enclosure and the enlargement of farms and an advantage in having industrious villagers to set an example of commercial habits to the tenantry. Agricultural improvements had quickened the demand for supplies and servicing such as clothing, footwear, smithing and wheelwrighting, which could not yet be met by rail transport, nor by existing market towns because they were too inflexible in outlook.[16]

Although, in the late nineteenth century, many planned villages had become very dependent on agriculture, they had frequently started out as industrial and commercial settlements starting with primary processing activities and diversifying into textile trades. There are a few specific references to planned villages near residences, such as Kenmore in Perthshire at the gates of the Marquis of Breadalbane's park and John Cockburn's well-known place at Ormiston in East Lothian, but on the whole there was not the same correspondence between seats and estate villages as in England. Landlords were not merely interested in exploiting mineral wealth as in England; they would support any industrial growth which would increase rents, so long as it was rural growth and social control could be exerted over the industrial workers. If an industrial village succeeded so well as to become a town they withdrew. The list of activities included linen and cotton manufacture, bleaching, brewing, milling, fishing, salt-boiling, the manufacture of coal tar, quarrying, mining, glass-making, lime-burning and all the usual range of crafts and trades needed to support the neighbouring farms. In the western highlands and islands the landlords also took an active part in the manufacture of kelp (a raw material produced by burning seaweed and used in soap and glass-making).[17]

There have been two major surveys of Scottish planned villages, one by Houston in which he reckoned the total as 150 for the period 1745-1845 and the other by Smout who arrived at 130 for the earlier period of 1730-1830. Houston excluded coal-mining and urban development; Smout omitted landlord villages not physically replanned; both included factory villages around Glasgow and Paisley. More recently a grand total of 268 planned villages has been reported.[18]

Smout distinguished between eight geographical groups of planned villages (see Figure 7.1). Group I were mainly places in which crofters were rehoused as a result of highland clearances; fishing was an important second occupation here. Group II is remarkable for its size and close spacing in fertile territory liberated from the highland raid; farming was much more prosperous than hitherto, to which linenweaving and fishing were often added. Group III mainly originated from the activities of the Commissioners of Forfeited Estates (properties belonging to Jacobite owners) and are a good example of the importance of social control, for the highlander above all was considered to be in need of moral improvement. The fourth group were mainly fishing and harbour settlements, some of them, like Tobermory and Ullapool, the responsibility of the British Fisheries Society. Group V was a linen group based on yarn sent out from Perth and Dundee and, like Group III, helps to explain the zone of nucleated villages with dispersed settlement distinguished by Thorpe. The factory villages mentioned above constituted Group VI, while the two groups in the Southern Uplands had diverse origins and occupations, including fishing, ship-

Figure 7.1: Planned Villages in Scotland

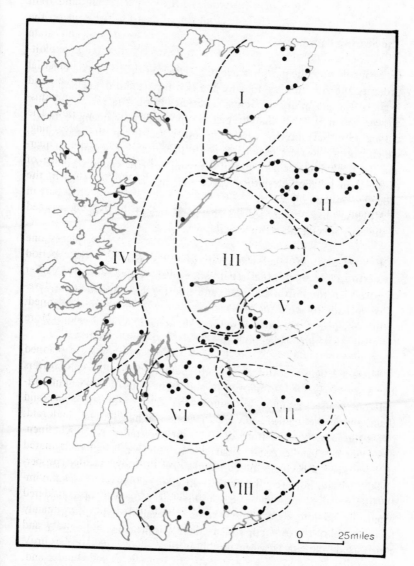

Note: See text for explanation of groupings

Source: Based on T.C. Smout 'The Landowner and the Planned Village in Scotland 1730-1830' in N.T. Phillipson and R. Mitchison (eds.) *Scotland in the Age of Improvement: Essays in Scottish History in the Eighteenth Century* (Edinburgh University Press, 1970), p. 102.

building, cotton-spinning, linen and woollen-weaving.[19]


## The Scottish Poor Law

Comparison with the narrow range of activities in English estate villages prompts the question as to why the Scottish landlord did not take fright at the possibility of rampant increases in poor rates. Part of the answer lies in the fact that he met the possibility of unemployment among farm servants by developing other sectors of the economy, which in England were frequently controlled by the urban middle class and the freeholding peasantry. But the two Poor Law systems were also different in practice, despite the fact that the Scottish Acts had been modelled on the English.

Mitchison has summarised the characteristics of the Scottish system in the early nineteenth century as follows:

> Firstly, that no relief was given to the able-bodied, the merely 'destitute'; secondly, that relief, when given, was not enough to support even the infirm and aged; and thirdly, that all possible efforts were made to avoid the 'evil' of assessment, or in other words that in most places the funds were those that could be raised voluntarily, mainly by church collections (p. 58).

There are signs that this generalisation did not hold true everywhere. The assessed parishes, a minority of about one in ten which were more generous, caused a minor, but unmeasured shift of labourers towards them; and in the highlands there are instances of new settlements being refused because of the potential effects on poor relief. After 1846 the new poor law caused assessed parishes to be the rule rather than the exception and this change raised payments to the poor in some areas.[20] On the whole, however, the marked differences between Scottish and English practices must have been influential. Moreover, in a country where the landlord classes appear to have prevailed fairly uniformly in their control of the rural population, there was little possibility of sharp contrasts developing between neighbouring townships on the English pattern.

## Highland Landlords and the Crofting System

Hunter has pointed out that by the mid-eighteenth century the political élite in Scotland, as in England, were distinctly unfeudal in outlook and were thoroughly immersed in trade and commerce. Also as in England, conspicuous consumption spurred them on, a habit which was relatively new in Scotland, especially north of the Highland Line, where status so recently had been based on military loyalty and feudal dues, rather than cash. This social system was already decaying in the early eighteenth century, as the north became important for the supply of cattle, sheep, wool, kelp and labour for lowland towns. But the older view that the defeat at Culloden in 1746, which provoked the abolition of feudal tenures, the proscription of the kilt and firearms and the dispossession of tainted lairds, also has merit in that it helps to explain the mid-century acceleration of trends already begun. By the first half of the nineteenth century, inflation, over-consumption and big arrears of rent due to the post-war depression had driven most highland landowners to a point where they had to embark on clearances or sell out and allow their successors, often lowlanders and even English, to do the same. Hence there was a lack of understanding between nineteenth-century highland proprietors and their tenants, similar to that which developed widely in Wales.[21]

## The Crofting System

While Scottish village communities outside the crofting counties belonged firmly to the estate system, inside the crofting areas there might be reason to suppose that circumstances were different, as small-scale farming and dual occupations are still surviving there. The seven crofting counties are Zetland, Orkney, Caithness, Sutherland, Ross and Cromarty, Inverness and Argyll, to which the 1886 Act and subsequent legislation applies and it is important to distinguish this smaller area from the whole of the area lying north of the Highland Line and to note the exclusion of substantial parts of the eastern and southern highlands. Moreover, within the crofting counties, crofting is much more important in the islands and the north-western coastline than elsewhere.

Crofting was a new development of the second half of the eighteenth century, arising out of the collapse of the clan system and complete reliance on a subsistence economy. Although much subsistence continued to be raised locally, crofting also relied on the sale of animals and wool and by-occupations such as fishing and kelp-burning, and later weaving and other secondary occupations. It also differed socially because the clan hierarchy was replaced by co-operation between independent households, through which were achieved certain necessary agricultural operations. These included souming (stinting of the common pastures), fanks (round-ups of animals) and in some areas re-letting of run-rig (arable strips).[22]

While crofting represents the survival of a peasant economy in a more meaningful sense than anywhere else in Britain, it is important to be clear as to why it survived. Very simply – perhaps too simply – it survived to 1886 because the highland landlords first of all found it convenient to let it do so and later on lacked the resources to make a clean sweep. Thereafter crofting has been protected by the state, presumably to ensure the maintenance of a minimum population in these distant parts of the realm. As noted above, the highland landlord, faced with declining rent rolls and a level of personal spending higher than before, was attracted to the solution represented by the clearances, the very word implying a stark choice between a semi-traditional economy and a commercialised economy of brutal simplicity.

The clearances were a method of removing impoverished crofters, to use the same land for large-scale sheep and cattle farming, bringing in well capitalised tenant farmers from further south who sold in the expanding wool and meat markets of industrial Britain. The clearances were not achieved without resistance from the original tenantry, but because the latter lacked security of tenure before the 1886 Act, the landlords were able to proceed without being hindered over much by the opposition. The extent of disturbance and brutality varied considerably from one estate to another, as did the reduction in population levels. There was a considerable amount of emigration – put at 50,000 in the period 1763-1775, before the clearances, when it was mainly voluntary. Some of the disturbed crofters sometimes migrated first on a seasonal basis then permanently to the lowlands and others were re-allocated different land, often of an inferior quality and quantity, but also often on the coast where fishing and kelp-burning were important occupations.[23]

Thus while the highland economy underwent a considerable phase of modernisation, the landlords did not extinguish the peasant class, because it provided the necessary labour for the kelp industry. The landlords expropriated this activity during the French wars and maintained it at a high level of productivity until technical changes in glass manufacture led to the decline of kelping in the 1820s. This decline was followed by intense efforts to promote emigration and to bring in sheep even to areas near the coasts. The urge to promote emigration was accelerated by the famine years of the 1840s and the change of the poor law in favour of the poor which occurred in 1846.

However, by the 1860s profits from sheep-farming were falling away, making the impetus for clearances a spent force, while profits from crofters' cattle-farming were much healthier and fishing provided many of them with a basic living. The contrast between 'congested, deprived and squalid townships (and) vast tracts of empty, uncultivated and not infrequently fertile land' continued to provide a stark physical manifestation of relative deprivation. This was pointed out to the Napier Commission in the 1880s and was the chief cause of the Crofters' War whose termination was associated with a government decree that crofters should have security of tenure and the benefit of tenants' rights over improvements.[24]

This modest victory of the peasantry over the landlords finds a faint parallel in the history of Wales but none in that of England unless the creation of county council smallholdings is counted as such.

The reluctance of the crofter to take part in modernisation has sometimes been interpreted simply as laziness and the inability to grasp the potentiality of an innovation. Carter has put forward the alternative explanation that while the landlord and his large tenant sheep-farmers were principally interested in profit maximisation on the basis of heavy capital expenditure, the crofter had other objectives. Not only did he lack the capital to engage in large-scale farming, he was more interested in maximising social solidarity than profits. The fact that the crofting system caught on in the eighteenth century in the span of a generation or two is instanced as an innovation accepted by the peasantry because it maximised social solidarity, while the adoption of potato-growing is an example of a rapidly accepted innovation that required a minimum of capital outlay, gave a good return on a small acreage and an opportunity to use family labour. Additionally, the crofter was frequently in debt to his landlord over arrears of rent. Any attempt to increase productivity was discouraged by the factor immediately demanding payment of debt. Even apart from the clearances, there was also the constant fear of eviction.[25]

Outside the crofting counties it is also possible to find examples of crofts surviving well into the nineteenth century and probably beyond, but again their marginal nature is apparent. Odell and Walton, referring to areas east of the Great Glen, note that most large farms were on the best land, with the spaces in-between filled with numerous small farms and crofts. In the lowlands, Third found similar evidence of large farms on good land and smaller farms limited to the muir frontage on clearly marginal sites. On the internal frontier of colonisation many crofter plots were taken into large farms once they were sufficiently improved by the crofter-squatters. In north-east Scotland, the Dukes of Gordon, Lord Seafield and the Duke of Richmond encouraged squatters to reclaim moorland and to exist on by-occupations such as day labouring on farms, slate-quarrying, and the cutting and carting of peat, living rent free in the meantime. Here is another instance of the Scottish landlord tolerating the peasantry when it suited him and moving them on when it did not (See figure 7.2).[26]

The marginal nature of the crofting system within Scotland as a whole is underlined by the linguistic, political and religious geography of the country. It is in the Highlands, especially the north west and the islands, that Gaelic has survived, despite its proscription in 1746. Here there is an interesting parallel with the Welsh peasantry, among whom the native language survived long after it had been abandoned by the gentry and some of the townspeople, and with the English peasantry who clung to dialect and other cultural traditions belonging to the countryside. As to religion, the Free Church, sympathetic to the plight of the lower classes, like the Primitive Methodists in England, was able to make the crofting counties its particular stronghold, despite difficulties in finding church sites, and this helps to account for the beginnings of community development in the mid-nineteenth century. Moreover, the crofter appears to have been radical and Liberal in his voting habits, thus following the path trodden by Scottish burgh populations, rather than that beaten by the Tory landlords and large farmers elsewhere in the country.[27]

## Conclusion

This account of Scottish rural society has shown that, although it contained superficial elements of comparison with hamlet England and the peasant system, notably much dispersed settlement and the survival of crofting, at its roots there existed a solid basis of concentrated landownership. While his policies differed in detail from those of his English counterpart, the laird operated in the Scottish context from motives and philosophies recognisably similar. Indeed it should not be forgotten that some Scottish estates were in English ownership. So the landed

Figure 7.2: Strathpeffer Crofting Area, Inland from Dingwall, Ross and Cromarty

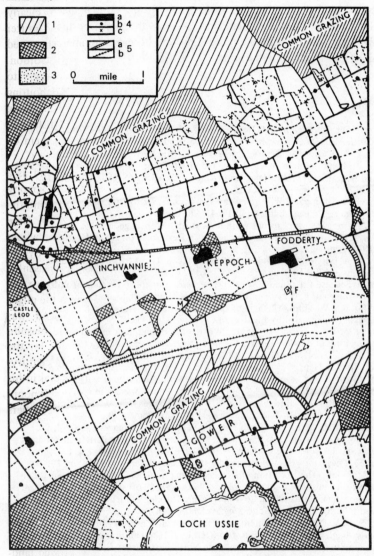

Note: 1 = Rough Grazing. 2 = Plantations. 3 = Estate 'policy'. 4a = Large farm steadings. 4b = Croft houses. 4c = Ruined or empty croft houses. 5a = Dingwall — Kyle of Lochalsh railway track. 5b = Old Dingwall — Strathpeffer railway track. Thick black lines are existing farm and croft boundaries; broken lines indicate field boundaries. A = Auchterneed; F = Fodderty Lodge; M = Millmain.
Source: J. Tivy's map in *Annual Report of the Scottish Field Association*, 1963.

classes in Scotland produced a rural landscape of large dispersed farmsteads and planned villages having greater freedom of action than their
counterparts in England. Crofting survived only on marginal land and
not in such favourable circumstances as the Fens or the Vale of
Evesham where smallholdings continued to be viable commercial operations into the twentieth century.

## Notes

1. See, for example, M. Hechter, *Internal Colonisation: The Celtic Fringe in
British National Development, 1536-1966* (Routledge, London, 1975), passim.
2. A.D. Carr, 'An Aristocracy in Decline: The Native Welsh Lords after the
Edwardian Conquest', *Welsh HR*, vol. 5 (1970-1), pp. 103-29 and A.C. O'Dell
and K. Walton, *The Highlands and Islands of Scotland* (Nelson, London, 1962),
p. 117.
3. H. Thorpe in J.W. Watson and J.B. Sissons, *The British Isles: A Systematic
Geography* (Nelson, Edinburgh, 1964), Ch. 19.
4. For a review of recent work in Scottish historical geography, see I.D.
Whyte, 'Scottish Historical Geography – a Review', *Scot. Geog. Mag.*, vol. 94
(1978), pp. 4-23.
5. A. Geddes, 'Scotland's "Statistical Accounts" of Parish, County and
Nation: c. 1790-1825 and 1835-45', *Scot. St.*, vol. 3 (1959), pp. 24-5.
6. See also C.P. Snodgrass (ed.), *The Third Statistical Account of Scotland:
The County of East Lothian* (Oliver and Boyd, Edinburgh and London, 1953),
p. 60; B.M.W. Third, 'Changing Landscape and Social Structure in the Scottish
Lowlands as revealed by Eighteenth-Century Estate Plans', *Scot. Geog. Mag.*, vol.
71 (1955), p. 89; and I.D. Whyte, 'Written Leases and their Impact on Scottish
Agriculture in the Seventeenth Century', *Ag. Hist. Rev.*, vol. 27 (1979), p. 1.
7. J.B. Caird, 'The Making of the Scottish Rural Landscape', *Scot. Geog. Mag.*,
vol. 80 (1964), pp. 73-4; E.J. Hobsbawm, *'Agriculture et Capitalisme en Ecosse
au XVIII^e Siècle', Annales: Economies, Sociétés, Civilisations*, vol. 33 (1978),
especially p. 581; F.M.L. Thompson, *English Landed Society in the Nineteenth
Century* (Routledge, London, 1963), p. 27; J. Hunter, *The Making of the Crofting
Community* (John Donald, Edinburgh, 1976), pp. 7 and 120.
8. H. Fairhurst, 'The Surveys for the Sutherland Clearances 1813-20', *Scot.
St.*, vol. 8 (1964), pp. 4-7 and 16 and 'The Rural Settlement Pattern in Scotland,
with Special Reference to the West and North', in R.W. Steel and R. Lawton
(eds.), *Liverpool Essays in Geography* (Longmans, London, 1967), pp. 196-9;
R.A. Gailey, 'The Evolution of Highland Rural Settlement with Particular Reference to Argyllshire', *Scot. St.*, vol. 6 (1962), pp. 159-60 and J.H.G. Lebon, 'The
Face of the Countryside in Central Ayrshire During the Eighteenth and Nineteenth Centuries', *Scot. Geog. Mag.*, vol. 62 (1946), p. 9.
9. R.A. Gailey, 'Settlement and Population in Kintyre 1750-1800', *Scot.
Geog. Mag.*, vol. 76 (1960), pp. 105-6; G. Kay, 'The Landscape of Improvement:
A Case Study of Agricultural Change in North East Scotland', *Scot. Geog. Mag.*,
vol. 78 (1962), p. 100; O'Dell and Walton, *Highlands and Islands*, p. 105; G.
Whittington, 'Was there a Scottish Agricultural Revolution?', *Area*, vol. 7 (1975),
pp. 204-6; I.D. Whyte, 'The Agricultural Revolution in Scotland: Contributions
to the Debate', *Area*, vol. 10 (1978), pp. 203-5; and A.J. Youngson, *After the
Forty-Five: The Economic Impact on the Scottish Highlands* (Edinburgh UP,
1973), pp. 12-13.

10. Caird, 'Scottish Rural Landscape', p. 72; Fairhurst, 'Rural Settlement Patterns', pp. 205-6; A. Geddes, 'The Changing Landscape of the Lothians 1600-1800, as revealed by old Estate Plans', *Scot. Geog. Mag.*, vol. 54 (1938), pp. 129-43; Lebon, 'Face of Ayrshire', pp. 10-15; M.C. Storrie, 'Landholdings and Settlement Evolution in West Highland Scotland', *Geografiska Annaler*, vol. 47B (1965), pp. 141-53; B.M.W. Third, 'Landscape and Social Structure' and ibid., 'The Significance of Scottish Estate Plans and Associated Documents: Some Local Examples', *Scot. St.*, vol. 1 (1957), pp. 39-64.

11. Kay, 'Landscape of Improvement', p. 100.

12. Caird, 'Scottish Rural Landscape', pp. 72-3 and 77; Kay, 'Landscape of Improvement', p. 104; R.N. Millman, *The Making of the Scottish Landscape* (Batsford, London, 1975), pp. 39, 94, 104 and 106; O'Dell and Walton, *Highlands and Islands*, pp. 124 and 151; I.M.L. Robertson, 'Changing Form and Function of Settlement in SW Argyll, 1841-1961', *Scot. Geog. Mag.*, vol. 83 (1967), p. 34, and G. Whittington and D.U. Brett, 'Locational Decision-making on a Scottish Estate prior to Enclosure', *Journal of Historical Geography*, vol. 5 (1979), pp. 33-46. For a good archaeological account of a clachan see the editorial note in *Scot. St.*, vol. 7 (1963), pp. 230-4.

13. Caird, 'Scottish Rural Landscape', p. 73. The mere passing of these Acts does not, however, necessarily imply that they were immediately (or eventually) put to extensive use – I.H. Adams, 'The Agricultural Revolution in Scotland: Contributions to the Debate', *Area*, vol. 10 (1978), pp. 198-203.

14. Adams, 'Debate', pp. 200-1; Fairhurst, 'Rural Settlement Pattern', p. 195; Millman, *Scottish Landscape*, pp. 89, 94, and 150-2; O'Dell and Walton, *Highlands and Islands*, p. 135. A standard work on this subject now under some challenge is: J.E. Handley, *The Agricultural Revolution in Scotland* (Burns, Glasgow, 1963).

15. This appears in the following pages of *Area*: vol. 7 (1975), pp. 204-6; vol. 8 (1976), pp. 237-9 and vol. 10 (1978), pp. 198-203.

16. T.C. Smout, 'The Landowner and the Planned Village in Scotland 1730-1830, in N.T. Phillipson and R. Mitchison (eds.), *Scotland in the Age of Improvement: Essays in Scottish History in the Eighteenth Century* (Edinburgh University Press, 1970), p. 75. See also J.M. Houston, 'Village Planning in Scotland 1745-1845', *Advancement of Science*, vol. 5 (1948), pp. 129-32 and M.C. Storrie, 'The Census of Scotland as a Source in the Historical Geography of Islay', *Scot. Geog. Mag.*, vol. 78 (1962), pp. 162-3.

17. Caird, 'Scottish Rural Landscape', pp. 78-9; Houston, 'Village Planning', pp. 129-32; R.H. Matthew and P.J. Nuttgens, 'Two Scottish Villages: A Planning Study', *Scot. St.*, vol. 3 (1959), pp. 116-8; Smout, 'The Planned Village', pp. 74-9, 89, 93 and 97 and 'Scottish Landowners and Economic Growth 1650-1850', *Scottish Journal of Political Economy*, vol. 11 (1964), pp. 220-7 and 232; J.D. Wood, 'Regulating the Settlers and Establishing Industry: Planning Intentions for a Nineteenth-Century Scottish Estate Village', *Scot. St.*, vol. 15 (1971), p. 42 and H. Woolmer, 'Grantown-on-Spey: An Eighteenth-Century New Town', *Town Planning Review*, vol. 41 (1970), pp. 237-50.

18. Adams, 'Debate', p. 201; I.L. Donnachie and I. Macleod, *Old Galloway*, (David and Charles, Newton Abbot, 1974), pp. 62-72; I.H. Adams, *The Making of Urban Scotland*, (Croom Helm, London, 1978), p. 59ff; Houston, 'Village Planning', p. 129; Millman, *Scottish Landscape*, pp. 16, 93 and 152-70 and Smout, 'The Planned Village', pp. 79-82.

19. Houston, 'Village Planning', p. 131; J. Prebble, *The Highland Clearances*, (1963, Penguin Edn Harmondsworth, 1969), pp. 56-7, 69, 101, 105-6, 135, 208-9; Smout, 'The Planned Village', pp. 83-5; W.H.K. Turner, 'Some Eighteenth-Century Developments in the Textile Region of East Central Scotland', *Scot.*

*Geog. Mag.*, vol. 69 (1953), especially, pp. 12 and 16; Wood 'Regulating the Settlers', and Youngson, *After the Forty-Five*, pp. 121-7.

20. Hunter, *Crofting Community*, p. 75; R. Mitchison, 'The Making of the Old Scottish Poor Law', *Past and Present*, vol. 63 (May 1974), especially pp. 58-61, 67, 72-3, 80-1 and 90; and ibid. 'A Rejoinder', *Past and Present*, vol. 69 (November 1975), pp. 119-21; Prebble, *Highland Clearances*, pp. 220-1 and G.S. Pryde, *Scotland from 1603 to the Present Day* (Nelson, Edinburgh, 1962), p. 148.

21. I. Carter, 'Economic Models and the Recent History of the Highlands', *Scot. St.*, vol. 15 (1971), especially p. 104; E. Cregeen, 'The Changing Role of the House of Argyll in the Scottish Highlands', in Phillipson and Mitchison, *Scotland in the Age of Improvement*, pp. 8-10; Hunter, *Crofting Community*, pp. 6-14; O'Dell and Walton, *Highlands and Islands*, pp. 103-4; Prebble, *Highland Clearances*, pp. 28, 108 and 249; Pryde, *Scotland from 1603*, p. 160 and Youngson, *After the Forty-Five*, pp. 19-21, 26ff. and 176.

22. J.R. Coull, 'The Economic Development of the Island of Westray, Orkney', *Scot. Geog. Mag.*, vol. 82 (1966), pp. 156-7; Cregeen, 'House of Argyll', p. 14; Millman, *Scottish Landscape*, p. 121; and H.A. Moisley, 'The Highlands and Islands: a Crofting Region?', *TIBG*, no. 31 (1962), pp. 83-4, 90-1; and ibid. 'Harris Tweed: a growing Highland Industry', *Economic Geography*, vol. 37 (1961), pp. 354-60.

23. Millman, *Scottish Landscape*, pp. 125 and 134; O'Dell and Walton, *Highlands and Islands*, pp. 141-2 and 159; Prebble, *Highland Clearances*, pp. 24, 28, 45, 95, 110, 141, 245 and 266; J.F. Scott, 'The Parish of Morvern', *Scot. Geog. Mag.*, vol. 70 (1954), especially pp. 84-5; D. Turnock, 'Glenelg, Glengarry and Lochiel: An Evolutionary Study of Land Use', *Scot. Geog. Mag.*, vol. 83 (1967), pp. 92, 94 and 97 and Youngson, *After the Forty-Five*, p. 177ff.

24. Hunter, *Crofting Community*, pp. 16-9, 33-4, 40ff., 73-6, 107-9, 128ff., and 162.

25. Carter, 'Economic Models', pp. 107-8; Cregeen, 'House of Argyll', p. 19; Hunter, *Crofting Community*, pp. 38 and 117; and Youngson, *After the Forty-Five*, pp. 164-5 and 173-4.

26. D.K. Cameron, *The Ballad and the Plough: A Portrait of the Life of the old Scottish Fermtouns* (Gollancz, London, 1978), pp. 158-9; I. Carter, 'Social Differentiation in the Aberdeenshire Peasantry 1696-1870', *Journal of Peasant Studies*, vol. 5 (1977), especially pp. 60-2; Donnachie and Macleod, *Old Galloway*, pp. 102-4; Kay, 'Landscape of Improvement', pp. 105-7; Millman, *Scottish Landscape*, p. 116; O'Dell and Walton, *Highlands and Islands*, pp. 151-3; J. Tivy, 'Easter Ross: A Residual Crofting Area', *Scot. St.*, vol. 9 (1965), pp. 69-75 and Whittington, 'Revolution?', *Area*, vol. 7 (1975), pp. 205-6. For an evocative fictional example of the residual nature of crofting in NE Scotland see L.G. Gibbon (pseud. = J.L. Mitchell), *Sunset Song* (1932; Jarrolds Edn, London, 1950).

27. Cameron, *Ballad and Plough*, p. 141; Hunter, *Crofting Community*, p. 94ff.; Moisley, 'Crofting Region', p. 92; H. Pelling, *Social Geography of British Elections, 1885-1910* (London, Macmillan, 1967), pp. 378-85; Prebble, *Highland Clearances*, pp. 63, 73, 199 and 216-7; and Pryde, *Scotland from 1603*, pp. 184-6, 197-8, 206 and 209.

# 8 RURAL WALES

'A study of modern Wales, and of modern Scotland as well, by pointing the contrast with England, might shed new light on the political characteristics of contemporary Britain, in which the rebirth of a sense of a local, regional or national community has been an important theme.' K.O. Morgan, *Wales in British Politics 1868-1922* (University of Wales Press, Cardiff, 1973), p. vii.

## Introduction

It is well known that rural Wales was (and is) a land of scattered dwellings and hamlets and of small farms, with a preponderance of chapel over church. These are characteristics which earlier chapters have shown to be typical of peasant areas in England. While this parallel holds quite well for the end of the nineteenth century, the situation was otherwise in Wales at the beginning, for then the gentry dominated Welsh society. The intervening years saw the peasantry, in alliance with nonconformist ministers and some of the middle class of the small market towns, gradually taking power from the gentry, despite a relatively static social distribution of landownership. They were more successful in some areas than others and Gareth Thomas has put forward a broad two-fold altitudinal model. Low lying areas of the Middle Borderland are seen as Tory, English and Established Church territory, leaving the much more extensive upland areas in the control of the Liberal-Radical, Welsh-speaking non-conformists.[1] This chapter explains the fundamental change in Welsh rural society and summarises evidence relating to Thomas' model.

Early medieval Wales was divided between the native tribal society of upland areas and the lowlands of the Border and coast, into which Anglo-Norman feudalism had penetrated, frequently accompanied by nucleated settlement and common field systems similar to those in England. Even in 1800 it was said that these latter areas maintained an agricultural society alien to the rest of Wales. The need to distinguish between feudalism and a tribal society has already been established in connection with the Highland clans, where, as in Wales, kinship had a degree of importance unknown in feudal England. Although the tribal system gradually decayed, and was finally abolished by the Tudor Acts

161

of Union, kinship remained a vital factor in Welsh rural society.[2]

Tribalism was associated with a clustered settlement pattern, but in the later middle ages these hamlets broke up under the pressure of a developing land market and an increase in the size of holdings. As in Scotland after 1700, the larger holdings were associated with dispersed settlement, but the typical Welsh farm nevertheless stayed small by comparison. Consolidation of holdings and estates in the fourteenth and fifteenth centuries was especially rapid in the bondlands, thus forming a broad counterpart to the lost villages of medieval England, where the lowest layers of rural society were the most easily uprooted. The land market should be noted as a factor distinguishing the Welsh peasantry from the 'purer' peasantries of Eastern Europe.[3]

The statute of Wales (1284), which signified English conquest, was followed in 1536 and 1543 by formal Acts of Union, whose declared purpose was to make government uniform in the two countries. Feudalism, which had already effectively died out in England, was abolished, thus bringing to an end the powerful Marcher lordships, along with English royal officials and the old Welsh 'royal' families in Wales proper. Power passed to a new class of lesser gentry who provided the eight JPs per-new-shire to administer justice and much else on the English model. Although interpreters could be used, English became the language of the courts in order to standardise the administration of the law. Thus although the gentry were Welsh they had to speak English and this set them on the, in a sense, fatal path of anglicisation, intermarrying with the English gentry, forsaking native culture, sending their young away to study in English schools and at Jesus College, Oxford. Economically, their power was reinforced by the adoption of primogeniture, which allowed the accumulation of considerable estates, while the lower landed classes clung to gavelkind (partible inheritance).[4] Thus was the wedge first inserted between the Welsh gentry and the peasantry.

## The Social Structure of Rural Wales

Nonetheless, in 1800, after two and a half centuries of power this gentry class seemed secure in its hold over Wales. In so far as they attended church, the country people were still members of the Established Church, in which the gentry appointed the clergy and Englishmen held bishoprics from afar. Welsh rural society is described in the same squire-dominated terms as the English estate system. For instance,

J. Morgan noted that 53 per cent of Denbighshire was owned by 54 people and the remainder by 1,432 smaller proprietors. Experience of English data for the same period suggests that this kind of distribution could very easily have left scope for a class of peasantry, especially if they were concentrated in particular localities, but in Wales the small freeholder is seldom mentioned.[5]

A more thorough analysis has been carried out by Howell, using the data collected by the New Domesday and subsequent surveys for the 1870s and 1880s to provide a comparison with Thompson's work on England. Howell points out that 'Estates of over 1,000 acres occupied 60 per cent of the total area of the principality. This concentration of land was even more marked than in England where estates of over 1,000 acres covered 53.5 per cent of the total area.'[6] As much of his subsequent argument is based on similarities between large Welsh and English owners, it is important to look closely at the full range of comparisons available in Table 8.1.

Table 8.1: Distribution of Land Between Estates of Different Sizes in England and Wales

| Estate categories by size (acres) | Containing percentages of land: | | | |
| | ENGLAND | | WALES | |
| | Individual size categories | Cumulative percentages | Individual size categories | Cumulative percentages |
|---|---|---|---|---|
| Over 10,000 | 24.0 | — | 13.52 | — |
| 3,000-10,000 | 17.0 | 41.0 | 30.64 | 44.16 |
| 1,000-3,000 | 12.4 | 53.4 | 16.30 | 60.46 |
| 300-1,000 | 14.0 | 67.4 | 14.84 | 75.30 |
| 100-300 | 12.5 | 79.9 | 12.09 | 87.39 |
| 1-100 | 12.0 | 91.9 | 10.47 | 97.86 |
| Other properties | 8.1 | 100.0 | 2.14 | 100.00 |

Sources: F.M.L. Thompson, *English Landed Society in the Nineteenth Century* (1963), pp. 32, 114-5, 117 and D.W. Howell, *Land and People in Nineteenth-Century Wales* (1977), p. 20 (both Routledge, London).
(Note the apparent inconsistency of the residual categories.)

While it is fair to acknowledge the greater concentration of land in Wales in estates of all sizes above 1,000 acres, it is equally necessary to acknowledge the lesser area of the really great estates of over 10,000 acres. Provided this is not an artefact of the smaller total extent of Wales or related in some way to the existence of Anglo-Welsh estates, the relative paucity of great estates may have been the weakness of Welsh agricultural management, as it is these estates above all which could have set the shining example of excellence to those lower down the scale. Added to this, the lower productivity of Welsh land meant that income available must have been much smaller than on comparative acreages in arable England. There were, in fact, only 31 Welsh peers according to Bateman's information quoted by Howell.

Despite their obvious strengths, there were also weaknesses in the position of the Welsh aristocracy and gentry. Their Englishness was often reinforced by that of English speaking clergy, by large parishes and the physical remoteness of many churches from their congregations. The fabric of churches was neglected, partly because of the appropriation of the tithe by laymen, an issue to become very fierce in the 1880s. The exclusion of dissenters from public office rankled and there were signs that freeholding dissenters were looking for opportunities to assert their independence of the gentry in other ways. Most of all, the Welsh gentry did not have a following of well-capitalised tenant farmers on the models of England and most of Scotland. One commentator after another remarks on the relatively classless structure of Welsh rural society below the rank of gentry and of the importance of kin rather than class, although Howell has pointed out that the common poverty of a semi-subsistence economy was also an important factor in the slow appearance of class distinctions.[7]

The common cause that held them together in opposition to the landlord is illustrated in an upland parish of north Montgomeryshire:

> Class distinction is comparatively weak in Llanfihangel . . . Almost every family until recently has held land direct from the landlord, and therefore the division between farmer and wage-earner has been less definite than in the neighbouring lowlands with their system of tied cottages.[8]

Here is an example that supports G. Thomas' altitudinal model.

In south-west Wales farm tenancies often passed between kin, as families moved to larger or smaller holdings as needs and resources changed during the life-cycle, thus conforming to the Chayanovian model. One size of holding merged imperceptibly with another and complicated economic and social relationships existed between labourers, cottagers and farmers of various sizes.[9]

One rough statistical indicator of the relative classlessness of Welsh rural society is the ratio of farmers to workers. For the whole of Wales in 1851 the proportions were 28 farmers to 16 relatives to 56 labourers. Owing to the considerable migration of labourers this ratio had become 36 : 20 : 44 by 1911. But, of course, this represents the picture only at given points in time. Many men worked as labourers for a portion of their lives after leaving home, but before taking a holding of their own, or when they were cottagers without full-time work at home. These relationships help to explain the relative lack of money wages in the Welsh economy, a factor likening it to continental peasantries.[10]

From one district to another the proportions could vary considerably. The parishes of north-east Wales in 1831 ranged from 25 to 90 per cent in the proportion of farmers employing labourers. In his work on that area, Rees Pryce[11] has distinguished between the following social classes associated with agriculture:

(1) Labourers, together with cottagers up to 20 acres, excluding those who employed two or more labourers who were regarded as members of Class 2.
(2) Medium-size farmers, 20-80 acres, mainly relying on sons and close relatives for manpower.
(3) Large farmers, over 80 acres, plus those in class 2 employing more than two labourers.

Even these large farmers could not compare with the large farms of arable Scotland and England, although the small farm image of Wales could be overdone, as in 1851 both Lancashire and West Riding had a larger proportion of small farms than Wales. The English speaking areas of Wales had bigger farms, a fact attributed not solely to their lowland nature but also to the predominance of primogeniture over gavelkind. Local influences, such as depopulation in south-west Carmarthenshire, could also bring about the enlargement of farms.[12]

With only a capital deficient peasantry in their way, could the Welsh gentry not have emulated the Scots? They had widespread economic interests extending into coal and lead-mining and one of the earlier writers, at least, believed them to have an interest in improvements.[13] It is true that Wales suffered from isolation and bad roads, although not as badly as the Highlands and Islands. On the Scottish mainland the building of military roads was sufficient to allow modernisation to start.

Lack of drive and commitment appears to be part of the answer. For example, in north Wales both in 1800 and the mid-century rack-renting was common, being associated with a failure to play a constructive landlord role in the sense of providing fixed capital in generous amounts. The land question, by no means unknown in England, was virulent in Wales and it served to direct attention away from technological progress towards opportunities for large numbers of labourers to become independent smallholders and, later, owners of land. The comparatively buoyant state of grassland farming at the end of the century encouraged the Welsh peasant to become an owner-occupier at a time when the general arable farmer in England was happy to be cushioned by his landlord. D. Williams has perhaps the most substantial answer to the problem when he states:

> The great landowners, who were prime movers elsewhere, were generally non-resident as far as Wales was concerned and took little interest in their estates apart from the collection of their rents. The smaller gentry lacked the necessary capital, and the holdings of individual farmers were too small to allow the introduction of improvements (p. 180).

The general absence from Wales of planned landscapes is a reflection of non-residence which was exacerbated by the employment of English and Scottish agents and perhaps by the fact that the Crown was the manorial lord in extensive areas of north Wales. The evidence laid before the Royal Commission on Land in Wales and Monmouthshire in 1896, while coloured by its origins, spotlighted insecurity of tenure and lack of tenant compensation for improvements, by then long taken for granted in arable England and Scotland but achieved by the crofters only a few years before. Here again are reasons to suspect a lack of landlordly interest and an absence of capital intensive effort on the part of tenants.[14]

Such was the state of debate before the publication of Howell's book, the first major survey of Welsh landownership in the nineteenth century. His view is that the large owners, i.e. those with over 1,000 acres, behaved much more in the English mould in relation to their tenants than has been generally supposed. Absenteeism is said not to have been a well-founded characteristic and although some agents spoke no Welsh, they were not unsupervised by estate owners. Over the century there was a gradual and considerable expenditure on improvements to farms, but this did not necessarily lead to increases in rent. Although tenancies were renewed annually, Howell supports Vincent's view that large numbers of them on the great estates were virtually hereditary.[15]

However, there are two caveats of importance. First, Howell's information comes from the records of a relatively few large estates, partly because papers from smaller estates have had a much poorer survival rate. Secondly, what information there is on the smaller estates strongly supports the traditional view of the Welsh landlord, who because of high land prices due to the 'land hunger' in the second half of the century, was less inclined to improve and much more inclined to raise rents on improvement or on taking over the estate after one of the more frequent sales after 1870. These sales were often occasioned by the selling off of outlying portions of the great estates, provoked in some instances by the declining social and political value of land. Added to this, the Welsh peasant farmer is seen to have been reluctant to spend money in order to farm well. He had little of the commercial attitude of the large English tenant farmer, who would take credit at the bank, since the former's main aim was to pay the rent and not to tempt the landlord to raise it. Howell's view is more balanced than those views based on the vast political propaganda surrounding The Land Question, but it does not set out to dispose of the major contrasts between English and Welsh experience, even though the benevolence of the very large owners is stressed.[16]

## Marginal Lands

Although Vincent, as the landlords' spokesman, regarded squatting on commons as trespass, it was widely practised in upland Wales, as population pressure drove people on to marginal land. Many squatters were dispossessed or allowed only a very insecure tenure, yet the movement was clearly considerable and probably a great deal more 'successful' than the crofter-squatters in Scotland. Enclosure commissions accepted as legal, squatting of over 20 years' duration. Nevertheless, there are parallels with situations in both Scotland and England. The use of marginal land makes the Welsh squatter comparable with the Scottish, as for instance in Aberdaron, in the Lleyn peninsula, where Careg Plas, a former demesne farm occupied good quality clay loam, while small-holdings nearby were confined to reclaimed moor. The comparison with English open villages held good in the sense that, for example, in the Gyffylliog area of north-east Wales, squatting was said to bring relief from supervision by the squire. There are impressions that the squatter population included outcasts from village society. More certain is that they were missionised by the nonconformists who built many a chapel in their midst, giving squatter hamlets esoteric names like Beulah, Zion and Nazareth. Not surprisingly in the circumstances, rude cottages in vernacular styles were the rule in such places, another point of comparison with the English open village. Taken in the round, this picture of the moorland hamlet gives strength to Gareth Thomas' altitudinal model.[17]

The widespread nature of squatting has been cited as a means of keeping the poor 'off the parish', and was accepted by the landlords as a lesser evil than high poor rates. Although Wales shared the English poor law with England and experienced considerable increases in poor rates in the early nineteenth century, there appears to have been very few 'close' parishes in Wales in the poor law sense of the term and landlords appear to have taken little interest in the housing of labourers.[18] It may be added that subsistence features of the economy (as in Scotland) may have been additional factors inhibiting the development of open and closed parishes on the English pattern.

Many of the moorland settlements, including some on estates, were associated with mining and quarrying. Subsistence holdings were occupied by the workmen, providing a duality of occupation similar to peasant communities in England. Sometimes landlords took a direct interest, as when Lord Penrhyn built a village without an alehouse for the Penrhyn slate quarry; and the Vaynol estate at Llanddeiniolen controlled squatting by allotting land in 3-10 acre holdings for the slate quarrymen.[19]

Other joint occupations were common in Wales, especially in the first half of the century before rural industry began to decline. Craftsmen and traders were often occupiers of land, no less than 66 out of a total of 203 occupied houses in one parish studied by Jenkins. The woollen industry, as in Yorkshire, gave rise to many dual occupations, being a largely domestic industry in the eighteenth century, and changing only slowly in the nineteenth, as it shrank to a low level of activity.[20]

## The Decline of the Welsh Gentry

It will be appreciated from the foregoing account that, while the gentry were superficially dominant in the early nineteenth century, there were basic weaknesses which fostered gradual decline in later decades. In this decline the rise of nonconformity played a major role, because it added sharp differences in religion to those existing in language and culture and in turn became a vehicle of political articulation, especially perhaps in The Land Question debate. D. Williams has pointed out that:

The chapel, where farmer and labourer, shopkeeper and industrial worker, were on an equality and conducted their own affairs, proved to be a school in democratic management. The Welsh peasantry had hitherto been remarkable for its servility, but this now disappeared.

Although it is easy to over-emphasise equality of status within the chapel, this statement strikes a real contrast between Wales before and after 1800, as the grip of the establishment, including the Established Church, was successfully challenged.[21]

From having small congregations meeting almost surreptitiously in isolated houses at the end of the eighteenth century, the nonconformists reached an estimated quarter of a million communicants by 1861 and over half a million by the first decade of the twentieth century. In the 1851 census 80 per cent of the population in attendance in places of worship was estimated to be nonconformist. However, it should not be overlooked that 48 per cent of the *total* population of Wales were unclaimed by any denomination, but a large proportion of this secular population lived in urban and industrial areas. In 1905, the Royal Commission on the Church and other Religious Bodies in Wales set up because of the disestablishment issue, reported 193,081 Church communicants to 551,679 nonconformist communicants (in a total population of 2,012,917 in 1901). Within the country there were variations, which, if studied closely, might correspond broadly with Thomas' altitudinal model.[22]

The disestablishment issue which had started far back in the nineteenth century, feeding to some extent on the Tithe Riots in the 1880s, dragged on after the Royal Commission reported. Eventually a disestablishment Act was passed in 1914, but implementation was held up until 1920 by the intervention of the war. This Act was regarded as a considerable victory for the Welsh peasantry and Welsh culture, although it came late in the day. As a result, politics and religion were finally severed and the Established Church is said to have become more Welsh, more democratic and less dependent on great landowners and squires.[23]

On the rising tide of nonconformity rode the revival of Welsh culture, assisted by many nonconformist ministers and the wider use of Welsh in chapel services. This served to underline the already existing anglicisation of the Welsh gentry. In the 1840s the Welsh establishment took the view that the Welsh language represented a barrier to moral progress, a view similar to that of the Scots establishment's attitude to Gaelic. The important difference between the two situations is represented in the fact that while about half the population of Wales in 1901 could speak Welsh, only 5 per cent of the Scots could speak Gaelic. It is not surprising to learn that English speaking areas between 1880 and 1910 voted more heartily for the Conservatives and, conversely, the upland areas, where the strength of Welsh was maintained partly by outward migration, were strongly attracted to Liberal Radicalism.[24]

The political defeat of the gentry is generally taken to have begun in the Annus Mirabilis of 1868, but there were significant issues and events before this. In the Corn Law debate of the 1840s the Welsh peasantry were persuaded to vote for repeal, on the ground that their prosperity depended on grass, while that of some of their landlords was based on corn-farming in England. In the 1850s and 1860s there were evictions which are supposed to have been based on differences in religion and politics. Although their number was exaggerated by Liberal propaganda, even Vincent agreed that they had occurred in some areas. Teetotalism, opposition to the militaristic policy of the Tories, excessive game preservation and the precarious tenure of chapels were other issues that drove the nonconformist peasantry into the Liberal fold.[25]

Although 1868 saw the election of many radicals, the ultimate breakthrough came twenty years later with a further extension of the franchise and the creation of county councils. This led to overwhelming Liberal voting in Parliamentary elections throughout Wales, until the advent of the Labour party and the decline of Liberalism generally, between 1910 and 1920. More than this, it robbed the old Tory squirearchy of power at the local level, in the councils and magistracy, where traders, farmers, schoolmasters and nonconformist ministers took over on a scale unparalleled anywhere else in Britain.[26]

This takeover left the Welsh gentry protesting for a while that opposition propaganda had been overdone, but the loss of political power based on landholding appears to have determined some of the Welsh gentry to sell out sooner than their counterparts in England. There were plenty of tenants eager to buy. After 1900 Englishmen like Lord Ancaster were busy selling off the Welsh portions of their estates and by 1910 the floodgates were open, whereas in England the deluge of sales did not occur until the early twenties.[27]

So it was that rural Wales emerged into the twentieth century with a society and economy in which the peasantry were dominant. As in the crofting areas of Scotland, social solidarity was still strong. For example, in south-west Wales, Jenkins has recorded a labour debt system in use right up to 1914. This system bound together the various levels in rural society. Thus cottagers were allowed to plant potatoes on farms for their own consumption, in return for which they worked for an agreed number of days without pay. The larger farms kept bulls, whose services were used at cow-places and one-horse places (the smaller sizes of farm), in return for the occupiers working on the big farms during the hay and corn harvests. In Wales generally the practice of boarding labourers and paying day labourers partly in kind (meals, etc.) survived later than in most parts of England. Even in the thirties, the peasant reluctance to spend money was illustrated by the wide use of child labour from within the family.[28]

## Conclusion

Wales shared with the crofting counties of Scotland the distinction of having virtually a two class rural society of landlord and peasantry with a widening gap between them. In the general farming areas of England and Scotland, particularly in arable districts, there were three social classes associated with farming — landlord, farmer and labourer. In the remaining parts of England and Scotland it is possible to distinguish a fourth sizable class, that of the family farm, interposing itself between the large farmer and the labourer and in many ways comparable with large numbers of the Welsh peasantry.

The English peasant system, the Scottish crofting areas (and outliers outside the crofting counties) and most of upland Wales shared an emphasis on the family as a unit of production, the relatively slow development of a full money economy and much evidence of social solidarity and the importance of kinship networks. Yet again these Gemeinschaft characteristics are found in the absence of effective participation by patriarchal landowners in the affairs of rural communities, when the clan and tribal systems disappeared. Where participation occurred in the greater part of Scotland, it signalled a rapid trend towards money relationships and specialised occupations and the decline of the family as a productive unit, which were reckoned by Tönnies as Gesellschaft-type developments. The Scottish laird was different from the English in that he concerned himself with an even wider range of modern economic activities, extending into labour-intensive manufacturing industries. This underlines the absence of a rural 'middle' class comparable with the English peasantry.

It also demonstrates the part played by the landed classes in the development of a Gesellschaft-type economy in Scotland, well illustrated by the Galloway examples of Sir William Douglas, a retired merchant, and James Murray, grandson of the fifth Earl of Galloway. Their interests extended through finance, agriculture, mining, industry and the development of communications and towns, including the new towns of Castle Douglas, Newton Douglas and Gatehouse of Fleet. They played their part too in Galloway politics in the second half of the eighteenth century, in the usual way of territorial magnates.[29] As we pass from rural to urban Britain, from an accent on the land to an emphasis on industry and commerce, the considerable influence of rural classes, whether labourer, artisan, peasant or landowner, should be borne in mind, for especially in the first half of the nineteenth century no sharp distinction can be made between urban and rural cultures.

## Notes

1. Gareth Thomas, 'Rural Settlement Patterns', Ch. V of E.G. Bowen (ed.), *Wales: A Physical, Historical and Regional Geography* (Methuen, London, 1957), p. 484. See also F.V. Emery, *The World's Landscapes: Wales* (Longmans, London, 1969) pp. 39-41 and 50; and W.T.R. Pryce, 'Approaches to the Linguistic Geography of North-East Wales, 1750-1846', *The National Library of Wales Journal*, vol. 17 (1972), *passim*.

2. E.G. Bowen (ed.), *Wales*, pp. 145-51; R.A. Dodgshon and R.A. Butlin (eds.), *An Historical Geography of England and Wales* (Academic Press, London, 1978), pp. 132-6; Emery, *Wales*, pp. 34-5; A.D. Rees, *Life in a Welsh Countryside: A Social Study of Llanfihangel yng Ngwynfa* (University of Wales Press, Cardiff, 1957), pp. 80-1 and D. Thomas, *Agriculture in Wales during the Napleonic Wars: A Study in the Geographical Interpretation of Historical Sources* (ibid., 1963), pp. 126-9.

3. See above, Ch. 3; Bowen, *Wales*, pp. 143-5; Emery, *Wales*, pp. 50-7 and G.R.J. Jones, 'Some Medieval Rural Settlements in North Wales', *TIBG*, no. 19 (1953), especially p. 65 and ibid., 'Early Territorial Organization in England and Wales', *Geografiska Annaler*, vol. 43 (1961), pp. 175-6.

4. Bowen, *Wales*, pp. 143-5; A.D. Carr, 'An Aristocracy in Decline: The Native Welsh Lords after the Edwardian Conquest', *Welsh HR*, vol. 5 (1970-1), pp. 116-17 126 and 129; K.O. Morgan, *Wales in British Politics, 1868-1922* (University of Wales Press, Cardiff, 1963), p. 5 and D. Williams, *A History of Modern Wales* (1950, rev. edn, John Murray, London, 1965), pp. 36-9, 44, 57, 79-83 and 87-9.

5. J. Morgan, 'Denbighshire's Annus Mirabilis: The Borough and County Elections of 1868', *Welsh HR*, vol. 7 (1974), p. 64; K.O. Morgan, *Wales in British Politics*, pp. 4-5 and Williams, *A History of Modern Wales*, pp. 95-7, 121, 127 and 132-7.

6. D.W. Howell, *Land and People in Nineteenth-Century Wales* (Routledge, London, 1977), p. 21.

7. E. Davies and A.D. Rees (eds.), *Welsh Rural Communities* (University of Wales Press, Cardiff, 1960), pp. 13-15, 165; Howell, *Land and People*, pp. 18, 91 and 153; D. Jenkins, *The Agricultural Community in South West Wales at the Turn of the Twentieth Century* (University of Wales Press, Cardiff, 1971), pp. 168-9; and Rees, *Welsh Countryside*, pp. 80-1 and 142-3.

8. Rees, *Welsh Countryside*, pp. 142 and 173.

9. Jenkins, *Agricultural Community*, pp. 48-58 and 105-9 and B. Kerblay, 'Chayanov and the Theory of Peasantry as a Specific Type of Economy', in T. Shanin (ed.), *Peasants and Peasant Societies* (Penguin, Harmondsworth, 1971), p. 154.

10. A.W. Ashby and I.L. Evans, *The Agriculture of Wales and Monmouthshire*

(University of Wales Press, Cardiff, 1944), pp. 74-5; D.W. Howell, 'The Agricultural Labourer in Nineteenth-Century Wales', *Welsh HR*, vol. 6 (1972-3), p. 262; R.A. Lewis, 'William Day and the Poor Law Commissioners', *Birmingham Historical Journal*, vol. 9 (1964), pp. 178-9.

11. W.T.R. Pryce, 'The Social and Economic Structure of North East Wales, 1750-1850' (unpublished PhD dissertation (CNAA), Lanchester Polytechnic, Coventry, 1971), Fig. 10 and pp. 188-90.

12. D.B. Grigg, 'Small and Large Farms in England and Wales: Their Size and Distribution', *Geography*, vol. 48 (1963), p. 272; Howell, *Land and People*, pp. 67-72 and W.S.G. Thomas, 'Lost Villages in South-West Carmarthenshire', *TIBG*, no. 47 (1969), p. 199.

13. A.H. Dodd, *The Industrial Revolution in North Wales* (University of Wales Press, Cardiff, 1933), pp. 39-44; D.W. Howell, 'The Economy of the Landed Estates of Pembrokeshire, c. 1680-1830', *Welsh HR*, vol. 3 (1966-7), p. 279.

14. J. Davies, 'The End of the Great Estates and the Rise of Freehold Farming in Wales', *Welsh HR*, vol. 7 (1974), p. 207; Emery, *Wales*, pp. 31 and 85-6; K.O. Morgan, *Wales in British Politics*, pp. 5 and 128; J.E. Vincent, *The Land Question in North Wales* (Longmans, London, 1896), pp. 1-4 and Williams, *History of Modern Wales*, pp. 180, 184 and 199.

15. Howell, *Land and People*, pp. 42, 45, 46, 61 and 80-1 and Vincent, *Land Question*, pp. 160-77.

16. Howell, *Land and People*, p. 49, 80-1, 89-91 and 147.

17. Bowen, *Wales*, p. 154; Davies and Rees, *Welsh Rural Communities*, Plate III and pp. 142 and 165; Howell, *Land and People*, pp. 29-31; Rees, *Welsh Countryside*, p. 20; D. Sylvester, *The Rural Landscape of the Welsh Borderland: A Study in Historical Geography* (Macmillan, London, 1969), pp. 187-8 and J.G. Thomas, 'Some Enclosure Patterns in Central Wales: A Study in Landscape Modification', *Geography*, vol. 42 (1957), pp. 28-31.

18. Bowen, *Wales*, p. 153; Dodd, *Industrial Revolution*, pp. 382-3; Howell, *Land and People*, p. 105; Williams, *History of Modern Wales*, pp. 200-4. Exceptionally, S. Thomas, 'The Agricultural Labour Force in some SW Carmarthenshire Parishes in the Mid-nineteenth Century', *Welsh HR*, vol. 3 (1966-7), p. 69, refers to Llandawke as a close parish.

19. F.A. Barnes, 'Settlement and Landscape Changes in a Caernarvonshire Slate Quarrying Parish', in R.H. Osborne, F.A. Barnes and J. Doornkamp (eds.), *Geographical Essays in Honour of K.C. Edwards* (University of Nottingham, 1970), p. 126; Dodd, *Industrial Revolution*, pp. 165 and 206; Emery, *Wales*, p. 107.

20. Dodd, *Industrial Revolution*, p. 10; Jenkins, *Agricultural Community*, p. 42-4, 58, 61, 81, 103 and 112 and M. Davies, *Wales in Maps* (University of Wales Press, Cardiff, 1951), pp. 53 and 72-3.

21. Davies and Rees, *Welsh Rural Communities*, pp. 52-3 and 181; Howell, *Land and People*, pp. 93-4; Jenkins, *Agricultural Community*, pp. 189-90 and 275-6; J. Morgan, 'Annus Mirabilis', p. 73 and Williams, *History of Modern Wales*, pp. 250-2.

22. K.O. Morgan, *Wales in British Politics*, pp. 11-2 and 314-5; H. Pelling, *Social Geography of British Elections 1885-1910*, (Macmillan, London, 1967), p. 347; Pryce, 'N.E. Wales', p. 268ff.; and Williams, *History of Modern Wales*, p. 246 and 250-2.

23. K.O. Morgan, *Wales in British Politics*, pp. 3, 45-6 and 271-3; and Williams, *History of Modern Wales*, pp. 259, 268.

24. Morgan, *Wales in British Politics*, p. 56 and 312; Williams, *History of Modern Wales*, p. 256 and Pelling, *Social Geography of British Elections*, pp. 346 and 369.

25. Jenkins, *Agricultural Community*, pp. 109 and 214-6; K.O Morgan, *Wales in British Politics*, pp. 58 and 84; Rees, *Welsh Countryside*, pp. 155-6; Vincent, *Land Question*, p. 9; and Williams, *History of Modern Wales*, pp. 212 and 259-62.

26. Jenkins, *Agricultural Community*, pp. 276-8; K.O. Morgan, *Wales in British Politics*, pp. 65-6, 107 and 249; and Williams, *History of Modern Wales*, pp. 261-5.

27. J. Davies, 'End of the Great Estates', pp. 188-95; Thompson, *English Landed Society*, p. 318; and Vincent, *Land Question*, p. 238.

28. Howell, 'Agricultural Labourer', p. 263; and Jenkins, *Agricultural Community*, pp. 48-58.

29. I.L. Donnachie and I. Macleod, *Old Galloway* (David and Charles, Newton Abbot. 1974), pp. 83-92.

# 9  TOWN AND COUNTRY: CONTRAST AND COMPARISON

'Towns are not like villages, subject, it may be, to the over-
sight and guidance of a single family, or of a single clergyman.'
R. Vaughan, *The Age of Great Cities* (Jackson and Walford,
London, 1843), p. 153.

## Introduction

Most of the dichotomies discussed in the first chapter were based on a
contrast between urban and rural communities and between agricultural
and industrial ways of life. Succeeding chapters have demonstrated very
wide variations between neighbouring rural communities, a fact which
undermines the basis of rural homogeneity within a rural-urban dichotomy. Consequently we might expect to find significant sociological
differences between and within towns which undermine the dichotomy
from the other side. Furthermore, there may be certain points of comparison between urban and rural communities which have been overlooked because of the common assumption that rural and urban conditions contrasted widely. In particular, the influence of the estate and
peasant systems, or something similar to them, in the development of
swelling urban communities has probably been ignored because they
have been thought of as belonging purely to the countryside.

Contact between town and country has usually been recognised only
in terms of a flow of people and food from the country to the town
and a flow of ideas and industrial goods in the other direction. These
flows are certainly important. During the period 1801 to 1911 the
population of Great Britain rose from 10.4 million to 40.8 million.
More significantly there was a shift of distribution from the country to
the towns, such that while the urban population was only 33.8 per cent
of the total population of England and Wales in 1801, it had reached
54.0 per cent by 1851 and 78.9 by 1911. To get this dramatic shift
into perspective, it is as well to bear in mind that in *absolute* numbers
rural population rose steadily from 5.8 millions in 1801 to 8.3 millions
in 1861 and only then began to decline, having sunk to 7.2 millions in
1901, thereafter turning upwards as suburban and ex-urban settlement
flowed out into rural administrative areas.[1] Nevertheless, the increase
in the urban population was considerably supported by the exodus

from the countryside of predominantly young adults who gave the towns a youthful age structure and a high birth rate.[2]

The flow of foodstuffs into Britain's growing industrial towns was obviously of crucial importance in an age when food imports from overseas were limited, among other things, by relatively high transport costs. This period lasted until about 1875. The reverse flow of manufactured goods grew steadily in importance as the century passed by. Rural self-sufficiency declined first in those products – like cotton goods – which were soon capable of mass manufacture, while heavier products, such as large agricultural machines were produced locally until much later. But it is in terms of ideas that the countryside's indebtedness to the towns is usually regarded as being completely one-sided. Medical knowledge, political attitudes, art, music and literature, indeed literacy itself all emerged from the town and diffused across the countryside. So obvious, strong and persistent was the flow that it is easy to overlook ideas, customs and attitudes which flowed from the country to the town. One of the objects of these last three main chapters of the book is to draw attention to the ways in which rural culture affected the growth of towns and life therein.

## The Contrast Between Town and Country

Having been at some pains to show that the boundary lines between urban and rural could have been no more clearly defined than vague zones of transition, it is nevertheless necessary to take account of contemporary thinking which worked on the assumption that town and country could be distinguished clearly enough to make discussion of their differences possible. During the early Victorian period, it was the large, rapidly growing manufacturing towns which seized the interest of leading social writers, most of whom agreed with and even anticipated Tönnies in showing a marked preference for the rural community, if only by implication, in expressing their fears about social control in the big towns.

Exceptions there were, however, such as Emile Durkheim, who in 1893 was proclaiming that the dynamic or moral density of towns was associated with their physical density. That is to say, the close proximity of large numbers of people both increased the possibilities of greater intimacy and the diversification of interests and functions in social life.[3] Towns were, therefore, superior to villages in the opportunities they provided for living fuller and richer lives.

Vaughan, too, as in the passage quoted at the head of this chapter, favoured urban life, arguing that rural isolation depressed the popular intelligence, while opportunities for association and social intercourse in the towns imparted greater knowledge, acuteness and power to the mind. It is significant that Vaughan took the closed village as his model of rural society, thus making the urban-rural contrast as wide as possible. It should also be pointed out that, as a nonconformist clergyman, he was unlikely to take sides with the Anglican clergy and gentry. However, in recognising that the town contained greater opportunities for formal and informal education, Vaughan also admitted that there were greater temptations to form vicious habits and to remain in a state of ignorance.[4]

Vaughan also drew a distinction between the large manufacturing centre and the small one. After remarking that in small towns and industrial villages 'the greater number of masters are prompted by interest, or by a higher feeling, to be observant of their workpeople', he contrasts Bolton with the nearby villages of Egerton and Turton. While the latter were under the surveillance of millowners, in Bolton working-class cottages were ill kept and unclean, even when the householder was in good employment.[5]

While Marx joined Vaughan in stating that urbanisation had rescued a considerable proportion of the population 'from the idiocy of rural life', other observers of the first half of the century played on short-comings of the urban population, as well as on the slum conditions in which increasing numbers were obliged to live. There was fear of social anarchy and a concern over immorality and irreligion which were well represented in Chalmers' essays printed in Glasgow in 1821-6. He argued (1) that the urban parish could be organised like a rural parish, if it were subdivided so that Christian influence would reach each area and (2) that the relationship between employers and the masses in manufacturing areas was distant and there was a clash of interests, whereas in such towns as Bath, Oxford and Edinburgh there was a more personal relationship, which was wholesome for social control.[6] This point has recently been repeated in relation to Exeter, a smaller town increasing in size over the century from 17,000 to 40,000, in which a working man was much more likely to be marked out if he made a nuisance of himself than if he lived in Leicester which grew from 17,000 to 200,000 over the same period.[7] 'In this matter (crime), as in other matters, it was the changed scale of things that gave an old problem the appearance of something new.'[8]

Much the same contrast between town and country was accepted by

Engels, despite his Marxist standpoint. It is not surprising, therefore, that he accepted the interpretation of crime figures put out at the time — that they were rapidly increasing and that crime rates were higher in towns than agricultural districts. He quoted for *c.*1830 the ratio of population and offences as 1 : 1043 in agricultural districts and 1 : 840 in certain manufacturing districts.[9]

Early writers in the *Journal of the Statistical Society* painted a similar picture. Taking 1.00 as the norm for England and Wales, Rawson calculated the following rates:

| | |
|---|---|
| Agricultural districts | 0.99 |
| Manufacturing districts | 1.14 |
| Mining counties | 0.45 |
| Wales | 0.31 |
| Middlesex | 1.61 |

Admitting that these figures reflected the effectiveness of the police, he nevertheless drew the conclusion that crime prevailed to the greatest extent in large towns. Fletcher reinforced this a few years later by declaring that the greatest increases in crime had occurred in the manufacturing areas.[10]

In 1852 a publication significantly called *Without Natural Police* emphasised the fear of anarchy and the fear for property, in referring to the effects of urbanisation over the previous half century, which had removed upper-class residents from the central areas of large towns.[11] Thus in Manchester in 1839 only five of the 30 magistrates lived in the central township and no less than 15 lived outside the newly incorporated borough altogether. In the small town, however, 'rich and poor lived in proximity and the superior classes exercised that species of silent but very efficient control over their neighbours'.[12]

One important way of exercising control was through the churches, of which there was probably a sufficiency in small towns, but not in the large. Increasingly it was thought, the working classes went to no church at all and were regarded as having fallen out of the pale of civilised influences. At any rate non-attendance, although of significant proportions in the countryside, was commoner in large towns of over 10,000 population in 1851 than elsewhere. Their index of attendance was 49.7, compared with 61 for the whole of England and Wales and 71.4 in rural areas and small towns.[13] Perhaps the reason for this falling off was that 'The Churchmen seemed primarily interested in order, the Nonconformists in liberty: what the working classes looked for was a mitigation of their poverty.'[14]

Between the late forties and the 1880s there appears to have been a slackening of the debate, perhaps because municipal reform and mid-Victorian prosperity reduced the worst excesses of poverty, poor sanitation and overcrowding. In 1881, Joseph Cowen, MP for Newcastle was able to speak in tones more confident even than Vaughan:

> Scattered populations are usually ignorant, and oppression is always most easily established over them. The power conferred by concentration may be abused, has been abused, but when regulated by vigilantly supervised representative institutions there is no fear either for the liberty of the individual or the community.[15]

However, the shock administered to Britain by its difficulty in winning the Boer War was followed by a period of social evaluation in which Masterman edited *The Heart of the Empire*, which in effect became the basis of Liberal policy in the reforming government of 1906. In this book contrasts were drawn between town and country:

> . . . the city population is cut off from the country, in a manner previously unknown. It has developed sympathies and passions of its own, differing in essential characteristics from those of a bygone age . . . In the old days, all classes lived together in small towns and villages, the employee boarding sometimes with, always near, his master. To-day we have East and West Ends, business quarters, manufacturing quarters, residential quarters, endless vistas of villadom, acres of Lambeth and Whitechapel.

The urban masses were seen as people lacking spiritual strength and therefore prone to a craving for material satisfaction.[16] The widening gap between town and country can be interpreted as part of the trend towards economic specialisation which progressed very rapidly during the nineteenth century and Marx himself put forward the idea that:

> The division of labour within a nation brings about, in the first place, the separation of industrial and commercial from agricultural labour, and hence the separation of *town* and *country* and the opposition of their interests. Its further development leads to the separation of commercial from industrial labour.[17]

**Town and Country: Comparison**

Despite the obvious contrasts between town and country, their differences can be overemphasised, as they were by Hall when he wrote:

> At the beginning of the nineteenth century, urban areas were com-
> pact and tightly packed: they ended sharply against open country-
> side. Physical definitions corresponded with functional ones: the
> town looked different from the countryside, and it performed
> different functions.[18]

While this statement is useful in reminding us of the difference between
the situation in 1800 and that post-1945, it should not prevent us from
seeking the useful comparisons which can be made between rural and
urban society in nineteenth-century Britain. Thompson was probably
nearer the essential truth, when he wrote, from the standpoint of
religious life, that:

> The further study of the open village as a community alongside the
> closed village and the growing town and combining features of both,
> will greatly aid our understanding of the nineteenth century as a
> whole.[19]

In a word, can the distinction between the estate and peasant systems tell us anything about urban development and life in towns in the
nineteenth century? In the remainder of this book evidence is marshal-
led which enables the answer to this question to be in the affirmative.

There are, of course, a number of important qualifications. The scale
of many urban communities was quite different from rural communities; the rate of growth was frequently much faster; the range of occupations was much greater; the influx of permanent long distance
migrants, such as the Irish and the East Europeans provided an element
totally outside the experience of rural areas. The same could be said of
the large units of employment and the corresponding growth of trade
unions.

There are also some considerable obstacles. Relatively little work has
been done from the chosen perspective. In particular, studies of urban
development tend to be biased towards the work of the aristocracy and
the large industrial enterprise, a bias similar to what was once the case
in rural history, for a similar reason — estate and company records survive better than those of the urban equivalent of the peasantry. The

recent growth of studies based on the census, while bringing the full social range into view, has not done much to correct this bias because most of the crucial economic activities and social relationships cannot be so discerned.

Despite these difficulties, it will be possible to demonstrate the importance of the perspective provided by the contrast between the estate and peasant systems because two of the key urban issues in the period were segregation and social control — could social control be maintained in view of the intensification of social segregation? The rural open-closed dichotomy was also very closely related to the same issues. Social control in estate villages on the part of the gentry, clergy and their allies was exercised partly by means of segregating the more deferential elements of the rural population from the remainder. In view of the fact that there was considerable coming and going between town and country, in terms of ideas, capital, migrants and so forth, it would be surprising if elements of the estate and peasant systems did not emerge from a study of nineteenth-century towns.

Carter has identified three groups of builders who provided urban housing: speculative builders, industrial employers and philanthropists.[20] As the two latter categories overlapped, it may be useful to use a two-fold division between the planned and the unplanned or the large and small scale. Such a dichotomy may be particularly useful in the first half of the century before by-laws imposed an element of planning even on the most profit-seeking speculative builder. Again, there is a deliberate attempt to draw an analogy between the rural estate system and the large scale, planned, or at least comprehensive, urban development, while the speculative, small-scale and unplanned developments may prove to be mainly the work of the peasantry's urban equivalent.

As the owners of country estates also had interests in urban and industrial areas, it will be possible to go beyond a mere analogy with the rural estate system, for many of the same individuals were involved in both urban and rural spheres. So far as industrial and social philanthropists are concerned, it will be shown that the model they used, whether implicitly or explicitly, was the rural estate village, influenced also by the urban example of the great landlords. It is with the concept of the urban peasant that difficulties can be more seriously anticipated. Nevertheless this concept is hardly new, having been used in 1963 by Vincent in an article on Rochdale where the term was used to describe the self-employed and other small capitalists.[21]

Subsequently, in discussing political consciousness in the nineteenth century, Vincent has stated that:

The essential division was between distributed property (mainly urban) and concentrated property (mainly rural), between capitalist agriculture and distributist petty production and exchange, between an urban 'free peasantry' and the great capitalists . . . Hence the perennial schizophrenia of the radical ethic, hovering between two sets of unstated assumptions about social structure, seething at inequality yet cherishing property and individual achievement . . . Their tone goes back in English history through the pamphlets of the 'freeholder interest' in eighteenth-century county elections, to the plain speakers of the Commonwealth.[22]

Vincent suggests, then, that the town should be seen as mainly an area in which the small capitalist prevailed, at least up to the end of the poll-book era in which he was interested (1872). Partly for this reason, it may not be wholly wrong to think of the urban peasant as subject to the full strength of market forces, since the large number of small builders, landlords and entrepreneurs would provide ideal conditions for competition. It is upon the basis of market competition spatially expressed that most of the geographers' models of urban residential space have been built. The large, country-based landowner, the large industrialist and the philanthropist, for a variety of reasons can be seen as quasi-monopolists, able by virtue of larger funds or inherited land to cut free from the constrictions of the market place and, indeed, to rise above it.[23]

With these considerations in mind we pass on to the final chapters of the book. Chapter 10 looks at social segregation and the role of landownership in the large town. The role of the large landowner is discerned with relative ease, but the identification of smaller developers is, on the whole, too difficult to press the analogy with the rural peasant system very far. In Chapter 11 the village takes the centre of the stage, partly in respect of the old-established industrial villages, but mainly with regard to the model which the estate village provided for those who planned the company town and garden city.

## Notes

1. C.M. Law, 'The Growth of Urban Population in England and Wales, 1801-1911', *TIBG*, no. 41 (1967), p. 130.
2. See R. Lawton, Ch. 9 in D.R. Mills (ed.), *English Rural Communities: The Impact of a Specialised Economy* (Macmillan, London, 1973).
3. J.A. Banks in H.J. Dyos and M. Wolff, *The Victorian City: Images and Realities* (Routledge, London, 1973), vol. 1, p. 109-110. He has pointed out that Tönnies drew his urban-rural boundary line *between* the small town and the city because he believed the small town to conform to rural mores.

4. R. Vaughan, *The Age of Great Cities* (Jackson and Walford, London, 1843), especially pp. 153 and 178.

5. Ibid., pp. 230-2.

6. T.B. Bottomore and M. Rubel (eds.), *Karl Marx: Selected Writings in Sociology and Social Philosophy* (Penguin, Harmondsworth, 1963), p. 137. Chalmers is quoted in B.I. Coleman (ed.), *The Idea of the City in Nineteenth-Century Britain* (Routledge, London, 1973), pp. 84-6.

7. Newton in Dyos and Wolff, *Victorian City*, vol. 2, p. 302.

8. W. Ashworth, *The Genesis of Modern British Town Planning* (Routledge, London, 1965), pp. 47-8.

9. F. Engels, *The Condition of the Working Class in England* (Blackwell, Oxford, 1958 edn), pp. 147-8.

10. R.W. Rawson, 'An Inquiry into the Statistics of Crime in England and Wales', *Journal of the Statistical Society*, vol. 2 (1839), pp. 337-8; J. Fletcher, 'Progress of Crime in the United Kingdom . . .', ibid., vol. 6 (1843), p. 224.

11. Hill quoted in Coleman, *Idea of the City*, pp. 132-4.

12. A. Redford and I.S. Russell, *The History of Local Government in Manchester* (Manchester UP, 1940), vol. 2, p. 32.

13. A. Rogers, *This was Their World: Approaches to Local History* (Longmans, London, 1972), pp. 141-2; Vaughan, *Age of Great Cities*, p. 300; E.R. Wickham, *Church and People in an Industrial City* (Lutterworth Press, London, 1957), pp. 14, 44, 85-93 and 110-1; Kent in Dyos and Wolff, *Victorian City*, vol. 2, p. 862; and K.S. Inglis, 'Patterns of Religious Worship in 1851', *Journal of Ecclesiastical History*, vol. 11 (1960), p. 80.

14. Mole in Dyos and Wolff, *Victorian City*, vol. 2, p. 831.

15. Quoted in Coleman, *Idea of the City*, p. 167.

16. C.F.G. Masterman (ed.), *The Heart of the Empire: Discussions of Modern City Life in England* (1901, Harvester Press, Brighton, 1973 edn), pp. v-vi, 8 and 287.

17. Quoted by Bottomore and Rubel, *Karl Marx*, p. 112.

18. P. Hall, *et al., The Containment of Urban England* (PEP, London, 1973), vol. 1, p. 75.

19. D.M. Thompson, 'The Churches and Society in Nineteenth-Century England: A Rural Perspective', *Studies in Church History*, vol. 8 (1972), p. 276.

20. In R.A. Dodgshon and R.A. Butlin (eds.), *An Historical Geography of England and Wales* (Academic Press, London, 1978), p. 391-2.

21. J.R. Vincent, 'The Electoral Sociology of Rochdale', *Econ. Hist. Rev.*, vol. 16 (1963-4), p. 82.

22. J.R. Vincent, *Pollbooks: How Victorians Voted* (Cambridge UP, 1968), p. 25. See also his Chapter II. The 'shopcracy' is a term of somewhat similar usage to 'urban peasant' and may be found notably in T.J. Nossiter, 'Shopkeeper Radicalism in the Nineteenth Century', in T.J. Nossiter *et al.* (eds.), *Imagination and Precision in the Social Sciences* (Faber, London, 1972), pp. 407-38. Note also Vincent's assumption that the estate system was predominant in the countryside.

23. D. Cannandine, 'Lords and Landlords', *New Society*, vol. 40, no. 757 (7 April 1977), p. 8.

# 10 SOCIO-SPATIAL SEGREGATION AND THE ROLES OF URBAN LANDOWNERS

'Even when the houses were brand new, they were suitable only for people who lived very similar lives, and whose conduct varied very little from a fairly restrictive norm.' K. Coates and R. Silburn, *Poverty: The Forgotten Englishman* (Penguin, Harmondsworth, 1970), p. 80, describing the working-class district of St Ann's, Nottingham, built in the mid-Victorian period and rebuilt in the 1970s.

## Segregation

Despite the fact that no really effective methods of measuring its increase have been devised, it is generally agreed that the growth of large cities has been accompanied by an intensification of socio-spatial segregation. In towns large enough to have developed distinctive residential zoning before industrialisation the effect was to invert the earlier pattern of high status residences in the principal streets with low status suburbs, because high income groups moved out and left the central areas to industry and commerce.[1]

It is also generally agreed that segregation has become much more complex, with the growth of urban populations and an increase in the range of urban functions. For the pre-industrial period, opinion wavers between a two-zone and a three-zone model. The two zones common to both models are (1) the central areas occupied by the merchants and master craftsmen and (2) the peripheral areas occupied by the labouring poor. In some towns, however, there may have been sufficient gentry to inhabit a distinctive high status, non-commercial district, possibly in association with a cathedral close.[2]

In the nineteenth-century town there developed specialist retail, wholesale, financial, administrative, transportation and industrial areas, most of them near the centre of the urban mass. Around this central business district, there developed concentric rings of housing, progressing up the social scale with distance from the centre (the Burgess model). These rings were frequently interrupted not only by natural features (e.g. river valleys carrying canal and railway routes, which attracted industry), but also by higher class sectors or wedges (the Hoyt model) and by the prior existence of older settlement nuclei (the Harris and Ullman model).[3]

Before passing on to look at the influence of landowners and specu-lators of varying size in a number of rapidly developing cities, it is necessary to recognise three general factors which were important in the reversal of the old patterns of segregation and in the intensification of the new. They may be described as the pollution factor, the journey to work and the specialisation factor.

The pollution of early industrial city centres has been very widely documented but what has not been brought out sufficiently is its impact on methods of social control. It is sometimes argued that mer-chants and industrialists lived at the place of their work well into the period of pollution because the transport system gave them little choice.[4] However, many of this class of person were well able to afford the kind of transport which could have carried them two or three miles each way each day between suburban house or country villa and factory or warehouse.

What would seem to have been a more vital consideration was the desire to continue to exercise the kind of social control over the work-force discussed in Chapter 9. By living on site, the entrepreneur could control his workpeople's behaviour outside working hours, as well as within; know whether they attended a place of worship and, if so, which one; and know their associates, respectable, political or other-wise. Removal to a suburb denied masters much of this information and the control which went with it. Hence they delayed making this move until well after the congested town centre, with its smells, noise, dirty humanity and much else, had become unpleasant as a residential environment. Reluctantly they gave up their Gemeinschaft-like associa-tion with their workpeople and settled for a pleasant place in which to live, worrying nevertheless that the working classes had been left 'with-out natural police'. The rural landowner retreated behind the park gates and left the open village much to its own devices, while in the same period the prominent urban employer was leaving his workpeople behind as he withdrew to the suburbs and the near-by countryside. Thus in both town and country segregation altered the forms of social control.

The journey to work began, of course, with the upper middle classes, but in due course the separation of home and workplace became a commonplace of industrial life and one which promoted the growth of a better transport system as well as ultimately being dependent on it. The early nineteenth-century association of workplace and residence has been most closely analysed for Chorley, where Warnes has described the scattered locations of different industries, each with its own work-force close by.[5] In the larger and more highly developed urban economy of Birmingham, Vance has pointed to various distinctions between mid-century industries which help to explain why some work-people lived close to their work and others not. Ties remained strong in the traditional gun and jewelry quarters where heads of households were prominent in the workforce. Where women and children made up a large proportion of employees, as in the button workshops and the brush trade, there was no clear spatial relationship between workplace and home. The same was true of factories set up for new products, as in the steel pen, iron woodscrew and brass trades, even if adult males were employed in large numbers. His main argument is that continued industrialisation brought about circumstances quite different from those which obtained in an earlier period, during which whole families were engaged in the same industry and lived in Gemeinschaft-like relationship to their employer and fellow workpeople.[6] So not only did the employer live apart from his work, but also his employees came to be scattered about the growing city.

In both the study of Chorley and that of Birmingham, the begin-nings of segregation by social class rather than occupation emerge. The latter form of segregation meant that people of different incomes lived near each other if they worked together. The more modern form of segregation has brought together people of similar income, *regardless* of occupation. This can be called the specialisation factor, for as industry and commerce became more complex, there developed a much greater range of occupations and of grades within occupations. Liberated by a better transport system from living near their work, as well as by the decline of entrepreneurial social control and paternalism, people chose to live with their own income group in property finely attuned to their pocket. And here they lived, according to Coates and Silburn, 'very similar lives' and their conduct 'varied very little from a fairly restric-tive norm'.

This specialisation factor has been stressed by Shaw, in his study of Wolverhampton from the censuses of 1851 to 1871, along with the developing importance of household composition (e.g. childless couples v. families) and minority group membership (e.g. the Irish).[7] These additional factors, largely independent of occupation, have also carried the late industrial city into forms of socio-spatial segregation more complex than those known in the eighteenth century. Thus the term 'specialisation factor' can be used not only of occupations, but also of housing districts. The more finely graded the income scale became and the larger the city, the more specialised could be the housing provision. During the nineteenth century then, there evolved a form of social control in the large city which was based on the behaviour of one's own social class, rather than the occupational group headed by the employer, his clerks and foremen.

Finally in this section on segregation, a word must be said about segregation *between* towns, for segregation did not only occur *within* towns. Just as the distinction between the estates and peasant village could be described partly as a form of segregation, so there was segregation between towns. Large cities tended to develop a wide cross-section of occupations and social classes; but many small and medium-sized towns, especially the newer creations of the period, tended to exhibit wide variations from the norm by virtue of their specialised functions. The emergence of railway towns, resorts, both inland and coastal, mining settlements, military establishments and company towns all contributed to the variety of urban social structures. Furthermore, they provide possibilities for the study of landownership, especially the large landlord or entrepreneur, in widely varying circumstances.

With these general considerations in mind, we now turn to a number of studies of large industrial towns, in which it is reasonable to assume that segregation increased during the nineteenth century. The roles of different kinds of urban developer are brought to the fore in the context of socio-spatial segregation.

## Large Industrial Towns

### Liverpool

Although this study, which is based on the 1871 census, admittedly omits the roles of developers, it makes a useful starting point because it is the most detailed and thorough study of socio-spatial segregation yet to be undertaken in any British city. Liverpool clearly illustrates elements of all three spatial models — the concentric, sectoral and multiple nuclei models. In broad terms there was a rise in socio-economic status from the centre to the periphery, yet distinctive sectors were also clearly discernible.

There were three notable working-class sectors, the largest of which ran out northwards from Dale St Ward through Scotland Ward to Everton and Kirkdale. Another one stretched southwards along the docksides to Toxteth Park and a third smaller sector ran eastwards from Lime Street Station. Intervening sectors were of higher status especially a south-eastern sector which included the Mount Pleasant district. In the more central parts of this sector density was relatively high with a preponderance of terraces, while at greater distances from the city centre villas reduced the mean density of population, thus demonstrating the existence of Burgess-type concentric zoning, as well as a sectoral pattern.

Liverpool in 1871 also illustrates clearly the importance of inmigration in building up socio-spatial segregation. Low status areas near the docksides contained many unskilled and semi-skilled labourers, a large proportion of whom lived in lodging houses in contrast to nuclear family households immediately inland. Ethnic differences reinforced segregation as there were distinctive Welsh and more particularly Irish districts. The Irish were not only ethnically distinct but also, being Roman Catholics, distinct in religious terms. In 1851, 24 per cent of the total population of the city were Irish born, but in some enumeration districts as many as 70 per cent or more of the heads of households were Irish.

While Lawton and Pooley did not study landownership, the Report on the State of Large Towns in 1844 commented on there being no very large landowners in Liverpool, with the exception of Lord Derby and Mr. John Leigh. To this factor the report ascribed the high density of building and the poor level of drainage, sewerage and building works. It might also be the case that the fine sorting of the population was the result of relatively unbridled effects of market forces operating in a world of small developers, as shopkeepers are reported to have been investing in working-class housing in the booms of the 1820s. More generally, investment funds for cheap housing came from lawyers financing speculative builders and groups of artisans working on a cooperative basis, as well as the shopocracy. All were agreed on the need to get a good return on capital invested, while the number of houses per landlord averaged between about four and nine houses in the wards of old Liverpool parish.[8]

*Leeds*

In Leeds, Ward drew a broad contrast between the two halves of the town on the basis that large compact farms and estates were common in the north, while smallholdings were typical of the south.[9] The latter had been associated with the early development of the woollen industry in which the dual occupation of farmer and clothier was usual. Either the pre-existing landownership structure favoured the growth of the industry, or large farms were split up (or both). In these areas residential development for working-class families came relatively early in the nineteenth century in a chaotic jumble related to property boundaries and little hindered by by-laws. Thus the peasant village of the eighteenth century became the working-class quarter of the nineteenth. Conversely, the larger estates of the northern townships of Leeds which came on the market later, were more spaciously laid out and more subject to by-laws. Presumably they attracted a better class of tenant.

## Bradford

In Bradford the larger holdings were similarly held back from the market, indeed over a longer period up to the end of the century; and the practice of entailing estates has been recognised as one reason for this delay. Mortimore[10] noted the influence of freehold tenure on the house market, first because it facilitated the subdivision of property into smallholdings of a type similar to south Leeds and secondly because builders, not being able to obtain leases, had to invest a certain amount of their capital in the land itself. While this situation favoured the terminating building societies, which operated in the lower middle class or better off part of the working-class market, it had the opposite effect on the poorest classes who depended on the speculative builder. Having invested money in land he was concerned to see a return on it as quickly as possible and was unhindered by the ground landlord who existed in some areas of the country and sometimes ensured minimal standards of layout and construction.

It is possible to link this situation with the widespread appearance in Bradford of the back-to-back house, clearly an economical way of using land and of building houses. The correlation of freehold with back-to-backs is strengthened by references to other West Riding areas, Manchester, Liverpool and Newcastle, the latter having pairs of tenements, which were, in effect, a vertical type of back-to-back. In contrast, at Huddersfield the 'through' type of house predominated and this was a leasehold town probably controlled by Sir J. Ramsden, the ground landlord.[10] No direct effects on segregation were recorded by Ward and Mortimore, but their work serves to emphasise that the style of housing, with which we are prone to associate certain social classes, can be much influenced by the landownership structure of an area, which itself was established long before the industrial period.

## Sheffield

Rowley's study of Sheffield,[11] although referring to the 1920s and 30s is particularly important because he specifically addressed himself to the role of landownership in urban growth. As he points out, if evidence can be found of the importance of landownership in post-1918 developments, how much more important must it have been in earlier decades when the market in land was much less articulated:

> It appears that social and political factors were strong forces in restraining landowners from selling land and to this extent landowners did not fulfil the role of 'economic man'. The notion of accessibility is also suspect, since development may be due to proximity to an existing road, or convenience, rather than to an overt awareness of accessibility . . . even the type of development may be strictly controlled and this has profound implications for studies in social segregation (p. 202).

By not fulfilling the role of 'economic man', Rowley actually means, as the rest of his argument shows, that although affected by market considerations, the large landlord was in the comfortable position, i.e. that of a quasi-monopolist, which enabled him to bide his time and take a wider view of the scene than the average small owner tempted by good fortune.

Rowley supported his thesis by evidence from the management of the Earl Fitzwilliam's Ecclesall estate, 2½ miles from the centre of Sheffield. Fitzwilliam was the 12th largest landowner in Britain in the 1870s, with 19,164 acres in Yorkshire, including 1,000 acres at Ecclesall. The family policy with regard to land was laid down in the 1850s and lasted until the 1920s: 'the sale of land was discouraged, although its development was encouraged, development in this part of the country meaning mineral exploitation and railway development'. From about 1900 onwards, there were a number of pieces of legislation, including taxation matters and the 1909 Housing and Town Planning Act which affected the context in which the Earl Fitzwilliam personally took decisions regarding the development of the estate. These were followed by a further Town Planning Act in 1925 and, in the same year, the Settled Land Act which allowed 'tenants for life', including Fitzwilliam, wider powers to sell their land. In this period of change Fitzwilliam considered a number of strategies, out of which two important policy decisions can be isolated. First was the decision to sell building rights, but to retain ground rents as a measure of control subsequent to sale. Secondly, there was involvement in Sheffield City Council affairs which also allowed Fitzwilliam to restrain sales until he was assured of the quality of urban development, including the retention of Ecclesall woods as an open space.

## Nottingham

In a recent article, Slater[12] has drawn attention to the general importance of landscape parks in the development of towns and, with particular reference to the small towns of Arundel and Warwick, has traced a
relationship between town and park not unlike that found on country
estates, with the desire for privacy, the securing of rural prospects,
demolition of houses, erection of model dwellings, the closure and the
realignment of paths, lanes, roads and streets. Nottingham was once
such a small town with a park attached to the castle in the ownership
of the Dukes of Newcastle. This section considers the park's impact on
massive urban growth.[13]

Nottingham's growth in the first half of the nineteenth century was
seriously restricted by the refusal of the burgesses to enclose the open
commons and fields and by the Musters family's ownership of land to
the east, as well as the inviolability of The Park, which is situated
immediately west of the central business district. From being almost a
garden city around 1700, Nottingham became a slum of 50,000 people
by 1851. Pleasant sites within the old town area being rare, there was a
considerable demand from the upper business and professional classes
for large houses in spacious and healthy surroundings. The Duke's
Park provided these conditions within walking distance of their places
of business, although out of sight of the town by virtue of the steep
sandstone ridge on which the Castle stands.

With the appointment of T.C. Hine as architect, the Duke of Newcastle responded to the demand, the first house in Hine's geometric
plan being built in 1854, to be followed by almost 600 others in the
period up to 1887. Everything was done to provide the best amenities
— broad, tree-lined streets, large plots, control over building styles, the
provision of water, gas, lighting and sewerage. Edwards writes that:

> The Park remained a purely residential area. There was not a shop,
> public house, bank or post-office, and the situation is the same
> today. Neither was there, nor is there today, a single commercial
> advertisement, only the tree-lined roads (p. 162).

> Among minor conditions householders may not build additionally
> unless the cost of labour and materials exceeds £2,000; they may
> not keep pigs, fowls, doves or pigeons; they may not expose the
> drying of clothes or other articles within the sight of neighbours;

neither may they utilise their property for functions other than residential (pp. 167-8).

Although much has changed inwardly by the conversion of houses into flats and a concurrent change in household composition, the Park Estate is still administered in certain respects separately from the rest of the City. Although the Dukes of Newcastle have no interest in the property the present owners, the University of Oxford, exercise much the same policy of preservation. Even in 1850 working-class housing was spreading across newly enclosed areas in close proximity to The Park and today these constitute some of the city's problem housing areas. This sharp discontinuity in townscape and the socio-economic status of inhabitants can be traced in a direct line from the aristocratic park of pre-industrial days.

*Birmingham*

There is a general similarity between the development of The Park Estate at Nottingham and the Calthorpe Estate at Edgbaston, Birmingham.[14] One difference, however, is in the size of the two estates, the Calthorpe Estate at 2,000 acres being several times larger than The Park. By 1914 2,841 houses had been built — between four and five times the number in The Park — and a good third of the land was still undeveloped.

Nevertheless the same aims were adopted by Lord Calthorpe as the Duke of Newcastle. He provided a grid of wide, sewered roads, beautified by the planting of trees and embellished by four churches built between 1833 and 1898. Industry, trade and commerce were excluded, building plans had to be authorised before construction began and the estate reserved the right to inspect properties twice a year. Consequently the 'right people' were attracted to Edgbaston, which for the later Victorian period has been described as 'the Council House at home' (p. 472). The estate housed a small knot of Nonconformist families whose élite status was enhanced by inter-marriage (nonconformity had a respectability in the city often denied to it in the village).

However, the élite were not on their own, as they appear to have been in The Park, for even Birmingham could not provide sufficient upper class families to fill such a large development. They constituted about a third of the leaseholders, the middle middle classes another third and the lower middle classes and the labour aristocracy the final third. 'In Edgbaston, segregation meant not only keeping industry out, but keeping tenants of different socio-economic status apart' (p. 474).

The lower status tenants were located on the margins of the estate where tram routes along major roads disturbed the peace, while the centre was reserved for the élite. To have done anything different would have been bad business practice. Nevertheless it is interesting to see a large landowner deliberately adopting a zoning policy consistent with modern forms of social stratification. Cannandine brings forward evidence to show that the lower income tenants were as equally proud of the status the estate enjoyed as their better off neighbours. They had been attracted to it by the address and by a desire to be near the leaders of society. Presumably, like the tenants in an estate village, they were predominantly of a respectable, deferential type.

While acknowledging useful insights which arise from the work of Firey, Hoyt and Burgess, Cannandine points out that 'Edgbaston's wedge shape was the result of the landownership pattern rather than any more general trends in Birmingham's urban expansion' (p. 482). In this, Edgbaston strongly resembled The Park at Nottingham.

## Camberwell

On the basis of what has been discovered about the open village, it was predictable that Camberwell would become for the most part a mediocre suburb, developed piecemeal and inhabited by the lower middle class, as indeed it had become by about 1900.[15] This parish of about 4,500 acres had once formed the basis for nine manors and in the Tithe Apportionment no less than 173 landowners are found sharing the 83.2 per cent of the parish which was tithable in 1837. The twenty biggest landlords owned well over four-fifths of the total but there do not appear to have been any resident gentry of consequence. The leading estate belonged to the Governors of Dulwich College, which comprised the whole manor of Dulwich, or about 1,500 acres and this, along with the relatively large estate of the de Crespigny family contained the best developments in the parish.

Dyos paints the development of Camberwell in a wealth of meticulous detail but declares a generalisation in the following terms:

It seems clear that even on the estates of the greatest suburban landowners there were always difficulties in the way of planned and orderly development. The more divided the ownership of land in a given area, however, the more likely did it become that the general layout of its streets would be intricate and ill-contrived. In general, the zigsaw of landed titles which had been produced by generations of dealings in the land market was reflected with remarkable fidelity by the superstructure of the suburb (p. 101).

Thus even the large estate owner, by bad luck or bad judgement in relation to the granting of leases might see his property pass down-market in a way which he had never intended. This risk throws Edgbaston and The Park, as successfully developed leasehold estates, into even sharper focus. Had there been larger and more expertly run estates in Camberwell there may have been more better class developments. On the other hand, this suggestion neglects a good many other variables, including the strength of commercial forces and the flow of lower-class families from nearer the city centre, which even impinged on Edgbaston before the end of the century and are described by Dyos in Camberwell:

> The general tendency was, it seems, for practically every district, except those strongly fortified against social change by sheer remoteness or by the configuration of the surrounding streets, to deteriorate in status as the relatively prosperous moved farther out and poorer families moved in (p. 191).

## The General Significance of Large Landowners

A number of at least partial generalisations can be drawn from these case studies in large cities. First, the pressure of population, being very considerable, created conditions in which Burgess-like rings of varying prosperity were potentially liable to form.

Secondly, however, large estates were often successful bastions against such pressures, at least for a time. In Nottingham and Birmingham they provided upper-class retreats much nearer to the city centre than the Burgess model would have predicted for the end of the century. In Bradford and Leeds larger estates tended to come on the market later when by-laws, as well as leasehold conditions exercised a beneficial influence on housing developments and in Sheffield the Fitzwilliams held on until the days of town-planning.

Thirdly, then, leasehold tenure appears to have been a potentially benign influence, if, for example, the link between back-to-backs and freehold tenure can be sustained. Moreover, the influence of the ground landlord could continue long after the building of a house estate and not merely at its inception.

Fourthly, the pre-existing pattern of landownership inherited from the rural past has been shown to have considerable importance. This in itself can be regarded as a strong rural influence on the development of the city, frequently ignored or unsuspected by historians anxious to emphasise the urban status of their burgeoning cities. The prior existence of the Calthorpe and Newcastle estates are of obvious significance, but so too was that of the village of farmer weavers in the West Riding or the cowkeepers of Camberwell.

This fourth generalisation can be underlined by reference to a late nineteenth-century survey of the tenures to be found in the towns of England and Wales.[16] It estimated that rather more than half of the urban population lived under ordinary freehold tenure, which was the usual tenure in a large number of small and medium-sized inland towns in England and was found elsewhere, generally in combination with other forms of tenure. A further 5 per cent, mainly in Lancashire and Cheshire, lived under freehold, subject to chief rents payable to a ground landlord, but whether this had an effect similar to a leasehold tenure is not clear. Leasehold tenures affected about 40 per cent of the population, 10 per cent being short leases (i.e. 99 years and under) and the other 30 per cent long leases. Short leases were said to deter improvements, but nevertheless it was said that far-seeing landlords, such as the Duke of Devonshire in Eastbourne and the Duke of Westminster in London, had made good use of their power to draw up effective leases. Leasehold tenures of both kinds were commonest in the towns not already mentioned, i.e. most of the large industrial cities, in London and the suburbs, in coastal towns, whether ports or resorts, and in Wales.

In Scotland the tenurial system was different from that in England and Wales. Nevertheless there are indications that, apart from the widespread occurrence of tenement buildings containing very small dwellings, it produced somewhat similar conditions to those in England and Wales. The feuing system was peculiar to Scotland and, theoretically, gave what the English might have called 'ground landlords' control' over urban development. Thus Adams writes:

> The superior (i.e. feudal owner), where he wished, could act as the absolute planning authority. However, one of the great weaknesses of the system was that the superiorities, which were marketable in their own right, gradually fell into the hands of large institutions and the standards demanded by the original superiors were often overlooked for commercial advantage (p. 187).

Thus while feuing restrictions have been cited as one of the substantial factors which helped to give middle- or upper-class status to several areas of mid-Victorian Edinburgh, including the famous Georgian developments in the New Town, investment in urban housing in Scotland was predominantly the responsibility of small savers, who bought from small speculative builders. As 85 per cent of the property was the subject of mortgage bonds, it was necessary to charge the highest possible rents. In Glasgow, the shopocracy have been specifically mentioned as the main investors in new working-class housing in the period 1850-1914, although company housing (e.g. railway companies) and housing erected by artisan building societies also played a significant part.[17]

While the state of research does not permit any definitive statements to be made on the role of landowners and developers, enough has been said to demonstrate their importance in the evolution of socio-spatial patterns in nineteenth-century cities and the necessity of distinguishing between great and small entrepreneurs as in the estate and peasant systems of rural Britain. Further studies could usefully take as one starting point the role of different tenurial systems, for these had an importance of their own, just as they had in rural history starting from very early times.

### New Industrial Towns

So far the discussion has turned on evidence from large industrial towns, which were well-established before the onset of industrialisation. Although the role of small owners has remained largely obscure, the ability of the large landlord to create marked socio-spatial segregation *within* a large town has been adequately demonstrated. Now it is necessary to introduce the concept of segregation *between* towns.

It has long been recognised that the eighteenth and nineteenth centuries saw the rise of a wide range of specialised industrial, residential and other types of town distinguished by function. It follows from this that they varied — and still do — in terms of the socio-economic composition of their populations.[18] The mining and shipbuilding towns, with an over-representation of the manual classes, were balanced by residential and resort towns and administrative centres such as the county towns not grossly affected by industrialisation. What roles did landowners have in these specialised towns?

Rapid population growth from a slender or non-existent base was characteristic of the selected towns (See Table 10.1), making percentage rates rather unreliable indicators. Unlike some of the smaller company towns, rapid growth was sufficiently sustained to lift towns like Govan and Middlesbrough to near the 100,000 mark and all the examples beyond 35,000, if Scunthorpe's later growth is included. It is important to notice that these towns are essentially creations of the second half of the century, and depended on the railway system for their growth.

Table 10.1: Population Growth of Selected New Industrial Towns (in thousands)

| Town | 1831 | 1841 | 1851 | 1861 | 1871 | 1881 | 1891 | 1901 | 1911 |
|---|---|---|---|---|---|---|---|---|---|
| Govan | | | | 8 | 19 | 50 | 63 | 82 | 90 |
| Partick | | | | 8 | 18 | 27 | 37 | 54 | 67 |
| Coatbridge | | | | 11 | 16 | 25 | 30 | 37 | 43 |
| Motherwell | | | | 3 | 7 | 13 | 19 | 31 | 40 |
| Clydebank | | | | | | | | 21 | 38 |
| Ebbw Vale | | | | | | 16 | 17 | 21 | 31 |
| Rhondda | | | | | | | 69 | 114 | 153 |
| Scunthorpe | | | 1 | 1 | 2 | 6 | 8 | 11 | 20 |
| Birkenhead | < 1 | 8 | 24 | 36 | 66 | 83 | 100 | 111 | 121 |
| Crewe | < 1 | < 1 | 6 | 8 | 17 | 24 | 29 | 42 | 45 |
| Swindon (New) | | < 1 | 2 | 4 | 8 | 18 | 27* | 45 | 51 |
| Barrow | | < 1 | < 1 | 3 | 19 | 47 | 52 | 58 | 64 |
| Middlesbro' | 1 | 5 | 7 | 19 | 40 | 56 | 76 | 91 | 105 |

*Large proportion of increase in previous decade due to boundary changes 1881-91. New Swindon and Old Swindon combined.

Crewe and Swindon remained railway towns with engineering workshops, Middlesbrough and Barrow were dependent on the transport function in their early days and the rapid growth of the other towns would have been hardly conceivable without modern industry operating at a scale made possible by railways. At Middlesbrough, Barrow, Birkenhead and Scunthorpe the discovery of iron ores and/or the growth of a series of iron-making and iron-using industries led to a reliance on heavy industry, leading to the occupational imbalance characteristic of all the new industrial towns. Coal-mining, iron and steel-making, shipbuilding and the railway industry lent themselves especially well to large-scale capital-intensive organisation and much vertical and horizontal integration.[19] It was from this economic situation that most of the political, social and even demographic circumstances flowed.

The dependence on a relatively few large employers had the effect of rendering towns of this kind peculiarly open to fluctuations in trade and decisions from head office, the latter especially in the railway towns and in the later years of the century. While unemployment occurred from time to time, especially in Barrow between 1875 and the end of the century, it was the upsurges in employment that created the greatest problems of congestion, lack of facilities and social discord. The extreme case is probably Barrow in the period 1870-5 when the population doubled from about 20 to 40 thousand, but Swindon almost doubled in the decade 1861-71, Middlesbrough grew nearly sixfold in the twenty years 1851-71 and the transfer of workshops to Crewe from Liverpool and Wolverton created sudden inrushes in the 1840s and 1859-60.[20]

Despite considerable efforts on the part of the construction industry, overcrowding, at least for a time, was the norm in the new industrial towns even when allowances are made for the general failings of the age in this respect. In Barrow the numbers per house rose from 6.7 to 7.32 persons in 1871-74, during the worst period of immigration, compared with 5.2 in Preston, 5.1 in Burnley, 5.5 in Lancaster and 5.4 in Openshaw in 1871. In Scotland, Coatbridge, Clydebank, Govan and Motherwell were among the 11 towns in which, in 1911, over 70 per cent of the population lived in one or two room tenements, compared with 62.5 in Glasgow and 37.2 in Edinburgh.[21]

The preponderance of the working class in the population, as implied by Welton's occupational data,[22] the sizes of the main enterprises and the reports of a poor range of service facilities were factors promoting the paternalistic social and political systems in the new industrial towns. Others were the nature of the 'crisis' birth of these communities and the control of land exercised by a few people (See Figure 10.1). In Barrow, for instance, it has been said that the wealthy outside owners, which included the Dukes of Buccleuch and Devonshire, were:

> Responsible for the lack of organic growth and of population, the initial design of works on the largest scale, the spectacular achievements, the temporary fantastic profits and the wide fluctuations which become typical of Barrow's economic life . . . Barrow in Furness, unlike Saltaire and Port Sunlight, was not designed as a model town, free from the evils all too evident in many existing urban agglomerations. It grew in response to the needs of local industrialists who found themselves in control of a growing community and exercised their government in the interests of their investments, tempered with a modicum of social conscience.[23]

At Crewe similarly:

Figure 10.1: Barrow-in-Furness, 1873, Demonstrating Monopoly in Landownership by Big Estates

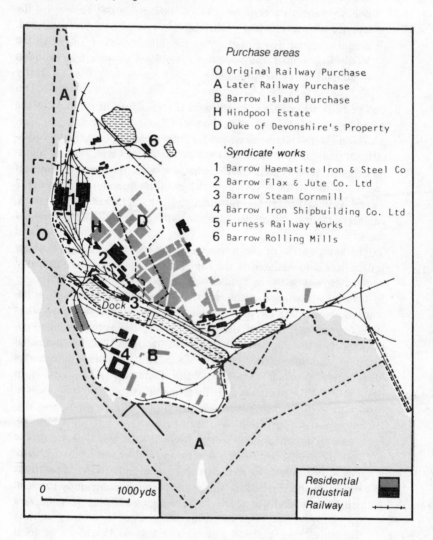

*Purchase areas*

O Original Railway Purchase
A Later Railway Purchase
B Barrow Island Purchase
H Hindpool Estate
D Duke of Devonshire's Property

'Syndicate' works

1 Barrow Haematite Iron & Steel Co
2 Barrow Flax & Jute Co. Ltd
3 Barrow Steam Cornmill
4 Barrow Iron Shipbuilding Co. Ltd
5 Furness Railway Works
6 Barrow Rolling Mills

0     1000 yds

Residential
Industrial
Railway

Source: Based on S. Pollard, 'Town Planning in the Nineteenth Century: The Beginnings of Modern Barrow-in-Furness', *Transactions of the Lancashire and Cheshire Antiquarian Society*, vol. 63 (1952-3), Map A

The Grand Junction Board was compelled by a mixture of principle, self-interest and necessity to adopt what might be termed a social policy towards its employees in the new colony at Crewe; in the absence of any efficient old-established system of government and urban economic organisation in the hitherto rural township of Monks Coppenhall, the company was obliged to undertake the task of building up a new community itself.[24]

The hallmarks of these towns were the regularity of street patterns, a housing 'hierarchy' reflecting the social hierarchy of occupations, the provision by the company of public utilities, public buildings, of educational and medical facilities, even policemen at Crewe, and of allotments and savings banks. In Crewe, there were four types of housing erected in the 1840s — villa style lodges for the superior officers, ornamental Gothic houses for the next in rank, detached mansions for engineers (four families per mansion) and labourers' cottages in terraces.[25]

The key position of the developing companies in relation to housing provision is demonstrated at the top end of the continuum of new and company towns by the companies' failure at Barrow and Middlesbrough. In Crewe and Swindon there are strong comparisons with the smaller company towns (see Chapter 11), but not so at Barrow. Although wide streets were laid out by the town council, the actual building of working-class housing was left in private hands and Barrow became a 'builders' and speculators' paradise'. Similarly, in Middlesbrough the 'dirty party' prevailed in town politics; there was said to be a high death-rate and the town was actually proud of its smoke.[26]

In this context, landowners like the Duke of Devonshire and the large companies might both have been expected to produce a planned environment of considerable worth. Why they did not always do so is not entirely clear, except that the scale and suddenness of the problem are obviously relevant. Nevertheless there were indications of paternalism similar to the rural estate village and the more consciously planned industrial villages and 'colonies' which are discussed in the next chapter.

## Resort Towns

The histories of resort towns, whether inland or coastal, make frequent reference to the activities of aristocratic landowners, whose interest was important in establishing the status of the resort as a refuge from industrial and commercial life (at least until the development of holidays for the masses).[27] Where the town was being created for the respectable classes it is to be expected that large landowners might persevere more than in the case of the large industrial towns described above. For this reason Barrett's comprehensive survey is particularly valuable. He distinguished a *majority* of resort towns in which growth was uncontrolled by a major owner or other agency. The minority included the well-known examples planned by one man, as well as a number that were less rigidly controlled by one owner, or a small number acting together, without an overall plan, yet with unmistakable signs of estate control. It is also necessary to distinguish between new resorts, large estate additions to existing towns and other estate developments.[28]

In his study of Llandudno, Carter[29] stressed the importance of the Mostyn family in developing the town as part of their general estate development after the creation of Sir Edward Pryce Lloyd as Baron Mostyn in 1831 and the acquisition of land by enclosure in the early forties. He distinguished between the 'priming decision' and 'secondary decisions'. The priming decision was taken by Lord Mostyn and he accumulated sufficient land for the venture. This gave the town a characteristic gridiron pattern of streets downslope from the old village on land Mostyn drained (See Figure 10.2). However, unlike some other owners quoted by Barrett, including the Newcombe Estate at Weston-super-Mare, Lord Mostyn left a good many of the secondary decisions to other entrepreneurs. For example, there was no attempt to provide the new town with appropriate central buildings. It was the Town Commissioners, created by the Improvement Act of 1854, who enforced building by-laws similar in character to those adopted by many towns twenty years later under the Public Health Act. Thus although careful attention, by the standards of the day, was paid to the principles of town planning, it was not in direct response to pressure from the Mostyn family. In other words it would be a mistake to assume from the evidence of a planned layout that a town's population lived under the paternalism characteristic of some of the planned towns of the nineteenth century.

Two points of comparison between new industrial and resort towns are, then, that both were more likely to come under the control of one company or owner where they grew from little or no 'pre-industrial' foundation and that both could outgrow the influence of their founders. However, by comparison with the large cities discussed earlier, Gesellschaft-like social relationships developed more slowly. Tönnies himself[30] recognised that small towns were not part of the Gesellschaft

Figure 10.2: Llandudno in 1849

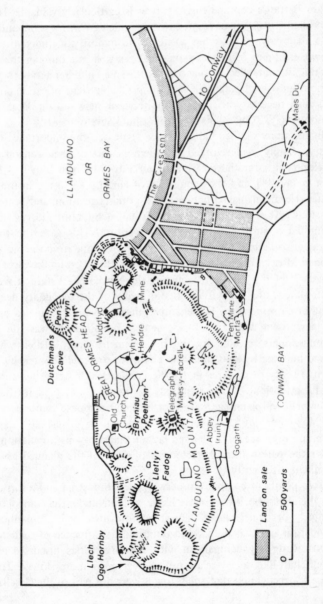

Source: From the map of 'Eligible Building land in Llandudno on the Gloddaeth Estate, belonging to the Hon. E.M.L. Mostyn, M.P., which will be sold by auction in lots . . . August 1849', by courtesy of Professor Harold Carter.

system, but some of those new towns were of considerable size and it was probably their newness which inhibited the growth of a shopocracy or urban peasantry as much as the relative size.

## Notes

1. The latest series of relevant studies are to be found in *TIBG*, new series, vol. 4, no. 2 (1979) pp. 125-319, which is devoted to the Victorian City; see also D. Ward, 'Victorian Cities: How Modern?', *Journal of Historical Geography*, vol. 1 (1975), p. 138; H. Carter in E.G. Bowen, H. Carter and J.A. Taylor (eds.), *Geography at Aberystwyth* (University of Wales Press, Cardiff, 1968), p. 227 (re Caernarvon); M. Shaw, 'The Ecology of Social Change: Wolverhampton 1851-71', *TIBG*, vol. 2, (1977), pp. 332-6; S.G. Checkland, 'The British Industrial City as History: The Glasgow Case', *Urban Studies*, vol. 1 (1964), pp. 41ff; D. Keir (ed.), *The Third Statistical Account of Scotland: The City of Edinburgh* (Collins, Glasgow, 1966), p. 19; A. Briggs, *History of Birmingham Vol II: Borough and City 1865-1938* (Oxford UP, 1952), p. 138; W. Ashworth, *The Genesis of Modern Town Planning* (Routledge, London, 1965), pp. 18-9; J. Langton, 'Residential Patterns in Pre-Industrial Cities: Some Case Studies from Seventeenth-Century Britain', *TIBG*, no. 65 (1975), pp. 1-4 and 9-11; and D. Cannandine, Victorian Cities: How different?', *Social History* vol. 1, no. 4 (1977) pp. 457-466.

2. Langton, *Residential Patterns*.

3. H. Carter in R.A. Dodgshon and R.A. Butlin (eds.), *An Historical Geography of England and Wales* (Academic Press, London, 1978), especially p. 385. The models of Burgess, Hoyt and Harris and Ullman are outlined in most textbooks of urban geography and urban sociology.

4. E.g. by Ward 'Victorian Cities', p. 139.

5. A.M. Warnes, 'Residential Patterns in an Emerging Industrial Town' in *Social Patterns in Cities*, Institute of British Geographers, Special Publication no. 5 (1973), especially p. 174.

6. J.E. Vance, 'Housing the Worker: The Employment Linkage as a Force in Urban Geography', *Economic Geography*, vol. 42 (1966), especially p. 319 and 'Housing the Worker: Determinative and Contingent Ties', *ibid.*, vol. 43 (1967), pp. 97, 108-9, 113-4, 116-21, 123 and 127.

7. Shaw, 'Ecology of Social Change', pp. 333-4.

8. Lawton in Dodgshon and Butlin, *Historical Geography*, pp. 351-4 and R. Lawton and C.G. Pooley, *The Social Geography of Nineteenth-Century Merseyside* (SSRC Report HR 1672 1975), especially pp. 48-9. Also *First Report of the Commissioners for Inquiring into the State of Large Towns and Populous Districts* (vol. 1, BPP, 1844), pp. 27 and 273 and S.D. Chapman (ed.) *The History of Working-Class Housing: A Symposium* (David and Charles, Newton Abbot, 1971), pp. 170 and 191-2.

9. D. Ward, 'The Pre-Urban Cadaster and the Urban Pattern of Leeds', *Annals of the Association of American Geographers*, vol. 52 (1962), pp. 151-5.

10. M.J. Mortimore, 'Landownership and Urban Growth in Bradford and its Environs in the West Riding Conurbation, 1850-1950', *TIBG*, no. 46 (1969), pp. 109 and 115-7.

11. G. Rowley, 'Landownership in the Spatial Growth of Towns: A Sheffield Example', *East Midland Geographer*, vol. 6 (1975), pp. 200-13, especially pp. 202-3 and 206.

12. T.R. Slater, 'Landscape Parks and the Form of Small Towns in Great Britain', *TIBG*, vol. 2 (1977), p. 325 especially.

13. K.C. Edwards, 'The Park Estate, Nottingham', Ch. 5 in M.A. Simpson and T.H. Lloyd (eds.), *Middle-Class Housing in Britain* (David and Charles, Newton Abbot, 1977).

14. Cannandine, 'Victorian Cities: How Different?', pp. 468-82.

15. H.J. Dyos, *Victorian Suburb: A Study of the Growth of Camberwell* (Leicester UP, 1961), especially pp. 40-1, 84-91, 99, 101, 126, 191-2.

16. *The Land*, The Report of the Land Enquiry Committee, vol. 2 Urban (Hodder and Stoughton, London, 1914), pp. 349-52, 373 and 407. This is based on information originally published in *BPP* 1887 (260), vol. XIII, *Select Committee Report on Town Holdings*, pp. 664-816 (Irish University Press Reprint, Urban Areas, Town Planning, vol. 5, 1969).

17. I.H. Adams, *The Making of Urban Scotland* (Croom Helm, London, 1978), pp. 166-7 and 187; Chapman, *Working-Class Housing*, pp. 74-5 and G. Gordon, 'The Status Areas of Mid-Victorian Edinburgh', *TIBG*, N.S., vol. 4 (1979), pp. 170, 184 and 186.

18. See, for example, *Census of Great Britain 1851*, BPP (1852-3), LXXXV, pp. xlix-xlx, where population data are presented by occupational classes of town. A good partial analysis of socio-economic differences is to be found in A.D.M. Phillips and J.R. Walton, 'The Distribution of Personal Wealth in English Towns in the mid-Nineteenth Century', *TIBG*, no. 64 (1975), pp. 35-48.

19. A. Briggs, *Victorian Cities* (1963, Penguin Edn, Harmondsworth, 1968), pp. 243-4, 247-51, 264-7; W.H. Chaloner, *The Social and Economic Development of Crewe 1780-1923* (Manchester UP, 1950), pp. 46 and 51; S. Pollard, 'Town-Planning in the Nineteenth Century: The Beginnings of Modern Barrow-in-Furness', *Transactions of the Lancashire and Cheshire Antiquarian Society*. vol. 63 (1952-3), pp. 88-9, 95 and 103; and E. Crittall (ed.), *Victoria History of the County of Wiltshire* (Institute of Historical Research, London), vol. 9 (1970), p. 105.

20. Pollard, 'Barrow-in-Furness', pp. 103 and 116; Chaloner, *Crewe*, pp. 46 and 51; and Briggs, *Victorian Cities*, pp. 264-7.

21. G.S. Pryde, *Scotland from 1603 to the Present Day* (Nelson, London, 1962), p. 260; Pollard, 'Barrow-in-Furness', p. 109.

22. T.A. Welton, 'Memorandum on Primary Occupations in the Principal English Towns in 1901', *Journal of the Royal Statistical Society*, vol. 66 (1903), pp. 360-5.

23. Pollard, 'Barrow-in-Furness', pp. 87 and 89 and S. Pollard, 'Barrow-in-Furness and the Seventh Duke of Devonshire', *Econ. Hist. Rev.*, vol. 8 (1955), pp. 221

24. Chaloner, *Crewe*, p. 45.

25. Ibid., p. 45-8, 52-6 and 63-4; Pollard 'Barrow-in-Furness', pp. 91, 93-4 and 98; Briggs, *Victorian Cities*, pp. 245-6, 253 and 256; and P.W. Kingsford, *Victorian Railwaymen: The Emergence and Growth of Railway Labour, 1830-70* (Cass, London, 1970) especially pp. 72-5, 121-2 and 170-81.

26. Pollard, 'Barrow-in-Furness', pp. 96-9, 105 and 115; and Briggs, *Victorian Cities*, pp. 263 and 268-73.

27. Ashworth, *Genesis*, p. 39; C. and R. Bell, *City Fathers: The Early History of Town Planning in Britain* (Barrie and Rockliff, London, 1969), pp. 98 and 103-4, for example.

28. J.A. Barrett, 'The Seaside Resort Towns of England and Wales', unpublished PhD Thesis, University of London 1958, pp. 48 and 51.

29. Carter in H. Carter and W.K.D. Davies, *Urban Essays: Studies in the Geography of Wales* (Longmans, London, 1970), especially pp. 72-5.

30. F. Tönnies, *Community and Association* (Routledge, London, 1955), p. 63 and 70-2.

# 11 THE ROLE OF THE VILLAGE IN INDUSTRIALISATION AND URBANISATION

'Rationality and self-interest had small room to flourish among men and women in the areas of working-class housing which grew up in knots round the factory or the pithead. This was a far cry from the capitalism of myriad small producers and consumers. It is not purely fanciful to see in communities of this type as many of the features which are held to go with *Gemeinschaft* as *Gesellschaft*. Industrialisation brought with it major regressive features judged by the measuring rods of modernisation.' E.A. Wrigley 'The Process of Modernisation and the Industrial Revolution in England', *Journal of Interdisciplinary History*, vol. 2 (1972), p. 259.

The work of the large landowner in a number of urban contexts emerged with reasonable clarity in the last chapter, but that of the urban peasantry remains unfortunately obscure. In the present chapter, however, the circumstances and the sources enable us to gain a view of both the peasant and estate systems making important contributions to the industrialisation and urbanisation of the country. A theme introduced in Chapter 1, that the rural-urban agricultural-industrial dichotomies are of limited value, reappears with some force, particularly with regard to the old-established industrial villages, whose existence has already been referred to in Chapter 6. It is also shown that the estate village made a contribution, for it was a model on which were based the industrial colony, the new factory village and the small company town — there were no clear demarcation lines between these types of settlement, partly because they drew on a common tradition, without their founders always being conscious of so doing. And while the values of the old peasant village may not be very apparent in modern society, those of the estate village have lived on in the tangible form of the garden city, the New Town and the council estate.

## Old-Established Industrial Villages

It will be evident from earlier chapters that there were good reasons why, in England at least, these belonged to the peasant system. There is no need, therefore to argue again that the activities of the peasantry extended beyond agriculture into the crafts and retail trades and into the manufacture of articles for sale outside the district concerned. That this situation was not merely a relic from the traditional past, but also a definite stage in the industrialisation and modernisation of the country has been recognised for a long time.

For example, Engels described the increasing trend towards specialisation that led to the peasant-textile worker becoming a village-based textile worker *only*, his household becoming dependent entirely on his wages. He also distinguished between the domestic stage in village industry and the beginning of the factory system there, with the consequent growth of population. The interaction between rural population growth — providing extra labour — and rural domestic industry — providing extra employment — has also been analysed recently as a phase of industrialisation termed proto-industrialisation.[1]

It is useful to distinguish loosely between four types of old-established, or peasant industrial village. First, there were those in which industry died out very early in the nineteenth century. Secondly, there were areas in which rural industry persisted, but was unable to expand at the same rate as industry in urban locations.

Thirdly, there are many examples of villages in the last category which were caught up and overrun by the superior growth of a nearby town. And lastly, there are a few instances where an old industrial village expanded to the point of gaining full urban status. Each of these types is now illustrated.

## Rural Industry Dying Out

Two examples of this situation are provided by quite different kinds of industry. When iron was produced with the aid of charcoal a flourishing iron-smelting industry, with about 60 principal sites, grew up in the Weald of Sussex, Kent and Surrey. Decline set in when the industry turned to coke for smelting purposes and the last works, at Ashburnham, closed in 1828.[2]

The straw hat and bonnet district of Buckinghamshire and Bedfordshire met a similar fate, but for totally different reasons and at a later date. The rural branch of the industry was the making of straw-plait by village women, which was subsequently made into hats and bonnets in Luton, St Albans and Dunstable. During the last quarter of the nineteenth century locally made plait was discarded by the hat manufacturers in favour of the much cheaper plait from China and Japan.[3]

*Rural Industry Persisting*

Two examples are again used here, one of an industry which contracted at a relatively early date, but nevertheless survived in some of the villages within the area. In the other case the industry was introduced only in the century from about 1750 and persists to-day on quite a considerable scale.

The first case is the woollen and cotton textile industry of the Craven district of Yorkshire, which while still strongly represented in some of the larger villages at the census of 1851, was gradually regressing on towns like Skipton and Keighley, but is still to be found in a few of the larger villages such as Addingham and Silsden.[4]

Secondly, in rural Northamptonshire the making of footwear replaced woollen textiles, silk and lace in the period 1750-1850, while in Leicestershire villages it followed in the footsteps of the declining hosiery industry after 1850. In 1905, 102,000 people in Northamptonshire were engaged in footwear factories and 22,000 in workshops which gives an indication of the scale of the industry and the fact that it then had a predominantly urban location, but had not died out in the villages. Rushden, Burton Latimer, Irthlingborough, Desborough, Irchester, Earls Barton, Higham Ferrers and Raunds were among the small towns and villages which sustained steady, sometimes rapid population growth on the basis of footwear manufacture. In Leicestershire a ring of villages encircling Leicester, and now in the middle of the commuter belt, obtained a good share of boot factories, of which in 1895 there were 96 outside the city and 235 within. In the west, Barwell and Earl Shilton acquired over 20 factories by 1911 and although affected by commuting are still free-standing industrial villages with considerable manufacturing employment of their own.[5]

*Industrial Villages Engulfed*

As mentioned in Chapter 10, Nottingham was a much overcrowded town in the first half of the century. Consequently some of the nearby textile villages, such as Sneinton, Radford, Lenton, Basford, Carrington and Hyson Green developed new districts in which better off working-class commuters came to reside. Urbanisation thus followed upon industrialisation. In the second half of the century they were absorbed into the borough and were completely surrounded by the urban mesh of greater Nottingham, but for a generation or two village conditions survived:

In the 'new' industrial villages there was room for the erection of more spacious dwellings and few houses were built back to back. Furthermore the artisans who moved to these villages were lace makers and mechanics who could afford to live in dwellings superior to those available at comparable rents in Nottingham.[6]

Although the circumstances of Nottingham's growth had an idiosyncratic twist, the general experience of villages being overrun by urban growth was repeated in many parts of the country. Reading, not normally the kind of town to be quoted in accounts of industrial growth, is a case in point, where the hamlet of Coley, half a mile west of the town centre, developed as a canal side working-class district, with many shops, facilities and sources of employment of its own, during the nineteenth century.[7]

## Village to Town

Many of the mill towns of Lancashire and the West Riding, not to mention mining settlements in north and south Wales and the Northumberland and Durham coalfield might qualify for this categorisation. Much depends on the definition, both of pre-existing village and urban status. St. Helens in Lancashire has a well-recorded history and may be considered an appropriate example.

There were four manor-townships in the area later occupied by the town of St. Helens; these were Eccleston, Parr, Sutton and Windle. St. Helen was the patron saint of the chapel-at-ease, of pre-Reformation foundation, which stood at the focal point of all four townships in a separate manor known as Hardshaw-within-Windle. Population growth around the chapel in the late eighteenth century led to the adoption of St. Helens as a place name, first for the immediate hamlet and later for the larger area. The fact that it was situated on the Prescot-Ashton turnpike must have been of prime significance in the establishment of a market near the chapel in 1780. By 1821 Windle township contained 4,820 people, the four townships together 10,603. In the next decade growth was rapid, especially in St. Helens itself which reached about 6,000 in 1831. This population growth was based on mining, glass manufacture, iron and copperworks, cotton-spinning, chemical works, watchmaking and an increasing array of service occupations. In 1861, St. Helens proper had a population of 18,396 out of the total of 37,961 and in 1901 the town boundaries contained 84,310 people. St. Helens was then unchallenged in its urban status.[8]

*Villages Various*

In some districts, several types of industrial village can be found. An example is the Renfrewshire district lying to the south of the Clyde, centring on Paisley and draining mainly into the river Cart. In 1695 about 80 per cent of the population (10,800) lived in settlements of less than 50 people and was engaged very largely in agriculture. By 1831, 86 per cent of a much larger population (98,100) was located in settlements of *over* 50 persons (including towns) and was engaged mainly in the cotton industry, following periods of activity in linen and silk gauze. Some of the rural cotton-workers lived in expanded, but old-established villages, including Lochwinnoch, Neilston and Eaglesham, others in new villages purposely built, like Johnstone and Thurnliebank. Since the mid-nineteenth century some of the textile villages have formed the nuclei of suburbs of Glasgow and Paisley, for instance, Pollokshaws. Others have attracted new industry to replace the now much shrunken textile industries. Within a twenty miles' radius of Paisley, therefore, village development varied considerably, contributing to both the industrialisation and urbanisation of the greater Glasgow area.[9]

This brief survey of old-established industrial villages is not authoritative, nor is it particularly analytical because it has been obliged to rely on studies undertaken with different objectives in mind. It has, however, demonstrated that villages were not cut off entirely from the main currents of social change in nineteenth-century Britain and it is therefore wrong to think of them as mere agricultural backwaters, whose only functions were to provide the towns with food, raw materials and healthy young workpeople.

## Industrial Villages of the Closed Type

Generally speaking, villages of this type were established during the eighteenth and early nineteenth centuries by industrialists who needed to provide housing accommodation for their workers in isolated locations which had been chosen for their accessibility to raw materials or power or transport facilities. The model they followed, in varying degree, was that of the rural closed village. To what extent the imitation was conscious, to what extent it was derived from the generally accepted mores of the period and to what extent it arose out of necessity is a very debatable matter, but the evidence suggests that all three factors were of significance.

The most complete survey of 'industrial villages' is that by Darley, who, discussing the motives of industrialists, has noticed this problem by acknowledging that they were more 'mixed' than those of rural estate owners, as there was nothing much to be gained from picturesque effects:

> Certainly the warring forces of expediency and conscientiousness fought a hard battle, but . . . it is clear that good materials were used . . . but their contribution to reform was more in the direction of their attention to education and recreation. They were not content to employ mere sweated labour in their factories and mills.

Nevertheless the common ground between landed gentry and philanthropic industrialist was demonstrated when Sir Francis Crossley, the carpet manufacturer, chose to buy for his retirement the model village of Somerleyton in Suffolk, built by Sir Morton Peto.[10]

The other considerable problem in this field of study is to attempt to establish some recognisable typology of settlements out of the wide variety of circumstances and the divergent approaches which have been made to them. First, another glance will be taken at the Scottish planned village, followed by some settlements which have been called colonies. Another important category is the mining village, which takes third place. Finally, we shall look at the textile villages built before about 1850. In terms of the continued development of ideas, the latter are the most important group of settlements, so much so that the distinction between them and the small company towns of the second half century is somewhat arbitrary.

## The Planned Villages of Scotland

These villages have been mentioned before in passing. Even excluding the mining villages, industrial development was one of the principal objectives of most of the planned villages in Scotland. Running through the literature of these villages there is the strong theme of paternalism which characterised the English estate villages, with a conscious seeking-out of tenants of good character. Mostly, the lead came from lairds, but in a group of about twenty villages in the Glasgow area the factory owners of places like Balfron, Deanston, Catrine and New Lanark were the figures of authority. Here the housing conditions were said not to be up to the standard of the lairds' foundations, but still much better than the usual Scottish industrial housing. In the villages of this group, industry (especially the textile industry) was well-established, in contrast to the typical planned village where it faded out in the early nineteenth century.[11]

Nevertheless it is possible to take the view that the typical planned village contributed something to the development of early town-planning ideas and this is the theme of a study of Grantown-on-Spey, founded in Morayshire by Sir James Grant in 1766.[12] Grant is said to have aimed to combine the best of town and country in a manner that would have been recognisable to Howard and ensured a better standard of housing than had previously prevailed in the area. While modern new towns have aimed to decentralise industry, however, Grant wished to develop industry to provide employment for those displaced from farming. There were several ways in which, like a new town development corporation, he set about attracting industry. He lent capital to likely manufacturers, provided premises, subsidised established industries, built roads, bridges and public buildings, provided water and removed nine or ten markets from other parts of the estate to Grantown, partly as a potential outlet for manufactured goods.

## Industrial Colonies

A significant number of industrial extensions to growing towns took the form of distinct factory villages or colonies on the edge of the town or separated from it by a few open fields. A good example is the Hillfields district of Coventry, begun in 1828 with the apparent intention of its being a suburb of villa residences for the well-to-do a mile out of the town. However, events proved otherwise, for it became almost wholly a colony of lower-class people living in terrace houses, employed at weaving and clock-making in domestic workshops included in the new development, along with shops, services and numerous pubs.[13]

Several distinct examples of colonies closely associated with towns have been discovered, not surprisingly, in Lancashire, where rapid urban expansion, the early growth of factories and the need for access to water power, railways or canals created favourable circumstances for this kind of 'colonisation'. Marshall has called this category of settlement a secondary colony, in distinction to the primary or clean slate type of colony. Of the latter he cites Belmont, on the moors north of Bolton, as well as Warthfold between Bury and Radcliffe and one mile away from both towns. Belmont and Warthfold were characteristic mill villages in which the owners took a paternalistic view of the residents' moral welfare. Examples of secondary colonies were to be found (1) around the margins of Blackburn, including Brookhouse (1845), begun by Hornbys the mill-owners (See Figure 11.1) and (2) near Bury, where on the eastern flank was Freetown, begun about 1822 and appearing as a substantial group of streets on the Tithe Map of 1837. By 1894 the 'colony had become absorbed into the more general urban mass (but) it retained a measure of self-conscious identity'.[14]

Figure 11.1: Brookhouses, Blackburn, *c.* 1845

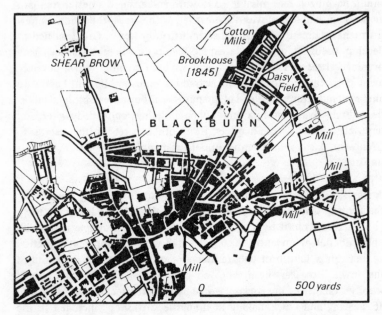

Source: Originally published in H.J. Dyos (ed.) *The Study of Urban History* (Edward Arnold, London, 1969) p. 227, having been redrawn by Lancashire Record Office from the Six Inch Ordnance Survey Map. Reproduced by kind permission of the County Archivist, Lancs. Record Office.

*Mining Villages*

Mining developments were probably the most common cause of new industrial settlements in the nineteenth century. In the case of lead-mining in the northern Pennines the isolation of mines was as significant as lack of accommodation in the nearest villages. Lodgings were made available in private houses, inns and boarding houses in old villages, especially in the eighteenth and early nineteenth centuries, as well as in lodging shops specially constructed by the mining companies for the most isolated or newest mines. Because the men worked a five-day week it was possible for them to commute on a weekly basis and spend two days at home.[15]

The permanent mining settlement pattern was based on a system of smallholdings of various sizes, this being an area where farmland was not in great demand. Moreover isolation was so great that there was a need to produce as much subsistence as possible on the spot. As lead-working expanded, pressure on land developed sufficiently to force more lead-miners into villages, but they remained a minority. This generalisation appears to have applied to the 650 square miles extending from Teesdale northwards to Derwentdale and westwards to Allendale and Alston Moor, including parts of the North Riding, Durham, Northumberland and Cumberland. Thus although much of the mining was in the hands of the London Lead Company, the Derwent Mining Company and other big entrepreneurs, the miner retained a considerable degree of independence in the tradition of peasant craftsmen elsewhere.[16]

Allenheads, Nenthead and Coalcleugh were new villages built by companies at heights of 1,237, 1,411 and 1,821 feet respectively, i.e. up to a thousand feet above the older villages containing lead-miners. The London Lead Company also rebuilt Garrigill and Middleton in Teesdale, as their declared policy from the early nineteenth century was to concentrate miners where possible in communities. In 1851 Nenthead had a population of 872 and contained company-built public buildings. By 1864, most of the miners working for the Derwent Company in the neighbourhood of Hunstanworth were living in the new company village, whose parish had a population maximum of 778 in 1861. From this peak lead-mining declined gradually until its eclipse at the end of the nineteenth century.[17]

The social life of these lead-mining communities reflects an interesting balance between paternalism by the companies – who, for example, had introduced compulsory education for children aged 6-12 by 1842 and succeeded in drastically reducing the number of public houses and toning down the traditional forms of merry-making – and a freedom of expression associated with open villages, nonconformist religion and poaching included.[18]

Although important locally, lead-mining was a very slender industry by comparison with coal-mining, which expanded rapidly in many parts of Britain. There was a close relationship between the size of colliery and size of village or town, and a crushing preponderance of miners within even large mining settlements has been widely noticed. Moreover colliery companies kept up the impetus in the building of new villages well into the twentieth century, as new, often deeper collieries were opened in fresh seams. For instance, in the period 1919-25, 10,033 colliery houses were built in England and Wales and 1,980 in Scotland.[19]

In mining, the paternalist tradition may have come directly from the fact that mineral rights were vested in landlords, many of whom had taken a direct interest in the industry up to the early nineteenth century. For example, in Alloa the Earl of Mar provided education and improved cottages for miners in that period, so it is perhaps not surprising that colliery schools were commonplace in Scotland by the mid-century. Early in the twentieth century three quarters of miners' dwellings in the Lothians and Ayrshire belonged to the employers and in Lanarkshire and central Scotland between a third and a half.[20]

Table 11.1: Example of Population Increases in Durham Pit Villages (Easington RD)

| Parish | Census 1801 | 1851 |
|---|---|---|
| Hutton Henry | 156 | 1,067 |
| Murton | 75 | 1,387 |
| Shotton | 250 | 1,607 |
| Haswell | 93 | 4,356 |
| Thornley | 56 | 2,740 |
| Wingate | 135 | 2,456 |
| Monk Hesledon | 150 | 1,495 |

In the Easington district of County Durham the sudden onrush of large-scale mining from about 1831 produced a sharp discontinuity both in the landscape and the life of a traditionally agricultural area:

In almost all cases the colliery settlements grew up alongside older villages, took their names and then expanded to a size previously unknown in the area. It tended to be the exception for agricultural hamlets to be absorbed . . . so that agricultural and mining communities tended to remain separate geographical entities.[21]

There are many coalfield areas where this description could still apply, but probably none more than the concealed coalfield running from east of Nottingham northwards to the Leeds-Selby area.

In his study of the south Wales colliery settlements over the period 1850-1926, P.N. Jones produced a morphogenetic classification based

Figure 11.2: A Part of the Map of Rhosllanerchrugog, North-east Wales

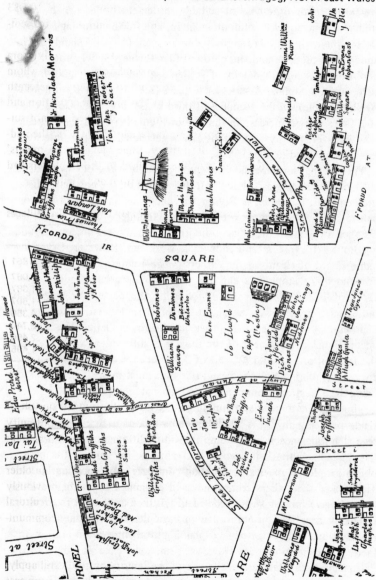

Note: In addition to the haphazard terraces, note the Wesleyan Chapel (centre), the pit-head (centre right), Joseph Griffiths' shop (bottom left) and the nicknames, which were typical of English, as well as Welsh villages of this period.

Source: Drawn *c.* 1835 by J. Platt; copyright National Library of Wales.

on (a) the phase of colliery development, its scale and duration (b) the pre-existence or otherwise of suitable settlement nodes (c) the availability of transport for commuting labour and (d) the building agencies. During the early phase of colliery development (1850-75) land was not under great pressure and the pattern of landownership was not of great significance except in details of settlement location and pattern, the latter often a haphazard series of terraces (see Figure 11.2 for a north Welsh example). In the second and third phases (1875-1900 and 1900-26), there was an increase in the size of the colliery and the degree of civic interference by way of by-law regulations, but the ubiquitous terrace continued to appear.[22]

Pre-existing settlements were not generally very old established, most of them being associated with ironworks on the northern edge of the coalfield. One such is Brynmawr which was uninhabited not long before 1820 when the iron ore works were founded. As they were some distance away from the village, the iron company left the job of building houses to traders and individual workmen. However, Brynmawr had a Board of Health at the earliest possible date in 1851, which was dominated by employers and the agent of the ground landlord, the Duke of Beaufort. After 1860, following the pattern of larger new industrial towns, power passed to the small tradesmen, who were the main employers in the town, other than nearby collieries. The lopsided occupational development of the town was still evident a century after the foundation, for in 1921 out of 3,229 occupied people, 1,640 were engaged in mining and quarrying, the next most important occupation being the 398-strong commercial and financial group.[23]

Jones listed three major building agencies in the south Wales coalfield: property investors, building clubs and colliery companies; and several minor agencies, including individual owner occupiers, speculative builders with their own capital and, at the end of the period, philanthropically motivated building companies and local authorities. The role of the colliery company was often limited to making a start in order to give other investors confidence, it then pulled out and concentrated on mining. This contrast with more deliberately planned settlements is an obvious factor in explaining much haphazard and unsatisfactory housing provision. However, some coherence was given to the larger developments towards the end of the century by the adoption of gridiron patterns on estates where large investors and building clubs erected the houses, except where property boundaries unfortunately produced obstacles to optimum lay-out.[24]

*Textile Villages*

New settlements in connection with the textile industries were far less common than in the case of mining, but their quality was generally higher and their influence on social planning far greater. Those in Scotland were influenced considerably by the planned village movement which was at its height when the need for new villages near water power sites in the greater Glasgow area occurred between 1780 and 1800. In the West Riding, Ripleyville was started about 1840 as a dyeworks settlement in the fields between Bradford and Bowling, dyeing being regarded as a noxious industry; and Saltaire was situated on the opposite side of Bradford. Near Halifax Akroydon (of the Akroyds) and Copley were also new planned textile villages. In Cheshire there was the well-known cotton village of Samuel Oldknow at Mellor, and in Derbyshire significant developments at Cromford.[25]

The bulk of these planned manufacturing villages were built before 1830, very largely out of economic necessity. Towns were still small, labour was still dispersed through thousands of agricultural or semi-agricultural villages, power and transport were often lacking where labour was to be found. Employers, with the possible exception of Robert Owen, did not start out with high ideals of producing a pleasant environment and good working conditions for their own sake. They saw the factory village as an extension of the factory, as a means of extending their control over workpeople to ensure a good standard of work. But they were pioneers and they developed a finer sense of responsibility pragmatically in the course of managing both factory and village.

Housing was a first necessity, but evictions could also be used as a means of enforcing factory discipline and competitions in cleanliness were seen as an aid to production. Likewise schools, mechanics institutes and chapels were a means of gaining obedience; and medical assistance and sick clubs were used to keep workers fully efficient. Drink was restricted as much because of its effect on work as on morals. The hated truck systems (food and clothing bought in company shops) were seen as a practical necessity in an isolated place. Where the local magistrates were not appointed by the country gentry, the vicious circle of power closed in on the worker, as the factory master became magistrate and policeman in one.[26]

With all their faults, limitations and paternalism, the new factory villages were a vast improvement upon the chaotic growth of the large existing towns and even smaller ones. They met a need for accommodation in mainly isolated places, thus of necessity combining certain characteristics of town and country. It was this combination which enabled them to make such an important contribution to the garden city movement and its forerunners.

## The Garden City Movement

With the benefit of hindsight, it is easy to see the garden city as a partial solution to the problem of suburbanisation and segregation. As the garden city was to have its own employment, it would cease to be a suburb and become a satellite, an economic satellite of a larger metropolis. As workers of different kinds would be needed a wider social range would be encompassed in the population. In providing pleasant living and working conditions the garden city would lose none of the physical advantages of the suburb, yet the tiring journey to work would disappear. While this concept of the garden city did not make its full appearance until 1898 and the first example at Letchworth began only in 1903, there was a long and involved ancestry behind it.[27]

The factory village of the first half of the century was a forerunner in the sense that relatively good accommodation was provided for workpeople in close proximity to their employment, with a wide range of facilities promoting a sense of physical and inner well-being. Before 1850 it is difficult to find references to open space on the scale that could enable the use of such a label as 'garden village'. Owen's provision of walks in the wild surroundings of New Lanark is probably the furthest early development in that direction.[28]

Bromborough Pool in the Wirral represented an important advance in the sense that, although it came into existence purely on grounds of economic necessity on an isolated site, '(It) is in every sense a garden village, with the cottages laid out in short terraces of four with wide spaces between each block and ample gardens at the back as well as at the front. The open space known as the Green was established at the start . . .' This was achieved by Price's Patent Candle Company in the mid-1850s.[29]

Bromborough has received much less attention than Saltaire, which was being built at the same time. This is unfortunate, because Saltaire can in no way be described as a garden village, despite the recreation space on the opposite side of the river. It was, however, a significant new departure in another sense. Sir Titus Salt, its founder, having made a fortune by early middle age, was not obliged by economic necessity to start a mill outside Bradford, when there were many suitable sites still left in the town. It is true that in economic terms the site he chose was brilliantly successful, with good access to road, river, canal and railway and he endowed it with a factory that became a model of efficient organisation. But his main avowed aim was to provide a model industrial town, free of the appalling conditions then prevalent in Bradford.

In his characteristically thorough way, he was the first man to use a social survey to ascertain the needs of the workers before they came into residence. He determined the number of houses required for differing sizes of family, the number of single workers requiring lodging-house accommodation and the number of old people, for whom he later built almshouses. Saltaire exudes Salt's paternalism in the hierarchical nature of its cottage architecture, the naming of streets after members of his family, his provision of chapel and school but no pub, and so forth. Nevertheless, his achievement must be recognised.[30]

After Bromborough Pool and Saltaire there was a pause of thirty or forty years before the building of the next pair of model towns, Bournville and Port Sunlight. These marked other significant advances, unlike the many pit villages of the second half of the century which appear to have made little contribution to the arts of town planning. Cadburys moved their factory from central Birmingham to Bournville in 1879 but it was 1895 before any considerable number of houses were built. Apart from being a garden city in all but name, with its founders giving much attention to the healthiness of the residents, Bournville also broke almost new ground by reserving 50 per cent of the accommodation for families who had no breadwinner working for Cadburys. The only partial precedent for this appears to have been Oldknow's village at Mellor in Cheshire around 1800 to which he attracted male employment in coal-mining, lime-burning, building and farming, in recognition of the fact that he mainly engaged women and children in his own textile mill. Although Cadbury resisted the temptation to become a feudal magnate, the setting-up of the Bournville Village Trust ensured a central management. By 1914 the population had reached 4,390.[31]

At Port Sunlight, which was begun in 1888 near Lever's soapworks on Merseyside, only a short distance from Bromborough Pool, the environment created was also that of a garden city. It is said to have been much more closely controlled by Lever than Bournville was by Cadbury. For instance he admitted preferring to build workers houses, to letting them spend their own share of the profits. It was more 'baronial', aped Versailles in its plan, and Lever only allowed a pub to be built when a majority of the employees voted in favour of one. Nevertheless Port Sunlight has an important place along with Bournville, New Earswick, built in 1904 by Rowntree at York, and the Hull Garden Village opened by Sir James Reckitt in 1908.[32] By this time

Howard's Letchworth Garden City had started to rise from the fields.

Its planning was based on the now familiar union of town and country and on the new concept of development trustees who were not to be deliberately associated with the chief employers. They were charged with the task of raising the money on the stock market at low rates of interest. Ground rents paid the interest, with a surplus going into the hands of the town council. But Letchworth did not become merely a superior type of suburb, since it was provided with a wide variety of employment, as well as a range of public buildings and other facilities. Two further ideas promoted by Howard did not get very far. He originally envisaged a town agricultural estate, using the refuse of the town, which was to support a population of 2,000, out of the total of 30,000. Howard had also hoped to build associated garden cities of similar size in a ring around a central city of twice their size, all connected across open country by rail links. This was unsuccessful, except in so far as Stevenage and Letchworth, along with the old-established towns of Hitchin and Baldock, form a constellation of interacting urban communities, being connected by frequent bus services as well as the railway.[33]

From the eighteenth century's new industrial villages of Mellor and New Lanark, there is then a continuous thread all the way down the years to the garden cities of Letchworth and Welwyn. The founders of the various new settlements discussed were influenced by traditional agricultural villages — or their perception of them — in two principal ways. First, although employment was to be industrial, locations were rural and various physical virtues of rural living were sought, especially by the builders of post-1850 settlements — access to open country and recreation space, clean air and water, plenty of light, an abundance of trees and other forms of vegetation both ornamental and useful. Secondly, societal values were also borrowed from traditional rural forms and in this there was a marked preference for the estate system. In some respects there was little choice, since the railway or mining company, the mill owner, the factory owner and the development trust were inevitably in much the same position as the rural landlord vis-à-vis their tenants. However, *paternalism* was a guiding philosophy which came to be applied out of more than mere necessity, as the difference between Cadburys and Lever nicely illustrates.

*Independence* as known in the open village flourished in two main kinds of urban or industrial situation. First, it was strong where there was a prior existence of small businesses, either in industry or commerce or both. In this respect the old-established industrial villages, the market towns and many cities had much in common. Secondly, given favourable conditions it could build up even in new urban communities over a significant period especially when there was substantial population growth. When manufacturing employment diversified, shops and markets accumulated in number and prosperity, newspapers and other organs of public opinion were established and the speculative builder appeared, then the paternalism of the early driving force, as described in Chapter 10, began to wither away.

## Notes

1. F. Engels, *The Condition of the Working Class in England* (1845, Oxford UP edn, 1958), pp. 12-3 and 28-9; F.F. Mendels, 'Proto-industrialisation: The First Phase of the Industrialisation Process', *Journal of Economic History*, vol. 32 (1972), pp. 241-61.

2. R. Millward and A. Robinson, *South-East England: The Channel Coastlands* (Macmillan, London, 1973), pp. 116-24.

3. C.M. Law, 'Luton and the Hat Industry', *East Midland Geographer*, vol. 4 (1968), especially Figs. 2 and 4 and p. 338; and D.J.M. Hooson, 'The Straw Industry of the Chilterns in the Nineteenth Century', *ibid.*, especially pp. 347-8.

4. Own fieldwork and R. Lawton, in D.R. Mills (ed.), *English Rural Communities: The Impact of a Specialised Economy* (Macmillan, London, 1973), especially pp. 169-75.

5. Own fieldwork and P.R. Mounfield, 'The Footwear Industry of the East Midlands', *East Midland Geographer*, no. 24 (1965), especially pp. 435-9; no. 25 (1966), especially pp. 10-13 and no. 27 (1967), especially pp. 154 and 162.

6. D. Gray, *Nottingham: Settlement to City* (Nottingham Co-operative Society, 1953), pp. 65-7 and 112-3; and R.A. Church, *Economic and Social Change in a Midland Town: Victorian Nottingham, 1815-1900* (Cass, London, 1960), p. 164.

7. P.E. Cusden, *Coley: Portrait of an Urban Village* (Reading Branch, WEA, 1977).

8. T.C. Barker and J.R. Harris, *A Merseyside Town in the Industrial Revolution: St. Helens, 1750-1900* (1954, Cass Reprint, London, 1959), pp. 3, 131, 168-71, 374, 427, 453-4 and maps.

9. N.A. McIntosh, 'Changing Population Distribution in the Cart Basin in the Eighteenth and Nineteenth Centuries', *TIBG*, no. 22 (1956), especially pp. 146 and 152-7.

10. G. Darley, *Villages of Vision* (Architectural Press, London, 1975), pp. 63 and 68.

11. T.C. Smout in N.T. Phillipson and R. Mitchison (eds.), *Scotland in the Age of Improvement: Essays in Scottish History in the Eighteenth Century* (Edinburgh UP, 1970), pp. 85, 87-9 and 96.

12. H. Woolmer, 'Grantown-on-Spey: An Eighteenth-Century New Town', *Town Planning Review*, vol. 41 (1970), pp. 237, 239-41 and 243-4.

13. R. Chaplin, 'Discovering the Lost New Towns of the Nineteenth Century', *Local Historian*, vol. 10 (1972), pp. 187 and 189-90. Information from the 1861 Census per Dr. A. Parton.

14. J.D. Marshall, 'Colonisation as a Factor in the Planting of Towns in NW England', in H.J. Dyos (ed.), *The Study of Urban History* (Edward Arnold, London, 1968), pp. 221-7.

15. C.J. Hunt, *The Lead-Miners of the Northern Pennines in the Eighteenth and Nineteenth Centuries* (Manchester UP, 1970), pp. 161-5.

16. Ibid., pp. 1, 5-6 and 165.

17. Ibid., pp. 138-9, 150, 186-92.

18. Ibid., Chs. 11 and 12 and W.S. Gilly, *The Peasantry of the Border: An Appeal on their Behalf* (London 1842, new edn, Bratton Publishing Ltd Edinburgh, 1973), p. 40.

19. R.P. Beckinsale and J.M. Houston (eds.), *Urbanisation and its Problems* (Oxford UP, 1968), p. 158; P.N. Jones, *Colliery Settlement in the South Wales Coalfield 1850-1926* (University of Hull, 1969), pp. 82 and 96-9; P.H. White, 'Some Aspects of Urban Development by Colliery Companies', *The Manchester School of Economic and Social Studies*, vol. 23 (1955), p. 272 and G.S. Stevenson, 'Portland Row, Kirkby-in-Ashfield', *Transactions of the Thoroton Society*, vol. 70 (1966), pp. 63-5.

20. W.H. Marwick, *Economic Development in Victorian Scotland* (Allen and Unwin, London, 1936), pp. 29-30, 161, 167 and 172-3.

21. W.A. Moyes, *Mostly Mining – a Study of the Development of Basington Rural District since Earliest Times* (F. Graham, Newcastle, 1969), pp. 74-5 and 98.

22. P.N. Jones, *Colliery Settlement*, especially pp. 61-5.

23. H. Jennings, *Brynmawr: A Study of a Distressed Area* (Alenson and Co., London, 1934), pp. 14-7, 73-7 and 84-6.

24. P.N. Jones, *Colliery Settlement*, especially pp. 40-8, 72, 77-8, 87, 90-1. See also Mills, *English Rural Communities*, pp. 20-4 and 137-44 and Dyos, *Study of Urban History*, p. 246.

25. For the most comprehensive list of industrial villages found so far, see Darley, *Villages of Vision*, pp. 137-149.

26. S. Pollard, 'The Factory Village in the Industrial Revolution', *English Historical Review*, vol. 79 (1964), pp. 513-31.

27. E. Howard, *Garden Cities of To-morrow*, (1902, Faber, London, 1946).

28. C. and R. Bell, *City Fathers: The Early History of Town Planning in Britain* (Barrie and Rockliff, London, 1969), pp. 182-5.

29. Tarn in Mills, *English Rural Communities*, p. 148.

30. Bell, *City Fathers*, pp. 189-95, R.K. Dewhirst, 'Saltaire', *Town Planning Review*, vol. 31 (1960-1), pp. 135-44; and own fieldwork.

31. Bell, *City Fathers*, pp. 206-8, W. Ashworth, *The Genesis of Modern Town Planning* (Routledge, London, 1965), pp. 120 and 132 and A. Briggs, *History of Birmingham, Volume II: Borough and City 1865-1938* (Oxford UP, 1952) pp. 158-60.

32. Ashworth, *Genesis*, pp. 132-42; Bell, *City Fathers*, pp. 208-12.

33. R. Thomas and P. Cresswell, *The New Town Idea: Urban Development, Unit 26*, (Open University Press, Milton Keynes, 1973), pp. 10-11.

# 12 EPILOGUE: LORD AND PEASANT TODAY

A title of this kind relating to modern Britain will strike the reader at first sight as totally discordant. Yet I am often asked what happened to the peasants? Moreover, there are still some very large estates and crofting still goes on in north-west Scotland. So, on a very speculative, intentionally provocative basis, some thoughts are offered which may help to link the foregoing study of nineteenth-century society with later developments.

Taking the estate system first, it exerts one of two influences on rural community development, depending on location. In the areas remoter from towns, the estate village tends, at least outwardly, to be a museum of itself, especially where property has remained in the hands of a few people, and on a good many shooting estates in Scotland. By virtue of recent and current planning policies, housing developments have been channelled into the bigger villages, i.e. mainly those which were open villages in the nineteenth century. Although this policy has been evolved on the basis of providing adequate services in a limited number of places, the result is much the same as could have been predicted on the basis of the open-closed model.

The other situation is where the once model village has found itself in the path of strong pressures for suburban or 'dormitory' development and has succumbed. It has usually done so on a totally different basis from the former open village. Instead of large numbers of three bedroom semi-detached houses, there will be limited numbers of individually designed detached houses, enhanced in desirability by the leafy environment surviving from estate days. Sometimes the big house has gone and smaller houses have been built on the site, sometimes it remains as a block of flats, with new houses in the grounds. Stable blocks, laundries, servants' quarters, gardeners' cottages, barns and granaries have all acquired a status which would have made the former inhabitants smile. And this status is protected by planning policies which prevent developments not in keeping with the character of the locality. Usually this means houses whose occupants could not afford a second car in which to take their children some distance to school. *Tout ça change, tout c'est la même chose!*

However, the estate system, I would suggest, has had the greatest influence on our present living conditions in the urban areas where most people still live. This is because a continuous thread can be traced from the English estate village and the Scottish planned village[1] through various factory villages and company towns down to the garden city movement, post-1918 surburbia and the New Towns. Welwyn, the second garden city, was designated as one of the first New Towns under an Act of 1946, thus making a direct link between the garden city movement and the New Towns. In 1973 there were 19 New Towns in Britain being managed by development corporations appointed by the government under the 1946 Act and five others designated as New Towns.[2]

The mode of appointment of these corporations invites an analogy with nineteenth-century company towns. In the absence of direct elections, accusations of paternalism and autocratic attitudes are unsurprising. The corporations are large landowners, have powers of compulsory purchase and easily come into conflict with pre-existing local authorities which have to carry on a muted existence.[3]

Town planning outside the New Towns also owes something to the ideals of the estate village transmitted through the garden city movement. In 1901 the Garden City Association was formed as an active voluntary body advancing the cause of decentralisation and in 1907 became the Garden City and Town Planning Association, now the Town and Country Planning Association. 'Town planning did not emerge out of the Garden City Movement, but was reinforced by it.'[4]

Outside the New Towns, the ideals of the town-planning movement have probably been most strongly felt on municipal housing estates which now provide accommodation for perhaps one third of the population. It is not merely the spacious layouts and the provision of amenities which seem redolent of the estate village. It could also be argued that on the council estate the housing department has taken over the role of the old time landowner, regulating not only the property but also the inhabitants, limiting lodgers, disallowing huts and preventing businesses from being run from council houses. Such rules and regulations go well beyond normal planning regulations, which in themselves are also a powerful aspect of paternal social control by the state. And finally, it should perhaps be pointed out that local authorities, like the estates before them, have operated on a large scale, particularly, of course, in the large cities where economies of scale have been there for the taking. So it is not uncommon to find that councils have bought big blocks of land from large landowners (such as the Fitzwilliam estate in Sheffield mentioned above, page 190), leaving the smaller patches of building land for the private developers and the owner-occupiers —

hence the frequent absence of facilities from housing estates of this kind.

But what of the peasantry and their values in this day and age? The trend towards larger farms which began in Tudor times has continued little abated and the numbers of viable smallholdings has continued to go down, despite a growth in demand for fruit, flowers, vegetables, eggs and pigmeat which in the first half of the present century looked set to rescue the peasantry. Both agriculture and horticulture have become capital-intensive industries (even the inaccurate use of the term 'industry' in this context now passes unnoticed). The decline of the large estates and the landlord-tenant relationship more generally, has led to owner-occupied farms becoming the norm, thus increasing still further the capital outlay required.

On the other hand, modern technology has dramatically reduced the farm labour force, so that in many parts of the country, especially the pastoral west, the family farm is the typical farm. Farmers themselves now provide over one third of the farm labour force, one of the observations which has led Winter to state that 'at no point in the development of agrarian capitalism have family farmers not existed'. His definition of a family farm is one in which 'the main feature . . . is that the capital, labour and management skills are chiefly provided by the family'. Otherwise it operates in much the same capitalist way as the larger, so-called capitalist farm.[5] This distinction seems not unlike that drawn between peasant and estate farms of the last century.

In addition to well-capitalised family farms, there are also many part-time farms. These are difficult to evaluate because they include retired industrialists and politicians at one extreme and dual occupationist crofters, often on the dole, at the other. Nevertheless, the careful observer will find examples of dual occupationists which appear to be in direct line of descent from the nineteenth-century peasantry, such as the following examples known to the writer:

publican and school bus driver;
joiner, antique dealer and undertaker;
two village tradesmen, grocer and painter, who share the work and crops on a fourteen-acre field;
Electronics engineer who runs a market garden;
carpenter and farm-worker who form a part-time tree-felling partnership (one of them also owns a wood);
farmers who own transport businesses;
agricultural contractors who have their own land as an operating base.

A few swallows do not make a summer, nor even a late autumn, although one should also bear in mind thousands of family shops, garages, pubs and building trade businesses. There is, however, an alternative approach to the identification of the peasant tradition in modern life. George Sturt's definition of the peasant system was one in which 'people derived the necessaries of life from the materials and soil of the countryside'.[6] Essentially this meant fending for oneself with the best of what came most easily to hand and the do-it-yourself movement appears to be a modern interpretation of this philosophy. Family labour is the essential element.

DIY is reinforced by the present taxation system, because the DIY man might otherwise have worked overtime in order to pay someone else to do the job. High levels of income tax also encourage 'moonlighting', the name given to tax evasion by self-employed persons and others doing 'private jobs' in their spare time for which they are paid in cash that does not have to be accounted for very scrupulously. Sir William Pile, chairman of the Inland Revenue, has guessed that this kind of tax evasion could account for as much as 7½ per cent of the entire economy.[7]

Moonlighters must be very close in attitude to the less respectable elements of the nineteenth-century peasantry – able to combine the use of their own labour with small amounts of capital, willing to seek out custom, sometimes dual occupationists, sometimes ignoring the paternalistic rules of the modern state such as safety regulations. They express their independence of, almost a nonconformity with the well-oiled machinery of the modern welfare state establishment represented by the trade unions, government departments and the major employers.

Is there a link between this line of thinking and the drive towards a property-owning democracy? DIY enthusiasts at least have more scope and more incentive when they live not as tenants, but in the hope of being the outright owners of their houses. With well over 50 per cent of houses in the owner-occupied sector in England and Wales, and Scotland now joining the race, it could be argued that we have become a nation of freeholders. The implications for social control are important. Property owners, the argument runs, look after their property and therefore respect the property of others, therefore the more property owners there are the more respectable society will become. This seems to echo arguments on which rested the franchises of the early and middle nineteenth century.

Finally, it is necessary to say a word about self-sufficiency perhaps the ultimate in DIY and also, like DIY, reinforced by the tax system. There has, of course, been a continuous tradition of digging the back garden and the allotment, kept alive by the English pattern of suburban housing, though threatened at one time by worship of the car and reliance on the supermarket. However, there is a more serious, even intellectual following for self-sufficiency, not only at the family level, but also at the national level. As Western Europe declines in the face of growing shortages of fuel and industrial raw materials, it could be that self-sufficiency will become a high priority. Edward Goldsmith has drawn attention to the 'fact' that:

> It is now generally known that it is not large-scale capital-intensive monoculture that produces the most food per acre. On the contary, very much more can be grown by labour-intensive methods on much smaller farms each producing a great variety of foodstuffs.
> To feed ourselves, in fact, we must transform our agriculture, radically reduce the size of holdings and return people to the land.[8]

A more realistic proposition would start from the fact that Britain's highly capital-intensive agriculture is the most efficient in the world, as measured by conventional standards. It derives this efficiency mainly from a high average farm acreage, a characteristic it owes mainly to the early start given to it by the estate system of the nineteenth and earlier centuries. However, this efficiency is also very dependent on tractor fuel, artificial fertilisers, weedkillers and insecticides. A revival then, in some suitably modernised form, of the peasant system seems to be most desirable to complement our large-scale monoculture. And as we deindustrialise, the balance between the two will be worked out in the agricultural revolution of the twenty-first century.

## Notes

1. For a conscious analogy between a planned village and the New Towns see H. Woolmar, 'Grantown-on-Spey: An Eighteenth-Century New Town', *Town Planning Review*, vol. 41 (1970), pp. 237-50.

2. R. Thomas and P. Cresswell, *The New Town Idea: Urban Development Unit 26* (Open University Press, Milton Keynes, 1973), pp. 14, 16 and 21.

3. Ibid., pp. 17-8, 22-4 and 50.

4. G.E. Cherry, 'The Town Planning Movement and the late Victorian City', *TIBG*, new series, vol. 4 (2) 1979, p. 315.

5. D.M. Winter, 'Family Farming and the Development of Capitalism', pp. 2, 5 and 15 (unpublished paper read to the Open University Faculty of Social Sciences, 23 May 1979, quoted by kind permission of the author).

6. G. Bourne, *Change in the Village* (Chatto and Windus, London, 1912), p. 87.

7. V. Keegan, *Guardian*, 28 March 1979, p. 17.

8. E. Goldsmith, *Guardian*, 25 April 1979, p. 21 (Edward Goldsmith is one of the founders of the Ecology Party and publisher of *The Ecologist*).

# INDEX

Only the villages that figure prominently in the text appear in the index. Readers should seek information about other villages through the appropriate county entries. Ancient counties have been used throughout.